W9-BZJ-207

R-2342-NA

July 1978

Sino-Soviet Conflict in the 1970s: Its Evolution and Implications for the Strategic Triangle

Kenneth G. Lieberthal

A Report prepared for

DIRECTOR OF NET ASSESSMENT, OFFICE OF THE SECRETARY OF DEFENSE

SANTA MONICA, CA. 90406

The research described in this report was sponsored by the Director of Net Assessment, Office of the Secretary of Defense under Contract MDA903-76-C-0119.

Reports of The Rand Corporation do not necessarily reflect the opinions or policies of the sponsors of Rand research.

THE LIBRARIES
COLUMBIA UNIVERSITY
WITHDRAWN
BURGESS-CARPENTER
& CLASSICS LIBRARY

Library of Congress Cataloging in Publication Data

Lieberthal, Kenneth.
   Sino-Soviet conflict in the 1970s.

   ([Report] - Rand Corporation ; R-2342-NA)
   1. Russia--Foreign relations--China. 2. China--
Foreign relations--Russia. I. United States. Dept. of
Defense. Director of Net Assessment. II. Title.
III. Series: Rand Corporation. Rand report ; R-2342-NA.
AS36.R3   R-2342   [DK68.7.C5]   081s   [327.51'047]
ISBN 0-8330-0049-7   78-13529

Published by The Rand Corporation

R-2342-NA

July 1978

Sino-Soviet Conflict in the 1970s: Its Evolution and Implications for the Strategic Triangle

Kenneth G. Lieberthal

WITHDRAWN

A Report prepared for

DIRECTOR OF NET ASSESSMENT, OFFICE OF THE SECRETARY OF DEFENSE

APPROVED FOR PUBLIC RELEASE; DISTRIBUTION UNLIMITED

Burgess

DK
68
.C5
L5

c.2

PREFACE

This report documents part of a project addressing the issue of the Sino-Soviet competition. The research was undertaken by The Rand Corporation on behalf of the Director of the Office of Net Assessment, Office of the Secretary of Defense. The report analyzes the evolution of Sino-Soviet relations since the Cultural Revolution in both bilateral and multilateral contexts, and it explains China's policies toward the Soviet Union in terms of the domestic political struggles that racked Peking during the 1970s. The final chapter applies the findings to the future and details the implications of the analysis for U.S. policy during the remainder of this decade.

This study should be of particular value to analysts of Chinese and Soviet foreign policy; to those interested in the history of Sino-Soviet relations since the Cultural Revolution and in future political/military contingencies in Sino-Soviet affairs; to formulators of U.S. policy toward the Soviet Union and China; and to specialists concerned with the interplay of foreign and domestic policy in China over the past half decade.

Other recent Rand studies that are relevant to this report include:

John Despres, Lilita Dzirkals, and Barton Whaley, *Timely Lessons of History: The Manchurian Model for Soviet Strategy*, R-1825-NA, July 1976.

Lilita Dzirkals, *Lightning War in Manchuria: Soviet Military Analysis of the 1945 Far East Campaign*, P-5589, January 1976.

Thomas Gottlieb, *Chinese Foreign Policy Factionalism and the Origins of the Strategic Triangle*, R-1902-NA, November 1977.

Arnold Horelick, *The Soviet Union's Asian Collective Security Proposal*, P-5195, March 1974.

Kenneth Lieberthal, *Strategies of Conflict in China During 1975-1976*, P-5680, June 1976.

Michael Pillsbury, *SALT on the Dragon: Chinese Views of the Soviet-American Strategic Balance*, P-5457, April 1975.

Michael Pillsbury, *Soviet Apprehensions about Sino-American Relations, 1971-1974*, P-5459, June 1975.

SUMMARY

Little has been written in the public domain about Sino-Soviet
relations since the onset of the Cultural Revolution in 1966. This
analytical neglect has left important and interesting questions virtually unexplored. How has each country perceived the threat from
the other, and to what degree have these perceptions changed over time?
What strategies has each adopted both bilaterally and multilaterally
to cope with these perceived threats? What kinds of debates over these
issues have taken place in Peking and Moscow, and how have these debates become intertwined with other policy issues in each country?
What do these factors tell us about the potential for change in Sino-
Soviet relations in the future and about the implications of this possible change for U.S. policy? This report and that by Thomas Gottlieb[1]
are designed to answer these questions on Sino-Soviet relations for
the period from the beginning of the Cultural Revolution through the
1970s. These two efforts, in turn, draw upon a larger body of research conducted at Rand largely under the auspices of the project on
Sino-Soviet competition and incorporate some of the wisdom generated
by these cognate efforts.[2]

Gottlieb's report analyzes Chinese factional conflict over Sino-
Soviet relations from 1966 through 1969, the years of the Great Proletarian Cultural Revolution. The current report, by contrast, takes
up the story since 1969--carrying it up to date and into the future.
Five concrete analytical questions inform the presentation in the body
of this report: (1) What bilateral strategies have the Soviet Union
and China adopted to deal with each other since 1969, and how have
these been implemented? (2) How has this bilateral relationship structured the policies of each country toward other states? (3) How have
Sino-Soviet relations become intertwined with domestic politics in the

---

[1]Thomas Gottlieb, *Chinese Foreign Policy Factionalism and the
Origins of the Strategic Triangle*, The Rand Corporation, R-1902-NA,
November 1977.

[2]See the Rand studies cited in the Preface.

People's Republic of China (PRC)?   (4) What are the probabilities of various types of change in Sino-Soviet relations during the coming years?   (5) What are the implications of the above factors for U.S. policy toward Sino-Soviet affairs?

Section I analyzes Soviet policy toward China from 1969 to 1978. The leaders in the Kremlin perceived their Peking counterparts as badly divided over the proper policy to pursue toward the Soviet Union. They therefore adopted a carrot-and-stick approach. The Soviets used the "border" negotiations that began in October 1969 to play out the "carrot" side of this two-pronged strategy. Moscow made an impressive series of proposals dealing with virtually all major dimensions of Sino-Soviet relations in these negotiations during the period October 1969 to August 1973. These offers, detailed in the text, kept pouring forth, even in the face of unremitting Chinese hostility in these talks. They were intended to provide those in China who desired a rapprochement with the Soviet Union additional ammunition to use as they discussed the better relationship that could be obtained.

The Kremlin brandished the "stick" in many ways. Militarily, the Soviets built up their capabilities in the China theater and initiated border incidents. Diplomatically, they advocated an Asian Collective Security System that would provide a vehicle for legitimizing Soviet involvement throughout Asia. Moscow made concerted additional efforts to isolate China both among the community of communist countries and in the larger international arena. The general Soviet economic and military presence in Asia also rapidly increased, as exemplified by the Soviet-Indian treaty of 1971. The Soviets during 1969-1973, in brief, tried to contain China diplomatically and militarily while offering potentially pro-Soviet leaders in the PRC a far more attractive alternative to the extant tension-filled state.

In the wake of the Chinese Tenth Party Congress in 1973, the Soviet leadership concluded that Mao Tse-tung would retain control over China's policy toward the USSR until his death. Therefore, no new offers were forthcoming during August 1973 to September 1976. Rather, the Soviets adopted the position that all previous offers remained open for negotiation and affirmed that the Chinese could at any time show their good faith by taking up seriously any Soviet offer that had already been put on the table.

This stance has continued to characterize the Soviet position since the death of Mao Tse-tung. In November 1976 Moscow renewed the border negotiations for the first time in several years so as to give the Chinese ample opportunity to signal any softening of their stance on issues of concern. The Soviets evidently received no such comforting sign in these talks, however. Moscow made another diplomatic effort to improve relations in February 1978--with equally disappointing results.

Section I of this report examines one additional potentially important dimension of Soviet policy toward China during the period under review--i.e., Soviet espionage directed against the PRC. The data problems in dealing with this issue are obviously immense, and little of certainty can be said. Still, there are reasons (examined in the text) to believe that Soviet espionage efforts may pose a significant threat to the political integrity of the PRC and, as detailed in Sec. II, the magnitude of this threat has been a subject of intense dispute within China itself during these years.

On the Chinese side, as analyzed in Sec. II, disputes over policy toward the Soviet Union have continued up to the present. Until Mao Tse-tung's death, moreover, these disagreements were inextricably intertwined with debate over a wide range of domestic policies. To complicate matters still further, these fused foreign/domestic policy debates also formed the grist of the struggle among all parties concerned to optimize their positions in the succession struggle.

The disagreements themselves centered on the related issues of the nature of the threat posed by the USSR and the best means to cope with that threat. Three major sets of arguments on these issues are apparent in the public media during 1973-1976. The first, advocated by the radicals and their followers, warned that the primary threat emanating from north of China's border was political--i.e., the threat of revisionism and subversion. The best solution to cope with this threat, therefore, would be to press home political campaigns and implement substantive policies geared to prevent the emergence of

revisionism within the borders of the PRC while also working hard to
ferret out all potential traitors at the highest levels of the Chinese
Party leadership.

The other two sets of arguments agreed on most particulars and
disagreed only on the tactical negotiating position to be adopted
toward the Soviet Union. These "moderate" arguments specified the
primary Soviet threat as military in nature and demanded that China
undertake a rapid buildup of its military power and, concomitantly,
expand as rapidly as possible its industrial base. This military-
focused threat perception thus had far-reaching programmatic consequences almost across the board for China's domestic policy in the
wake of the Cultural Revolution.

The only disagreement in the "moderate" camp centered around how
best to win the breathing space necessary to strengthen China before
a Soviet military onslaught. The "soft" moderates advocated sending
an occasional signal to the Soviets that China might be willing to
establish a better relationship so as to undercut the hawks in Moscow
at least to the degree that the Soviet leadership would find it impossible to reach a consensus on the momentous decision on whether to
attack China. The "hard" moderates, by contrast, argued that the
Soviets scorn the weak and respect only the strong. The Chinese,
therefore, should put up a bold front, for bluff and bluster would
succeed in holding at bay the Russian Bear whereas compromise would
only increase the chances of a Soviet attack. Through an examination
of the politics of this period, Sec. II traces the course of this
debate during the years concerned, analyzes its interaction with a
range of domestic issues and factional political battles over time,
and attempts to pinpoint the individuals who made up each of these
three groups. The analysis concludes that the radical faction consisted of Chiang Ch'ing, Wang Hung-wen, Chang Ch'un-ch'iao, and Yao
Wen-yuan; the "soft" moderate position until Mao's death reflected the
views most prominently of Hua Kuo-feng, Teng Hsiao-p'ing, and Yeh Chien-
ying; and the "hard" moderate stance could be attributed to Chi Teng-
k'uei, Li Hsien-nien, and T'an Chen-lin, among others. Teng Hsiao-
p'ing has shifted from the "soft" to the "hard" position since Mao
Tse-tung's death. Thus, the October 1976 purge of the "Gang of Four"

leaves Chinese policy in the hands of people who view the Soviet threat
in military terms and who pin China's hopes for security on rapid development of the PRC's industrial and military capabilities, although
disagreement remains between the "hard" and "soft" moderate views
over the tactical strategy to use with the USSR. Structural dimensions
of the situation (explained in the text), however, make it virtually
impossible for the soft moderates to carry the day completely. Importantly, also, this analysis indicates that there are no truly "pro-
Soviet" elements in the Chinese leadership--debate now centers solely
around the question of how best to ward off the Soviet threat to the PRC.

Substantively, this internecine conflict in China produced policies that reflected at various times the preferences of each of the
three contending perspectives outlined above, depending on the shifts
in politics in the Forbidden City. The Gang of Four predominated in
early 1974, for instance, whereas the "hard" moderates came into greater
prominence in the latter half of that year. The fact that Mao Tse-tung
personally strongly opposed any signs of compromise with the USSR forced
the "soft" moderates to assume a lower profile, and thus their views
rarely found expression in actual Chinese policy toward the Soviets.
The most notable exception, the Chinese release of the captured Soviet
helicopter pilots in December 1975, is examined in detail in the text.
Since Mao's death, the conclusion of a border river navigation agreement
in October 1977[3] reflects the continuing vitality of the soft moderate
position within the Chinese political spectrum. Section II analyzes in
depth the twists and turns of the interaction among the people repre-
senting these different perspectives from the Tenth Party Congress until
1978.

These Chinese policy decisions were taken against a background of
PRC willingness to participate in border negotiations, although there
is no evidence that the Chinese have ever very seriously negotiated
any part of the border question in these talks. Militarily, the Chinese
took strong measures during 1969-1971 to increase their defense against
a Soviet attack. This military program tapered off in 1971 for a variety
of reasons discussed in the text, although there is every likelihood

---

[3]*New York Times*, October 8, 1977.

that, with the death of Mao Tse-tung and the victory of the hard and soft moderates over the Gang of Four, a more feverish pace of military development is now in the offing.

Section II also reviews the PRC's multilateral effort to defend itself against the Soviet Union. On the world stage, China has largely pursued a strategy appropriate to a resource-scarce country under threat. It has sought to make friends almost everywhere, losing no opportunity to warn others of the need to maintain vigilance in the face of Soviet aspirations for hegemonism. Through these diplomatic efforts, the Chinese have tried to encourage other powers to pursue policies that would direct Soviet resources away from China's border to the maximum extent possible. This has, in short, been a policy of weakness, albeit one that has been accompanied by a good bit of rhetorical bluff and bluster. China has correctly viewed the United States as the most important building block in putting together the anti-Soviet international structure that it seeks.

Section III analyzes the possibilities for Sino-Soviet relations in the mid-term future and the implications of the findings of this report for U.S. policy. This section argues that, for a wide range of reasons, the chances of either war or friendship in Sino-Soviet relations are very slim. If the relationship for any reason should move toward one end of the "war-friendship" continuum, moreover, it is war that clearly emerges as the more likely possibility. Why would either side start a war? Almost certainly because it felt it "had no choice" in the context of a crisis set in motion by any number of events (detailed in Sec. III) growing out of the political successions in each country. A war that neither side initially planned to start, in brief, is more probable than one in which a carefully calculated decision to begin hostilities is made in the absence of some rapidly escalating preceding crisis.

This report analyzes a range of possible changes in U.S. relations with both the Soviet Union and China to determine their probable effect on the Sino-Soviet leg of the three-country triangle. This analysis concludes that the United States should recognize that it cannot fine-tune Sino-Soviet relations by means of Washington's actions toward either or both of the other parties. Indeed, few possible U.S. policies would significantly affect Sino-Soviet relations at all.

Relatedly, the triangular relationship is now sufficiently gelled that the United States cannot reap major benefits in its bilateral relations with either party by "playing the triangle." Bilateral far more than multilateral issues will determine the degree of progress, stagnation, or retrogression in Sino-U.S. and Soviet-U.S. relations. While focusing on its bilateral interests with each country, neverthe-less, Washington must remain sensitive to the fact that officials in Moscow and Peking might view U.S. policies against the background of the triangular relationship.

In sum, the time is past when the United States could attempt with confidence to manipulate the Sino-Soviet-U.S. triangle. The contours of that basic set of relationships are now fairly firmly established in stable mutual perceptions and concepts of national interest. Because the United States is well-served by a Sino-Soviet relationship that hovers between rapprochement and war, moreover, U.S. officials should take comfort from the fact that the various forces at play will almost certainly produce precisely this type of Sino-Soviet interaction during the coming years. This, in turn, should allow the United States to pursue bilateral relationships with each of these two major countries in ways designed to maximize U.S. interests, broadly defined.

ACKNOWLEDGMENTS

I benefited greatly while writing this study from my discussions with colleagues at Rand and elsewhere. At Rand, I owe a special debt of gratitude to Jeremy Azrael, John Despres, Lilita Dzirkals, Anna Sun Ford, Thomas Gottlieb, Arnold Horelick, Benjamin Lambeth, Nathan Leites, Steven Levine, and Richard Solomon. Other people who sharpened my thinking on the issues in this report include A. Doak Barnett, Philip Bridgham, Arthur Cohen, Carol Hamrin, James Lilley, Charles Neuhauser, Michael Pillsbury, William Rope, J. Stapleton Roy, and Allen Whiting. I also want to thank Lisa Diaz for her excellent research assistance at various stages of this work.

Most of those listed above contributed to my thinking primarily by challenging arguments and forcing me to consider more thoroughly the issues at hand. All the above-mentioned colleagues in this important sense helped to improve the quality of this analysis, yet probably none of them holds views on this complex issue that are identical with my own.

CONTENTS

I. SOVIET STRATEGY TOWARD CHINA, 1969-1978

BACKGROUND

In March 1969 two violent border clashes in the vicinity of
Chenpao Island sent shock waves through both China and the USSR.[1]
This mutual bloodletting riveted the world's attention once again on
a conflict between the two communist giants that had been building
since the 1950s. The close Sino-Soviet relationship of the 1950s had
turned sour by the early 1960s over issues of both political and military significance. By 1964, territorial issues had explicitly entered
the dispute and formal talks convened during that year to resolve these
issues. These talks occurred simultaneously with the better-known
exchange of open polemics between the Central Committees of the Chinese
Communist Party (CCP) and the Communist Party of the Soviet Union (CPSU).
However, they ultimately made as little progress toward resolving the
points in contention as did their better-known analogs. Even before
Nikita Khrushchev's fall in October 1964, then, political, military,
and territorial issues had become entangled in the rapidly deteriorating Sino-Soviet relationship.

Around 1965, the Soviet Union decided that prudence required that
it develop a major military presence along the Sino-Soviet border.[2]

---

[1]There is an ample literature available on these border clashes,
which occurred on March 2 and March 15, and on the details of the
territorial issues that divide the two countries. The major review of
both is Thomas Robinson, "The Sino-Soviet Border Dispute: Background,
Development and the March 1969 Clashes," *American Political Science
Review*, Vol. LXVI, No. 4, December 1972, pp. 1175-1202 (also published
by The Rand Corporation as RM-6171-PR, August 1970). See also the following works: An Tai-sung, *The Sino-Soviet Territorial Dispute*, Westminster Press, Philadelphia, 1973; Dennis Doolin, *Territorial Claims in
the Sino-Soviet Conflict*, Hoover Institution, Stanford, 1965; Neville
Maxwell, "The Chinese Account of the 1969 Fighting at Chenpao," *China
Quarterly*, No. 56, October-December 1973, pp. 730-739; Neville Maxwell,
"A Note on the Amur-Ussuri Sector of the Sino-Soviet Boundaries," *Mod-
ern China*, Vol. 1, No. 1, January 1975, pp. 116-126; and George
Ginsburgs, "The Damansky/Chenpao Island Incidents: A Case Study of
Syntactic Patterns in Crisis Diplomacy," *Asian Studies: Occasional
Paper Series*, No. 6, Southern Illinois University, 1973.

[2]See A. Doak Barnett, *China and the Major Powers in East Asia*,
The Brookings Institution, Washington, D.C., 1977, pp. 48-49.

It is not completely clear either how firm this decision was or how far-reaching it was intended to be. The USSR had evidently taken some low-key measures in the security realm prior to 1965 to cope with the changing nature of its relationship with the PRC.[3] Since 1966, moreover, it is possible that Moscow has made a *series* of major decisions to prolong, broaden, and make more permanent the size and nature of the Soviet military presence along its border with China rather than having anticipated as early as 1965 the full scope of the commitment now evident. There is no question, however, that during 1965 the USSR decided to fortify a Sino-Soviet border that had many Chinese troops stationed within several hundred miles of the line but almost no Soviet military presence.[4] Not surprisingly, this Soviet effort eventually produced a Chinese response (detailed below), the net effect of which was to militarize the dispute to the point where leaders on both sides subsequently have had to take national security into serious account in almost all of their deliberations about each other.

The Cultural Revolution in China added its own complications to Sino-Soviet relations. Peking's foreign policy degenerated into virtually unmitigated stridency. Radicals replaced a coherent and differentiated policy with virulent attacks on all things foreign, and the Soviet Union not surprisingly bore the brunt of many of these verbal assaults. For a period, radical leftists took over the Foreign Ministry. The Soviet embassy in Peking itself came under seige for several weeks.[5] On the border, Red Guards and others harassed and insulted Soviet border guards.

---

[3] For example, around the spring of 1960 (the dating is not precise in the source) the Soviet Union's intelligence services allegedly recatalogued China from a "People's Democracy" to a "non-Communist country in the Far East" and increased accordingly their attempts to gather intelligence on the PRC. Oleg Penkovsky, *The Penkovsky Papers*, Doubleday and Company, New York, 1965, pp. 71 and 73. *The Penkovsky Papers* were written under the aegis of the Central Intelligence Agency but were based on data obtained directly from Oleg Penkovsky: *New York Times*, December 25, 1977.

[4] The pre-1965 disposition of military forces along this border is reviewed in Robinson, 1972, op. cit., pp. 1183-1185.

[5] The high point of radicalism in Chinese foreign policy occurred during June-August 1967, when Yao Teng-shan and other leftists seized

The Soviets viewed the Cultural Revolution purge as directed primarily at removing all the "healthy forces" in China who might someday "come to their senses" on the Soviet issue. They watched with dismay as China seemed to sink into an anti-Soviet paroxysm and reacted by hedging their military bets with an arms buildup near the Chinese border and by making clear that they considered Mao Tse-tung "and his clique" to have deserted all semblance of Marxism. From that time until Mao's death, the Soviets consistently voiced open support for all efforts to remove Mao from leadership of the Chinese Party.[6]

Reactions of frustration and anger over the Cultural Revolution could well be expected from Moscow. The Cultural Revolution seems in addition, however, to have given the Soviets a glimpse of the policy preferences of the radical left in China and a foreboding that these violently anti-Soviet cadres could in fact someday inherit the Chinese revolution. This was a sobering thought, for it meant that the USSR might eventually face, along the longest national border in the world, a vociferously and irreconcilably hostile, seemingly "irrational" country, armed with nuclear weapons. Although the Soviets had viewed previous politics in Peking as a struggle between pro- and anti-Soviet groups, they had never before felt that the latter could emerge victorious after Mao's demise. The Cultural Revolution, in Soviet eyes, became a possible preview of the nightmare yet to come.

Soviets never though anti-Sovit group would win

---

control over the Ministry of Foreign Affairs. Melvin Gurtov, "The Foreign Ministry and Foreign Affairs in the Chinese Cultural Revolution," in Thomas Robinson (ed.), *The Cultural Revolution in China*, University of California Press, Berkeley, 1971, pp. 334-352. For a brief description of the seige of the Soviet Embassy in late January to mid February 1967, see Thomas Robinson, "Chou En-lai and the Cultural Revolution in China," ibid., p. 267.

[6]The most comprehensive Soviet analysis of Sino-Soviet relations since 1945 appears in O. B. Borisov and B. T. Koloskov, *Sino-Soviet Relations, 1945-1970*, translated and edited by Vladimir Petrov, Indiana University Press, 1975; an updated Soviet version of this volume is O. B. Borisov and B. T. Koloskov, *Soviet-Chinese Relations, 1945-1973*, translated by Yuri Shirokov, Progress Publishers, Moscow, 1975. The former has the more complete analysis of Chinese politics during the Cultural Revolution (pp. 278-346). The latter is the version referred to in the remainder of this report.

At least some Chinese leaders remained chary of provoking the USSR during the Cultural Revolution and took measures to lessen the risks of inadvertent incidents.[7] This concern largely explains the unusual lengths to which Peking went to assure continuing control over the events in China's provinces bordering the USSR.[8] China faced a range of very difficult alternatives in foreign policy toward the end of the Cultural Revolution, however. In oversimplified terms, the PRC could direct its main defense effort against the United States, which at that time was deeply embroiled in the Vietnam War; it could adopt a dual adversary strategy, permitting confrontation with the world's two most powerful countries; or it could improve relations with the country that had been its major enemy since 1949 to strengthen its position against its former ally. Given the extraordinarily high potential costs of each one of these policies, especially in the context of Peking's vicious internal politics since mid-1966, it is not surprising that the Chinese could not develop an agreed-upon policy for dealing with the USSR as of the closing days of the Cultural Revolution. The Soviet invasion of Czechoslovakia in August 1968 and the continuing U.S. escalation in Vietnam, moreover, heightened the sense of risk inherent in all of China's potential policies. Thus, while on the Soviet side the Cultural Revolution left a legacy of relative agreement on the proper policy to pursue toward China, in Peking, Soviet policy continued to be a divisive issue.[9] Consequently, China's policy toward the USSR during the subsequent years tended to lack the consistency of the Soviets' China policy, for many of the "foreign policy" actions undertaken by the PRC during the 1970s in fact reflected

China's policy lacks consistency

---

[7]Chou En-lai seems to have been one of these. Robinson, 1971, op. cit., p. 267.

[8]See, for example, the May 25, 1967, order of the Military Affairs Committee to the Inner Mongolian Military District, *CCP Documents of the Great Proletarian Cultural Revolution*, Union Research Institute, Kowloon, 1968, pp. 447-455. After the Cultural Revolution, the Military Affairs Committee was redesignated as the Military Commission.

[9]The most comprehensive available analysis of these divisions in China over Soviet policy during the Cultural Revolution is Thomas M. Gottlieb, *Chinese Foreign Policy Factionalism and the Origins of the Strategic Triangle*, The Rand Corporation, R-1902-NA, November 1977.

the attempts of one group of Peking leaders to influence and constrain the options available to others in the Chinese hierarchy.[10]

The March 2, 1969, armed clash over Chenpao (Damansky) Island[11] may have been one of these instances of Chinese factional politics' influencing foreign policy. Too little is known, unfortunately, to pinpoint this with certainty. On January 23, 1969, the Chinese changed their border patrolling procedure so that every unit that visibly pa-trolled territory near the disputed boundary had a backup unit that remained hidden from Soviet view.[12] On the fateful morning of March 2, the Chinese sent a border patrol out onto the ice near Chenpao. A Soviet patrol came out to confront it, and the Chinese group headed for the island itself instead of going back to its own shore. The Chinese backup patrol was hidden on the island and opened fire on the Soviets when the latter pursued the initial patrol group to Chenpao. It re-mains unclear exactly who began the firing, but even the Chinese ver-sion as told to Neville Maxwell has all the earmarks of a preplanned ambush.[13] Additional evidence, such as the seemingly greater Chinese preparedness to make propaganda over this bloody clash, tends to sup-port the thesis that the Chinese anticipated--and precipitated--this conflict.[14]

_____

[10]Section II of this report analyzes this aspect of China's Soviet policy.

[11]As noted above, two major border clashes occurred on and near Chenpao Island during March 1969 (the use of the Chinese name, here and elsewhere, does not reflect any judgment on the merits of the competing Chinese and Soviet claims to territories in dispute). The first, on March 2, seems to have been initiated by the Chinese. The second, on March 15, seems to have been essentially a retaliatory action by the Soviets. Both involved heavy casualties. For detailed descriptions of these, see Robinson, 1972, op. cit., pp. 1187-1191. An Tai-sung (op. cit., pp. 91-102) also provides good overviews of these events.

[12]Maxwell, 1973, op. cit., p. 734.

[13]Ibid., pp. 734-735. Maxwell asserts that it was the Soviets who opened fire, but the concealment in advance of the Chinese cover patrol on Chenpao and the subsequent retreat of the Chinese forces to Chenpao (where they could be sure they would be pursued) rather than back to their own bank suggest that the Chinese had in fact prepared a trap for their Soviet adversaries.

[14]For a more complex analysis of the possible explanations for this difference in media coverage, see Ginsburgs, op. cit., passim.

The Chenpao Island clash brought Sino-Soviet relations to a
crisis point. It predictably heightened fears in Moscow and forced
active consideration of appropriately drastic action. China, still
severely divided internally, could hardly have contemplated major
Soviet military actions against the PRC with equanimity. The Chinese
military, at that time heavily involved in internal administrative
and political work, must have been particularly sensitive to this
question. If the Chinese side did in fact provoke this clash, then
who within China decided to do it--and why?

Thomas Robinson dissects this question in terms of various possible cleavages in China--center/local, among factions in Peking,
and so forth. Robinson concludes that China's actions around Chenpao
Island in March 1969 cannot be explained in factional terms on the
basis of currently available data.[15] Harold Hinton, by contrast,
suggests a factional explanation that ties together Mao and Lin Piao
in bringing about the March 2 clash.[16] Finally, Roger Brown also
bases his explanation of this event squarely on a factional analysis
but argues that Mao, Chou, and their allies provoked the March 2 clash
as a means to counter Lin Piao and to highlight the overriding danger
from the USSR on the eve of the Ninth Party Congress so as to justify
the Mao/Chou prescription for a fundamental reorientation of China's
foreign policy. The clash itself, with the predictable Soviet retal-
iation almost two weeks later, created the necessary anti-Soviet hys-
teria to allow Mao et al. to carry the day at the Ninth Congress.[17]

The above scenarios are intricate and fascinating but leave many
questions unanswered. Brown, for instance, assumes that Mao and Chou
were willing to risk provoking a war with the USSR to create a crisis
atmosphere at the Ninth Congress--a rather drastic way of nudging

---

[15]Robinson, 1972, op. cit., p. 1192.

[16]Harold Hinton, *Bear at the Gate,* American Enterprise Institute
for Public Policy Research, Washington, D.C., 1971.

[17]Roger Glenn Brown, "Chinese Politics and American Foreign Policy:
A New Look at the Triangle," *Foreign Policy,* No. 23, Summer 1976, pp.
5-7.

an ongoing policy debate in a particular direction. In addition,
the Chenpao Island incident predictably produced a war scare on
the eve of the Ninth Party Congress—and this could only have the
effect of increasing the power of the People's Liberation Army (PLA)
headed by Lin Piao. All evidence—Lin's political report to the Ninth
Congress, his formal designation as Mao's heir at this convocation,
the high percentage of military leaders in all organs (Central Committee, Politburo, Standing Committee of the Politburo, etc.) elected
at and directly after this Congress,[18] and Chou En-lai's greatly decreased public stature in the months following the Congress—suggests
that Lin emerged in a very strong position at the conclusion of this
meeting. As Philip Bridgham has demonstrated,[19] the seeds of Lin's
ultimate demise were sown at this Congress; it would have taken a
subtle dialectician indeed, however, to have concluded that Lin Piao's
position and prospects had been weakened during April 1969 rather than
strengthened. Moreover, it seems certain that the Chenpao Island
clashes contributed to Lin's strength at the meeting—a consideration
that makes the Brown reconstruction of Chinese politics concerning
this clash less than compelling.

It is unlikely that the data will ever become available to allow
a definitive reconstruction of events in China leading to this clash.
Perhaps, indeed, as Allen Whiting has argued, Chinese deterrence
strategy includes a carefully controlled and limited preemptive strike
against an enemy that China fears is heading toward a major military
confrontation with the PRC.[20] In this case, the March 2, 1969, Chinese

Lin Piao heads PLA

Lin's strength up after the clash.

---

[18]The Ninth Congress elected the new Central Committee; the First
Plenum of the Ninth Central Committee convened on April 28 and elected
the new Politburo and Standing Committee of the Politburo. The Ninth
Congress passed a Party Constitution that designated Lin Piao as Mao
Tse-tung's successor; and the First Plenum elected Lin as the sole vice-
chairman of the CCP. Documents of the Ninth Congress and the First
Plenum are in *Peking Review*, No. 18, April 30, 1969, pp. 16-49.

[19]Philip Bridgham, "The Fall of Lin Piao," *China Quarterly*, No.
55, July-September 1973, pp. 428ff.

[20]Allen Whiting, *The Chinese Calculus of Deterrence*, University
of Michigan Press, Ann Arbor, 1975, pp. 238-240.

action at Chenpao may have reflected a decision that commanded agreement among all key actors in Peking.

In any case, the armed clash at Chenpao jolted both Moscow and Peking into wide-ranging policies designed to contain the threats posed by each other. Section II analyzes the strategy the Chinese developed. On the Soviet side, the Kremlin initiated a complex strategy to deal with its China problem: Bilaterally, it brought Peking into negotiations aimed at improving state-to-state relations while continuing to bolster its own military forces in the area; multilaterally, Moscow attempted to isolate Peking within the four major international groupings with which the Chinese might seek to identify-- the communist bloc, Asian states, developing countries, and the great powers.

THE BILATERAL DIMENSION

Negotiations

The Soviet leadership has had to contend with an unremittingly hostile China since 1969. Peking launched a crash program of war preparations directly following the March clashes,[21] and at no time from that date to the present has the PRC given significant indication of its desire to improve relations in a meaningful way with the USSR.[22] The Soviet Union, nevertheless, until 1973 held firm to a policy that gave a prominent place to the border negotiations--meetings in which the Soviet side made a series of one-sided concessions over a period of almost four years without eliciting any corresponding response from the Chinese. Why did Moscow persist in a course that had so little ostensible payoff?

---

[21] The most thorough available review of the PRC's preparations for war with the USSR during the first year following the Chenpao Island clashes is contained in Lu Yung-shu, "Preparation for War in Mainland China," *Collected Documents on Mainland China*, Taipei, Taiwan, 1971, pp. 895-918. Weapons procurement from the late 1960s through 1974 is reviewed in Sydney H. Jammes, "The Chinese Defense Burden, 1965-1974," *China: A Reassessment of the Economy*, Joint Economic Committee, Washington, D.C., July 10, 1975, pp. 459-466.

[22] See Sec. II of this report.

Analyses in the USSR in the early 1970s indicated that the Chinese leadership in fact remained split over the Soviet issue.[23] Although as of 1969 Mao's strongly anti-Soviet position had prevailed, Moscow believed that if it could pursue the right policies, it might be instrumental in bringing to the fore Chinese leaders who opposed the Chairman's views on this issue. This Soviet analysis suggested that Moscow would be wise to use the negotiations as a forum for laying out its vision of the benefits of an improved Sino-Soviet relationship in the future so as to undercut the Chairman's harsh characterization of the USSR's desires and intentions. It should persist in doing so, moreover, even if the Chinese refused to negotiate any of the Soviet offers already put forward, as the goal was to sketch out the contours of a fundamentally different relationship. This, indeed, is precisely what the Soviets proceeded to do, even in the face of continuing Chinese recalcitrance.

Soviets negotiate to restructure relations.

Thus, at the first session of the border talks, which convened from October 20 to December 14, 1969, the Soviet delegation proposed discussion of the whole range of Sino-Soviet differences in the belief that the two sides should work cautiously toward a border settlement by way of successes in other areas such as trade, cultural exchanges, and the level of diplomatic representation. The USSR also offered China some form of nonaggression agreement.[24] In the face of Chinese intransigence, however, the only agreement reached in the course of the twelve meetings during these months was to adjourn until early January for both sides to consult with their governments.[25]

Soviets want to negotiate broad range of issues. '69 session

Having laid out this basic position during the October-December 1969 negotiating session, the USSR then maintained a steady stream of new offers--and refinements of previous proposals--during each of the successive negotiating sessions until the CCP's Tenth Party Congress

---

[23]See, for instance, Borisov and Koloskov, op. cit., and *Pravda*, October 16, 1973, cited in *Foreign Broadcast Information Service (FBIS)/ USSR*, October 18, 1973, p. C-10.

[24]*Pravda*, December 22, 1972, cited in *Current Digest of the Soviet Press (CDSP)*, Vol. XXIV, No. 51, January 17, 1973, pp. 11-12.

[25]Hong Kong, *Ta Kung Pao*, November 6, 1969; *New York Times:* November 20, 1969; December 21, 1969; and December 31, 1969.

in August–September 1973. When the Soviet team returned to the border talks in early January 1970, for instance, it tabled a significant new package that sought to solve the territorial question by handing over certain islands in dispute along the Ussuri (including Chenpao Island) and expressing a willingness to negotiate Chinese claims in the Pamir region (thus implying that these claims had at least a shred of legitimacy) in exchange for the PRC's dropping all further territorial demands and withdrawing their insistence on Soviet recognition of the "unequal" nature of the previous treaties defining the border. This session of the talks ended without progress on April 22.[26] Four months later, nevertheless, the Soviet government made several additional proposals. It offered to hold talks to work out a draft interstate accord on mutual nonaggression that would include bans on nuclear weapons, on warlike propaganda, and on preparations for hostilities against the other side, to which the Chinese did not respond directly.[27] It also offered to convene a summit meeting.[28] When it became clear that the Chinese would remain unresponsive to these proposals, Moscow suggested that both sides simply reaffirm their adherence to the 1950 Sino-Soviet Treaty of Friendship and Mutual Alliance.[29]

In 1971, the Sino-Soviet border talks seem to have convened in only one session that lasted through the first half of the year. This session met from mid-January until the summer with a break in late March–early April for Soviet chief negotiator Ilyichev to attend the Twenty-Fourth Congress of the CPSU. No formal meetings were held after Lin Piao's death in early September. The Soviet Union made additional offers to China during this 1971 session.

Soviets willing to give some islands for dropping other claims.

war

reaffirm treaty

Lin Piao's death '71

---

[26] *London Observer*, January 18, 1970, cited in *FBIS/PRC*, January 19, 1970, pp. A-3-4; *New York Times*, March 1, 1970.

[27] *Zycie Warszawy*, June 23-24, 1974, cited in *FBIS/Eastern Europe (EE)*, June 23, 1974, p. G-10.

[28] *Mirovaya Ekonomika i Mezhdunarodnyye Otnosheniya*, No. 12, December 1975, cited in *FBIS/USSR*, January 14, 1976, p. C-5; *Pravda*, April 28, 1976, cited in *FBIS/USSR*, April 29, 1976, p. C-4.

[29] Budapest Radio to Europe, July 24, 1971, cited in *FBIS/Hungary*, July 26, 1971; Budapest, *Magyarorszag*, July 25, 1971, cited in *FBIS/Hungary*, July 29, 1971, p. C-4.

On January 15, Moscow moved significantly beyond its earlier offer to discuss with China the formulation of a "draft accord" on nonaggression or a reaffirmation of the 1950 Sino-Soviet Friendship Treaty. Now the Soviet negotiators tabled a full draft of a "special treaty on the nonuse of force," the provisions of which ruled out both the use and threat of conventional, nuclear, and missile forces in solving disputes between the USSR and the PRC. The Soviets proposed, moreover, that this draft be acted on "immediately,"[30] and Alexei Kosygin met with Chinese ambassador Liu Hsin-ch'uan on January 18,[31] almost certainly to add point to their offer. China refused to sign a separate treaty on the nonuse of force and proposed instead to include a suitable provision in the text of an intermediate accord on maintaining the status quo along the border. The two sides then negotiated a mutually acceptable text for this article in an accord-- at which time the whole enterprise foundered over Chinese insistence that the article on nonuse of force be tied to Soviet acceptance of the PRC concept of "disputed areas."[32]

During this session the Soviet Union also agreed to accept the Thalweg principle in demarcating the boundary along border rivers between the USSR and China.[33] This is a principle that one source says the Soviets had in fact accepted to demarcate the eastern boundary in the border talks of 1964, but which the Chinese never formally agreed

---

[30]*Pravda*, December 22, 1972, cited in *CDSP*, Vol. XXIV, No. 51, January 17, 1973, pp. 11-12; *Pravda*, April 28, 1976, cited in *FBIS/USSR*, April 29, 1976, p. C-4; *Zycie Warszawy*, June 23-24, 1974, cited in *FBIS/EE*, June 28, 1974, p. G-10.

[31]*Pravda*, January 19, 1971, cited in *CDSP*, Vol. XXIII, No. 3, February 16, 1971, p. 25.

[32]*Zycie Warszawy*, June 23-24, 1974, cited in *FBIS/EE*, June 28, 1974, pp. G-10-11.

[33]*Zycie Warszawy*, June 23-24, 1974, cited in *FBIS/EE*, June 28, 1974, p. G-8; Harold Hinton, "The United States and the Sino-Soviet Confrontation," *Orbis*, Vol. XIX, No. 1, Spring 1975, p. 33; *Washington Star News*, November 2, 1971. Subsequent events made clear that this excluded the area around Hei Hsia Tzu, where acceptance of the Thalweg would have given China possession of the large island at the confluence of the Amur and Ussuri that lies just off of the Soviet municipality of Khabarovsk.

to. Now the Soviet negotiators tabled a draft accord that defined the boundaries as running along the main channel of navigable rivers and along the middle of the beds of the non-navigable rivers. The Chinese did not accede to this demarcation,[34] presumably because it did not leave them in control of Hei Hsia Tzu,[35] but also possibly because the Chinese had claimed territory on the Soviet side of some of the boundary rivers as "disputed areas."

Either before or after their Twenty-Fourth Congress, the Soviets made yet another potentially significant proposal in offering to conclude a new border treaty rather than simply amending the existing accords.[36] Moscow had previously carefully maintained that although Chinese claims had no basis in international law, the USSR would consider minor adjustments so long as they did not serve as the prelude to still more Chinese demands.[37] While not changing this basic stance, the Soviets now adopted a somewhat more accommodating position by permitting negotiation of a new accord that could replace the former treaties, even though these earlier agreements remained fully legitimate in Soviet eyes. The Chinese, however, remained intransigent. Chou En-lai met personally with Soviet ambassador Tolstikov and the head of the negotiating team, Ilyichev, on March 21, just before they left to attend the Twenty-Fourth CPSU Congress.[38] Presumably, Chou wanted to make China's position on refusing the Soviet offers completely clear before these men returned to Moscow.

The following year, negotiations did not commence until late March. On March 20, 1972, Brezhnev sent Ilyichev back to Peking for

---

[34] *Zycie Warszawy*, June 23-24, 1974, cited in *FBIS/EE*, June 28, 1974, p. G-8.

[35] Jay Taylor, *China and Southeast Asia: Peking's Relations with Revolutionary Movements*, Praeger, New York, 1976, p. 167; *Washington Star*, November 2, 1971.

[36] *Pravda*, July 1, 1971, cited in *FBIS/USSR*, July 2, 1971, pp. D-1-7; Taylor, op. cit., p. 167.

[37] *London Observer*, January 18, 1970.

[38] Moscow Domestic Service in Russian, March 23, 1971, cited in *FBIS/USSR*, March 23, 1971, p. A-18; Taylor, op. cit., pp. 167-168.

a new round of talks and also took the highly unusual step of making public--in a speech to a trade union conference--the major proposal that Ilyichev carried with him. This consisted of word of Moscow's willingness to establish relations with China on the basis of the five principles of peaceful coexistence. Brezhnev also made public that the Soviet Union had put forward concrete proposals on the settlement of the border problem, on a nonaggression treaty, and on a general improvement in relations "on a mutually advantageous basis" (probably indicating various types of economic proposals).[39]

Moscow's acceptance of the "peaceful coexistence" formula in fact amounted to an important concession. In November 1970 China had changed its own attitude toward "peaceful coexistence" from its earlier insistence that these principles characterize only relations between states with differing social systems to acceptance of these as the basis for relations among all states regardless of social system.[40] Still, however, the Soviet Union clung to its insistence that socialist states base their interaction on the principles of proletarian internationalism--which, according to the Brezhnev Doctrine, clearly include the obligation to interfere in the affairs of a fraternal state should that state stray too far from the scientific path of socialism as viewed from Moscow.[41] Peaceful coexistence, by contrast, explicitly prohibits interference in the internal affairs of another state. While Brezhnev was careful in his speech to make clear that he still believed China to be socialist, he declared, in effect, that for China the Soviet Union would give up the right of interference that it *de facto* claimed for all other communist states, and he accompanied this doctrinal concession with a reaffirmation of Soviet willingness to conclude a nonaggression treaty with Peking. China, however, remained intransigent.

----

[39]Moscow Domestic, March 20, 1972, cited in *FBIS/USSR*, March 21, 1972, p. J-15.

[40]The Chinese had adopted a more ambivalent, in-between formulation in their New Year's Day editorial of 1970; *Peking Review*, No. 1, January 2, 1970, p. 7. For the November 1970 assertions, see Ch'iao Kuan-hua's remarks at the Yugoslav National Day reception on November 27, cited in *Peking Review*, No. 49, December 4, 1970, p. 23.

[41]*Pravda* Editorial, August 22, 1968; *Izvestia*, August 23, 1968.

1973 witnessed two Soviet offers to the Chinese--in March and June. On March 6, the Soviets attempted to break the impasse over continuing Chinese insistence on prior agreement on withdrawal of troops from disputed territories by offering to combine *simultaneous* negotiations on the various issues with new Soviet concessions in important areas. To maximize chances for reaching some early agreement, Moscow proposed that both sides first negotiate only the eastern boundary.[42] Furthermore, Moscow resubmitted its version of the eastern border on maps, and this new version reflected the earlier Soviet acceptance of the Thalweg principle for all river boundaries except around Hei Hsia Tzu, where the USSR still claimed that the border ran through the smaller Kazakevichego Channel to the south and west of the island.[43] This new demarcation gave the Chinese possession of most of the islands in dispute between the two countries. Peking, nevertheless, remained unmovable,[44] and on April 5 Alexei Kosygin conceded that little progress had been made.[45]

The Soviet package of mid-June had three components: a "concrete nonaggression treaty that prohibits both the threat and use of any kind of force"; relations based on peaceful coexistence; and reiteration of Soviet willingness to convene a summit meeting at any time.[46] This amounted, it seems, to a strong reaffirmation of earlier Soviet offers, conceivably with some new details not made public. According to Leonid Brezhnev, the Chinese did "not even deign to respond" to these offers.[47]

The Soviets had by mid-1973 also tabled offers that included: expansion of trade based on long-term agreements and on the resumption of deliveries of full sets of industrial equipment; cooperative

---

[42] Moscow in Mandarin to China, February 20, 1976, cited in *FBIS/ USSR*, February 23, 1976, p. C-1.

[43] Neville Maxwell, Rand seminar paper (unpublished), pp. 22-23.

[44] Moscow in Mandarin to China, February 20, 1976, cited in *FBIS/ USSR*, February 23, 1976, p. C-1.

[45] *Los Angeles Times*, April 26, 1973.

[46] *Pravda*, September 25, 1973, cited in *CDSP*, Vol. XXV, No. 39, October 24, 1973, pp. 4-5.

[47] Ibid.

arrangements between the two academies of science; extensive contacts in the public health and sports spheres; renewed ties between the friendship societies; exchanges of newspaper correspondents; and so forth. However, "the Chinese side either failed to reply to or rejected all the Soviet Union's proposals."[48]

Thus, by the eve of the CCP's Tenth Party Congress in August 1973, the Soviet Union had utilized the forum of the border negotiations to lay out a wide range of proposals aimed at improving Sino-Soviet relations. They used the border negotiations as the major vehicle for making these offers because, they argued, the border dispute itself was more a reflection than a cause of Sino-Soviet animosity and thus it would best be resolved as the overall relationship improved.[49] These offers actually aimed, however, primarily to communicate with people in China who favored improved Sino-Soviet relations and to provide them with ammunition for their arguments with their colleagues in the Forbidden City.

The Soviet analysis of splits within the Peking leadership thus explains why Moscow continued to make unilateral concessions in the bilateral negotiations over a period of four years even though the Chinese refused to negotiate any of the Soviet offers put forward. It does not, however, explain the timing of these offers.

Clearly the initial Soviet offers were timed simply to put a maximum range of issues on the table as quickly as possible before negotiations faltered. Even here, however, Moscow proved sensitive to the broader diplomatic significance of the negotiations themselves. For instance, on the very day that the negotiations began, Andrei Gromyko met secretly with Richard Nixon and Henry Kissinger in Washington and firmed up plans for the SALT negotiations to commence.[50]

---

[48] Ibid. The exact timing of these offers is not clear, although the wording suggests that most were made in March and/or June 1973.

[49] A knowledgeable Soviet scholar argued this case strongly in a conversation with me during 1976.

[50] The date was October 20, 1969. On the Gromyko meeting with Kissinger and Nixon, see Marvin Kalb and Bernard Kalb, *Kissinger*, Little, Brown and Company, Boston, 1974, pp. 114-115.

The implications of each of these sets of negotiations for the other were not inconsequential, and it is likely that the "coincidence" of dates was more than just that.

As time went on, the USSR more blatantly timed its offers to serve broader political purposes. The Soviet proposals during the summer of 1970 may well have been keyed to affect political discourse in China during the jockeying preceding the critical Second Plenum of the Ninth Central Committee.[51] This raises an interesting but ultimately unanswerable question concerning the quality of Moscow's intelligence on the Chinese political process at this time. Even if the Kremlin did not know the concrete issues being discussed at the moment, for instance, could it learn of the upcoming convocation of a major Party gathering through, for example, having an agent in the bureaucracy who was involved in the administrative process to prepare for such a meeting? Interpretations of the motivation behind the timing of the Soviet proposals in early 1971 pose similar types of problems. Was the Kremlin tuning its policy to affect a debate in Peking over the desirability of a Sino-U.S. rapprochement? In this connection, had Moscow's China specialists "read" correctly the implications of the picture of Edgar Snow standing alongside Chairman Mao in the December 25, 1970, issue of *People's Daily*? Did Soviet intelligence supplement these data with information concerning Mao's invitation (transmitted through Edgar Snow) to Richard Nixon to visit Peking?[52] Indeed, might the Soviets have been aware of the secret exchange of letters taking place between Peking and Washington[53] as of the time that Moscow made its new initiative to the Chinese on January 15?

After 1971, guesswork concerning the rationale for the timing of Soviet offers becomes considerably less hazardous. Of the four

---

[51]The Second Plenum convened from August 23 to September 6, 1970. For documentation on this meeting, see *Jen-min Jih-pao*, September 10, 1970; *Peking Review*, No. 37, September 11, 1970, pp. 5-7; and *Chinese Law and Government*, Vol. 3-4, 1972-1973, pp. 31-42.

[52]Edgar Snow, *The Long Revolution*, Vintage Books, New York, 1973, p. 170.

[53]Kalb and Kalb, op. cit., p. 236.

4 sets of proposals

sets of proposals put forward during the course of 1972-1974[54] by

Moscow, three clearly sought to affect Soviet-U.S. summitry. The first

72-74 concerns to affect U.S.-Soviet summitry.

of these, in late March 1972,[55] may have been designed to foster an

aura of Sino-Soviet reconciliation between Nixon's dramatic February

visit to China and his May journey to Moscow.[56] The timing of this

offer should have maximized Chinese incentives to show some flexibility,

lest Brezhnev feel during the summit that Moscow really could hold out

no hope of an improved relationship with Peking and should bargain with

the United States accordingly. PRC recalcitrance, moreover, could also

be turned to Soviet advantage, by making Moscow appear to the United

States and others as the more reasonable party in the dispute. Similar

concerns dictated the Soviet offers of June 14, 1973,[57] and June 25,

1974[58]--the 1973 offer being made one day before Brezhnev met with

Nixon in Washington and the 1974 offer occurring just 48 hours before

Nixon's final summit trip to Moscow. The only major Soviet offer dur-

ing 1973-1974 not clearly tied to Soviet-U.S. summitry was that of

March 6, 1973,[59] which may have been designed to create some momentum

toward Sino-Soviet détente following the Vietnam accord to which both

---

[54]The 1974 "proposal" in fact seems to have assumed more the form of an ultimatum over release of the Soviet helicopter pilots that the Chinese had captured in Sinkiang in March 1974: TASS, August 18, 1974, cited in *CDSP*, Vol. XXVI, No. 33, September 11, 1974, p. 16; AFP, September 11, 1974, cited in *FBIS/PRC*, September 11, 1974, pp. A-5-6. Section II provides more details on this helicopter pilot incident and its ramifications in Sino-Soviet relations during 1974-1975.

[55]For details, see Moscow Domestic, March 20, 1972, cited in *FBIS/USSR*, March 21, 1972, p. J-15.

[56]President Nixon visited the PRC on February 21-28 and visited the USSR on May 22-30.

[57]*Pravda* and *Izvestia*, September 25, 1973, cited in *CDSP*, October 24, 1973, pp. 4-5; Borisov and Koloskov, op. cit., p. 357; *Mirovaya Ekonomika i Mezhdunarodnyye Otnosheniya*, No. 12, December 1975, cited in *FBIS/USSR*, January 14, 1976, p. C-5.

[58]See footnote 54 above.

[59]Moscow in Mandarin to China, February 20, 1976, cited in *FBIS/USSR*, February 23, 1976, p. C-1; Maxwell (unpublished seminar paper), op. cit., pp. 22-23.

Moscow and Peking had affixed signatures four days earlier.[60] This was the first international accord signed by both Moscow and Peking (other than bilateral trade agreements) since the Cultural Revolution.

The temporal connection of the 1972-1974 offers with Soviet-U.S. summitry need not mean that the Nixon-Brezhnev meetings provided the only basis for the timing of these initiatives. The June 1973 proposals, for example, may have resulted in part from Soviet awareness that a major Chinese Party Congress would soon convene and a desire to be as forthcoming as possible in stating the Soviet negotiating position during the preparations for that meeting.[61] Likewise, it bears repeating that while the timing of these later initiatives was almost certainly affected by essentially opportunistic considerations going beyond direct Sino-Soviet bilateral relations, the *substance* of the offers was consistent with the continuing Soviet effort to communicate the USSR's willingness to engage in a far-reaching rapprochement with the leadership in Peking should leaders who were willing to tread this path come to the fore in the Forbidden City.

By the Tenth Congress of the CCP in August-September 1973, the Soviet Union had tabled a considerable range of initiatives in these bilateral negotiations with China. Moscow had cleared away some of the obstacles to reaching an eventual agreement by accepting the five principles of peaceful coexistence as the basis for Sino-Soviet relations, embodying the Thalweg principle in its demarcation of the border where this was delimited by rivers (except around Hei Hsia Tzu), proving responsive on the issue of a treaty barring the threat or use of any kind of force, and expressing its willingness to sign a new border treaty. At the same time, the Soviet side had demonstrated its desire to follow through on better relations by proposing a summit

---

[60]The Vietnam accord was concluded on March 2, 1973; *New York Times*, March 3, 1973.

[61]The Tenth Congress of the CCP convened from August 24-28, 1973. Documentation is in *Peking Review*, No. 35-36, September 7, 1973. Soviet commentary on the Congress suggested that Moscow was sensitive to the fact that the Soviet position could influence the strength of potentially pro-Moscow elements in Peking--see especially *Pravda*, October 16, 1973, cited in *FBIS/USSR*, October 18, 1973, pp. C-1-10.

meeting, restoration and development of economic, scientific, and
cultural relations between the two countries, and a range of approaches
to settling the actual boundary dispute in a piecemeal fashion. As
noted above, the Kremlin enunciated these offers--many of which amounted
to genuine concessions--in a piecemeal fashion over a period of four
years in the face of virtually absolute Chinese intransigence.

To be sure, Moscow had not yielded on the core Chinese demands.[62]
The USSR adamantly refused to pull back its forces from "disputed"
areas along the border; it made clear that it would not accept the
position that the Sino-Soviet treaties that had defined the border
during the 19th century had been "unequal"; and it persisted in its
demand that the border negotiations take both the treaties and the
actual situation, rather than the treaties alone, as the basis for a
final settlement. In several places, most importantly in the Pamir
region of Sinkiang, the "actual situation" evidently placed territory
in the possession of the Soviet Union that the treaties had left in
China's hands.[63] Even so, Moscow had gone a long way toward trying to
lay the groundwork for a compromise border settlement and improved
relations on a broad basis by the time of the Tenth Party Congress of
the CCP in the late summer of 1973.

In the wake of the Tenth Congress, however, the USSR reluctantly
concluded that any Chinese leaders who preferred a Sino-Soviet rapprochement of some dimensions would not be in a position to begin to move
toward that prospect until after Mao Tse-tung's demise.[64] This

---

[62]The basic Chinese demands are spelled out clearly in a "statement" of the Ministry of Foreign Affairs on October 7, 1969, and a
"document" of the Ministry of Foreign Affairs on October 8, 1969.
Texts in *Peking Review*, No. 41, October 10, 1969, pp. 3-4 and pp. 8-15,
respectively.

[63]Maxwell (unpublished seminar paper), op. cit.

[64]Soviet commentary on the Tenth Congress made clear that Moscow
still regarded the Chinese leadership as badly split over many major
issues, not least of which was the Chinese rapprochement with the
United States. This same commentary, however, noted that Mao Tse-tung
and his "clique" seemed at least temporarily to have maintained a strong
hold over Chinese politics. *Izvestia*, September 12, 1973, cited in
CDSP, Vol. XXV, No. 37, October 10, 1973, pp. 3-4; *Pravda* and *Izvestia*,

conclusion prompted the Kremlin to adopt a new stance in the border negotiations. Moscow now made clear that it would make no more concessions until it had received a response from the Chinese that suggested that Peking was ready to allow some positive movement in their bilateral relationship. If the PRC should give some indication that the time for substantive negotiations was at hand, China would find the Soviet Union prepared to respond positively to the new situation.[65]

What would the Soviet Union consider to be an adequate sign of China's willingness to negotiate seriously? This question arose concretely when the Chinese suddenly, and evidently without prior notice to Moscow, on December 27, 1975, released the Soviet helicopter pilots that Peking had accused of espionage and had held captive since March 1974. The Chinese made this move in a highly conciliatory way, but they accompanied it with some of the most strident anti-Soviet rhetoric in the long history of their denunciation of the USSR.[66] Did the helicopter pilot release, then, indicate that Peking was ready to move forward in its relations with the Soviet Union? Or should Moscow keep more tuned to the criticism in the Chinese media?

The Soviet answer, which came quickly and has subsequently been reaffirmed, stated that Moscow had put forward significant and concrete proposals in the bilateral negotiations and that the Chinese should indicate their willingness to take up one or more of *these* Soviet proposals for serious discussion if Peking would like to signal unambiguously its desire to work for an improved relationship. This

September 25, 1973, cited in *CDSP*, Vol. XXV, No. 39, October 24, 1973, pp. 4-5; *Pravda*, October 16, 1973, cited in *FBIS/USSR*, October 18, 1973, pp. C-1-10.

[65]See, for example, Belgrade TANJUG Domestic Service in Serbo-Croatian, May 5, 1975, cited in *FBIS/USSR*, May 5, 1975, p. C-1; Moscow in Mandarin to Southeast Asia, December 30, 1975, cited in *FBIS/USSR*, January 2, 1976, pp. C-2-3; *Pravda*, April 18, 1976, cited in *FBIS/USSR*, April 19, 1976, pp. C-1-6.

[66]The Chinese statement announcing the release of the helicopter pilots is given in *Peking Review*, No. 1, January 2, 1976, p. 7. As noted above, Sec. II of this report contains a detailed analysis of the mode of the Chinese gesture and the motivations of various groups in Peking with regard to this issue.

response implied that in lieu of such a sign, the Soviet Union would not make additional offers to improve relations with China.[67]

The Soviet Union has maintained basically this stance since the death of Mao Tse-tung on September 9, 1976. Moscow's initial approach consisted of an almost total cessation of polemics against China, combined with clear statements to the effect that the Soviets remained willing to improve relations if and when the new Chinese leadership should signal its readiness to do so. Thus, for instance, a *Pravda* article by Aleksandrov, a pseudonym used for authoritative statements on the Kremlin's China policy, reviewed some of the past Soviet offers to China and asserted that there was no reason why relations should not improve between the two countries.[68] At the same time, the CPSU sent telegrams to China to express condolences on Mao's death, and Brezhnev personally congratulated Hua Kuo-feng on his appointment as the new CCP Chairman—thus providing the first known instance of attempted Party-to-Party communications in over a decade.[69] Relatedly, on November 27, 1976, Moscow sent Ilyichev back to Peking for the first publicly announced session of the border negotiations in over two years.[70] A resumption of harsh treatment of China in the Soviet media starting in the spring of 1977 has not signalled any change in this fundamental approach.[71] Indeed, on February 24, 1978, the USSR again took the diplomatic initiative, calling for a "joint statement on the principles of mutual relations." A negative Chinese response on March

---

[67] Moscow in Mandarin, December 30, 1975, cited in *FBIS/USSR*, January 2, 1976, pp. C-2-3.

[68] *Pravda*, October 1, 1976, cited in *CDSP*, Vol. XXVIII, No. 39, October 27, 1976, pp. 1-3, 24.

[69] The Chinese rejected both communications on the basis that Party-to-Party relations had long ago been completely severed. Hong Kong, *Hsin Wan Pao*, November 2, 1976, cited in *FBIS/PRC*, November 4, 1976, pp. N-2-3.

[70] *New York Times*, November 28, 1976. These talks adjourned, reportedly without having made any progress, on February 28, 1977: *New York Times*, March 1, 1977.

[71] See, for example, the Aleksandrov article in *Pravda*, October 1, 1977, cited in *CDSP*, Vol. XXIX, No. 39, October 26, 1977, pp. 11-12.

6[72] evidently triggered a 5000 mile, thirteen-day trip by Leonid Brezhnev to review defenses along the Soviet-Chinese border several weeks later.[73]

Clearly, the death of Chairman Mao and the purge of the highest ranking radicals in the Chinese Communist Party in late 1976 has ushered in a period when the potential for change in Sino-Soviet relations is greater than at any time during the past decade. Might the Soviets still make some dramatic new offers to China to move their relations off dead center? What is the range of opinions within Peking concerning the future of China's relations with the USSR? Given our knowledge of events over the past decade, what is the range of probable outcomes in Sino-Soviet relations during the next few years? What are some of the less likely--but still possible--scenarios? The remainder of this report seeks to answer these questions and to spell out their implications for U.S. policy.[74] But first, the Soviet strategy toward China since 1969 must be outlined in greater detail.

The Military Dimension

The Soviet Union has not, of course, confined its bilateral relationship with China to the negotiations just outlined. As noted above, ever since the eve of the Cultural Revolution, Moscow has devoted substantial resources to increasing its military presence around the PRC's periphery. This has involved a several-pronged effort.

Most directly and visibly, the USSR has vastly increased its military strength on the Sino-Soviet and Sino-Mongolian borders (the latter through a Soviet-Mongolian mutual defense treaty).[75] The deployment of additional forces along these borders continued through the end of 1972, at which time Moscow had well over 40 divisions stationed in what

---

[72]The diplomatic interaction is detailed in *New China News Agency*, March 25, 1978, cited in *FBIS/PRC*, March 27, 1978, pp. A-6-8. On Brezhnev's trip, see *New York Times*, March 27, 1978.

[73]*New York Times*, April 10, 1978.

[74]These questions form the crux of Secs. II and III of this report.

[75]This 20-year treaty was signed on January 15, 1966. The text is in *Pravda*, January 18, 1966, cited in *CDSP*, Vol. XVIII, No. 3, February 9, 1966, pp. 7-8.

could be called the "China theater." Since 1973, the effort may have
focused more on upgrading these forces and consolidating undermanned
divisions, as available figures for manpower deployment in the area
have shown no increase (and for numbers of divisions have shown an
ostensible decline) since that date.[76] Longer-term Soviet efforts
to develop Eastern Siberia, in addition, affect logistics and other
capabilities in the region in a way that makes it impossible to dis-
tinguish strictly military from civilian activities. Clearly, the
major efforts now in train to carry out this development effort (including the construction of additional rail connections over a part
of this distance) are significantly increasing the USSR's military
capabilities in the area.[77]

Moscow has combined this effort along the Sino-Soviet and Sino-
Mongolian borders with a parallel attempt to augment its military
capabilities all along the periphery of China. Its Pacific fleet
has experienced significant growth and now includes missile-firing
submarines. The USSR has also established an impressive naval

---

[76]Roughly accurate figures on the Soviet buildup along the Chinese
border areas are contained in the annual *Military Balance*, Institute
for Strategic Studies, London, for the years concerned. Joseph Alsop
dates a larger percentage of the Soviet buildup in the "China theater"
to before the March 1969 border clashes: See the *Washington Post*,
July 11, 1969.

[77]The current Soviet Five Year Plan envisions major investments
in Central and Eastern Siberia, especially in the extractive industries and in the transport facilities necessary to link these areas
more closely into the economy of European Russia. This plan will,
therefore, entail the transfer of substantial capital and human resources to the area north of the Chinese border, increasing thereby
the Soviet Union's sensitivity to any threat to the security of this
vast region. Construction of the Baikal-Amur railway line is, moreover, a major component of this plan. This line, which will run to
the north of the Trans-Siberian railroad, will greatly improve both
the logistical capabilities of the Soviet armed forces in the area
and the security of their major rail transport capability. The Trans-
Siberian along substantial stretches runs perilously close to the
border with the PRC. On the Five Year Plan investment allocation and
the Baikal-Amur line, see Brezhnev's Report to the Twenty-Fifth Party
Congress, *Pravda*, February 25, 1976, cited in *CDSP*, Vol. XXVIII, No.
8, March 24, 1976, p. 17; and Kosygin's Report to the same Congress,
Pravda, March 2, 1976, cited in *CDSP*, Vol. XXVIII, No. 11, April 14,
1976, p. 14.

presence in the Indian Ocean,[78] while using its diplomacy in the Middle East (not very successfully) to try to improve both its logistical access to the Indian Ocean and its ability to shift military resources from one ally to another as necessary throughout the area.[79] Vietnam now represents the largest military force in Asia south of the Yangtze River[80] and Moscow is trying to cement its relations with the leaders in Hanoi. If the USSR should gain access to the port facilities at Cam Ranh Bay, the Soviet Navy's position would be dramatically strengthened throughout the Western Pacific.

Without exploring the specific distribution of forces and their concrete capabilities, therefore, it can be said with confidence that over the past eight years the USSR has developed a capacity--either independently or in league with states it has cultivated--to menace China from the east and south as well as from the north. While the major land threat remains concentrated in China's north, naval and missile assaults can now be launched from around the eastern and southern peripheries. Thus, Moscow has combined its diplomatic overtures to Peking with highly visible and clearly threatening actions to bring military force to bear in this relationship. It has done this, of course, in the context of a rapidly increasing Chinese military presence on Peking's side of the border. How Soviet military power might be brought into play and under what circumstances is considered in Sec. III of this report.

---

[78] On the Soviet naval threat to China from around the PRC's eastern and southern peripheries, see Francis J. Romance, "Peking's Counter-Encirclement Strategy: The Maritime Element," *Orbis*, Vol. XX, Summer 1976, pp. 437-459.

[79] Avigdor Haselkorn has constructed an interesting and controversial argument to the effect that the Soviet Union tried to put together a collective security system that would lay the basis for mutual strategic support among three subsystems: those of the Warsaw Pact, the Middle East, and India. Avigdor Haselkorn, "The Soviet Collective Security System," *Orbis*, Vol. XIX, Spring 1975, pp. 231-254.

[80] Guy Pauker, *Prospects for Regional Hegemony in Southeast Asia* (Statement Presented to the Subcommittee on Future Foreign Policy Research and Development of the House International Relations Committee), The Rand Corporation, P-5630, April 1976.

THE HIDDEN FACTOR: SOVIET SUBVERSION IN CHINA

There is one final element of Soviet bilateral strategy toward
China that leads directly into a thicket of problems about data--
that is, the question of Soviet subversion. There are two major
aspects to this question: Soviet attempts to subvert the minority
peoples who live along the Sino-Soviet border, and Moscow's efforts
to subvert relatively higher ranking members of the Party and military
apparatuses in the PRC. The former is an obvious continuing cause
of concern to Peking, which has taken strong measures to increase the
native Han population in these sensitive regions.[81] It is the latter,
however, that poses the most intriguing questions for the analyst of
Sino-Soviet affairs.

There is no hard evidence available that allows one to determine
with confidence whether or not the Soviet Union has maintained illicit
contact with any people high in the Chinese bureaucracy. Probably
Moscow previously enjoyed such access. Kao Kang, the leader of the
heavily industrialized northeast region and a Politburo member, for
instance, is alleged to have reported regularly on the attitudes of
the top Chinese leadership toward the Soviet Union.[82]

Subsequent complicity has been alleged, most notably with the
purge of Minister of Defense P'eng Teh-huai in the summer of 1959 for
attacking the Great Leap Forward with backing from Moscow. During the
middle of the Lushan Conference at which P'eng voiced strong opposition
to many of Mao's Great Leap Forward policies, Khrushchev denounced the
Great Leap strategy in a speech in Bucharest. This *prima facie* case of

---

[81]See, for instance, June Teufel Dreyer, "The Role of Ethnicity
in the Sino-Soviet Dispute," paper presented to the Tri-State Modern
China Seminar, University of Pittsburgh, September 17, 1977.

[82]Nikita Khrushchev's recollections assert this. *Khrushchev
Remembers: The Last Testament*, Little, Brown and Company, Boston,
1974, pp. 243-244. A more complex argument about the interpenetration
of Soviet and Chinese leadership factions during the early 1950s is
presented in Roy Grow, "The Politics of Industrial Development in
China and the Soviet Union: Organizational Strategy as a Linkage
Between National and World Politics," Ph.D. Dissertation, University
of Michigan, 1973. See also Richard Thornton, *China: The Struggle
for Power, 1917-1972*, Indiana University Press, Bloomington, 1973.

collusion was bolstered by several supporting items: P'eng had returned from a trip to the USSR shortly before the Lushan Conference, and thus he had enjoyed the opportunity there to voice his grievances to the Soviet leaders; on June 20--after P'eng's return but before the Conference convened--Moscow abruptly cancelled its nuclear sharing agreement with the PRC, which *de facto* provided P'eng with ammunition to use at Lushan to dramatize the costs of alienating the Soviet Union; and lastly, another member of the "military clique" purged at Lushan was Chang Wen-t'ien, former Chinese ambassador to the Soviet Union and a man with a long history of political squabbles with Chairman Mao Tse-tung. More concrete evidence of actual Soviet collusion with P'eng and others to undercut Mao at Lushan has never been provided, but the above bits and pieces are tantalizing.[83]

Since 1959 not even the above suggestive types of evidence are available on Soviet penetration of the Chinese civilian or military hierarchies. Still, the Soviet Union throughout the 1950s enjoyed

---

[83] Few major Chinese events have generated as full a literature as has the purge of P'eng Teh-huai. The strategies of Mao Tse-tung and P'eng Teh-huai at the crucial Lushan meeting remain obscure, however, in spite of a wealth of specific information available on events before, during, and after the meeting. The Soviet connection fits in with all of the available data but still may have been vastly overplayed by Mao Tse-tung to paint his opponent with the brush of treason. A summary of the available documentation on the Lushan meetings is presented in Kenneth Lieberthal, *A Research Guide to Central Party and Government Meetings in China, 1949-1975*, International Arts and Sciences Press, White Plains, 1976a, pp. 141-149. Much of this documentation appears in *The Case of P'eng Teh-huai*, Union Research Institute, Hong Kong, 1968. The major secondary literature on this affair consists of David Charles, "The Dismissal of Marshal P'eng Teh-huai," *China Quarterly*, No. 8, October-December 1961, pp. 63-76; Linda Perkin, "The Chinese Communist Party: The Lushan Meeting and Plenum, July-August 1959," M. A. Essay, Columbia University, 1971; and J. D. Simmonds, "P'eng Teh-huai: A Chronological Reexamination," *China Quarterly*, No. 37, January-March 1969, pp. 120-138. Frederick Teiwes has made the most thorough review of the evidence available on the P'eng Teh-huai affair in an as yet unpublished manuscript, "The Dismissal of P'eng Teh-huai and the Campaign Against 'Right Opportunism,' 1959-1960," Seminar Series Paper for the Contemporary China Centre of the Australian National University, July 23, 1976. Numerous other authors have given their own interpretations on this affair in more broadly gauged books about Chinese politics of this period.

broad access to Chinese bureaucrats, especially in the military-
related heavy industrial sectors.[84] Within the military itself,
Soviet involvement with China was most intense in the air force, a
relationship that has been maintained (albeit on a greatly reduced
scale) through all the subsequent ups and downs of Sino-Soviet relations.[85] Given KGB standard operating procedures in Eastern Europe
and in non-communist countries, it would be remarkable indeed if the
Soviet intelligence apparatus had not tried to recruit agents in
China and among Chinese students studying in the USSR. Additionally,
major leadership splits and political instability provide a relatively fertile ground for such recruitment--and the upheaval of the
Cultural Revolution, followed by several major waves of purging and
rectification since 1969[86]--have left a large pool of Chinese in
authoritative positions who have had reason to believe that the system
had gone radically off the track during recent years.

One brief example may demonstrate the potentially wide-ranging
repercussions of a successful Soviet liaison with a high-level Chinese
leader. Following the death of Lin Piao after his purported coup and
escape attempt to the USSR, the Chinese circulated internally the so-
called "571" document. They claimed this to be the plan drawn up under
the aegis of Lin Li-kuo--Lin Piao's son and one of the heads of the
Chinese Air Force--for Lin Piao's attempt to seize power by military
force if all else failed.[87] Two things are noteworthy in this document:

---

[84]This is detailed in Borisov and Koloskov, op. cit., and Hans
Heymann, Jr., *China's Approach to Technology Acquisition: Part I:
The Aircraft Industry*, The Rand Corporation, R-1573-ARPA, February
1975, esp. pp. 9-12.

[85]Since the early 1960s this relationship has consisted primarily
of Chinese Air Force related purchases from the Soviet Union. See
Heymann, op. cit., and Michael Pillsbury, "Patterns of Chinese Power
Struggles: Three Models," unpublished paper prepared for the Modern
China Seminar, Columbia University, March 27, 1974.

[86]Politburo level purges in China are briefly reviewed in Sec. II
of this report.

[87]A partial text is reproduced in Michael Y. M. Kau (ed.), *The
Lin Piao Affair: Power Politics and Military Coup*, International Arts
and Sciences Press, White Plains, 1975, pp. 80-95. The Chinese assert
that Lin Li-kuo had some assistance from co-conspirators in drawing up
this plan.

that Lin counted on the air force rather than the ground forces for initial support in this military attempt; and that this military effort, which was to be based in East and Central South China, would rely on Soviet actions north of the border to tie down the troops loyal to Mao in North China and prevent their effective use against the insurgents. Naturally, each of these elements could have been inserted by the victors to further tarnish Lin Piao's reputation and that of the air force, which Lin had favored in his last years.[88] Indeed, the entire document may well have been forged by the victors.

Nevertheless, it is striking to note the incentives for Lin Piao to make some sort of contact with the Soviets in 1971: He was rapidly losing ground to Chou En-lai as Mao's probable successor; he required Soviet military assistance in his most pessimistic contingency plan; and he opposed the opening to the United States.[89] Thus, Lin may actually have planned to establish contact with the Soviet Union--and may even have implemented this part of his plan before his purported assassination attempt against the Chairman on September 11.[90]

What if Lin Piao established such contact? It could not have been done by Lin personally, of course. What information would the Soviets require before agreeing to play their part in the plan? Might Lin have told them which military commanders had become so completely

---

[88]Air force procurement had surged ahead of that of the other Chinese armed forces since the late 1960s. It suffered severe cuts right around the time of Lin Piao's fall in September 1971. Jammes, while analyzing the overall rise and decline in Chinese military procurement, comments specifically that "Much of the decline [following Lin's death] reflects a sharp curtailment of acquisitions of aircraft." Jammes, op. cit., p. 463.

[89]On Lin Piao's opposition to China's potential turn toward the United States as early as the Cultural Revolution period, see Gottlieb, op. cit., passim. For the early 1970s, see Taylor, op. cit.

[90]Although the "571" document called for seeking some support from the USSR, the Chinese have never alleged that Lin and his conspirators actually established a liaison with the Soviet Union. Peking does, of course, point to the fact that Lin died while on a plane headed for the USSR to "prove" Lin's treasonous relationship with Moscow.

disaffected that they had joined in a cabal to overthrow Mao and Chou
En-lai? Assuming that the "571" document is authentic and unaltered,
how could Mao be certain that this type of information had not been
passed to Soviet intelligence? How could the military commanders concerned know whether they had been compromised? What other information
might have been passed by these men who had clearly become desperate
in their bid for power? The period from late 1971 to 1973 must have
been tense indeed as the Chinese leadership tried to ferret out Lin's
co-conspirators without compromising national security even further.
One wonders whether Soviet organs could still retain information on
any member of the Lin Piao conspiracy that has so far escaped detec-
tion--information that might be used for blackmail at an appropriate
time as the twists and turns of the Chinese succession work themselves
out. These are obviously low probability contingencies and yet they
cannot safely be completely excluded from an analysis of the dynamics
of the Soviet strategy toward China in the past--or in the future.[91]

Lest the Lin Piao affair now appear too removed to be relevant
for contemporary politics, it is worth noting that the purge of the
"Gang of Four" in Peking on October 6, 1976, also involved some of the
same elements that had invited earlier Soviet meddling. This purge
netted Mao Tse-tung's nephew, Mao Yuan-hsin, among others. The younger
Mao had been political commissar of the Shenyang Military Region and
a leading Party official in the heavily industrialized Manchurian
province of Liaoning. Reports directly following the purge indicated
that Mao Yuan-hsin had sought to move some troops loyal to him into
the region of the capital shortly before Mao Tse-tung's death, but that
he had been blocked in this request (presumably by Li Teh-sheng, the
commander of the Shenyang Military Region).[92] Again, therefore, a
major Chinese power struggle with high stakes involved military forces
and included important moves by highly disaffected leaders, this time
in Manchuria, bordering on Soviet Siberia. There is no indication of
any Soviet involvement in this latest political turmoil in China, but

---

[91] Section III of this report focuses on future Soviet strategy
toward the PRC.

[92] Tokyo, Kyodo News Agency, October 20, 1976, cited in *FBIS/PRC*,
October 20, 1976, p. E-2.

these developments highlight the continuing conditions that might make possible Soviet suborning of pivotal Chinese leaders.

On a somewhat less dramatic level, even a Soviet informant on the clerical staff at a sufficiently high level of the Chinese Party bureaucracy could provide an invaluable stream of information on the terms of current disagreements over foreign policy and the timing of major central meetings. These could, in turn, greatly assist Moscow as it decides what kinds of approaches to make to China and when to take specific initiatives.

In sum, an important but hidden part of Soviet strategy toward China may have involved subrosa contacts with well-placed individuals in the CCP apparatus or military bureaucracy. The recurrent political purges and radical shifts in policy in Peking have provided potentially fertile ground for this type of activity, although presumably the Chinese counterintelligence effort is also impressive. Most likely, once Mao had again consolidated his power after the disaster of the Lin Piao affair (i.e., by the Tenth Party Congress), the Soviets decided to "bank" this resource (if they had it at all in the first place) to preserve it for possible use if the succession to Mao should provide a critical opportunity.

MOSCOW'S MULTILATERAL STRATEGY TOWARD CHINA, 1969-1978

The Soviet Union has also pursued a part of its China policy through multilateral diplomacy during the 1970s. This effort has aimed primarily at isolating China from her potential allies, both in Asia and elsewhere. On this broader diplomatic level, the USSR's success has been limited, at best.

Among Communist Countries

Within the communist bloc, Moscow tried repeatedly to convene a meeting that would expel China from the socialist community, without success. In June 1969, the USSR proved unable to convince an International Meeting of Communist and Workers' Parties held in Moscow to castigate Peking, even at the height of the border tensions between

the two countries.[93]   At an oft-postponed meeting of European Communist Parties that convened in early 1976, Moscow again failed to
secure any agreement on the China issue.[94]   Indeed, this latter convocation formally endorsed the right of each country to pursue its own
path to socialism without interference from others—a far cry from
what the Kremlin had originally hoped to achieve at the conference.
Paradoxically, then, this 1976 meeting seemed to mark the end of the
tightly knit socialist bloc that had existed at least in theory since
the end of the 1940s—a demise that had been proclaimed by vice premier
Teng Hsiao-p'ing in his speech at the United Nations on April 10, 1974.[95]

Soviet inability to isolate China within the bloc has stemmed from
a range of causes.   In part, China's active and reasonably flexible
bloc diplomacy has played a significant role.   China virtually christened
its policy of sending ambassadors back to posts after the Cultural Revolution in May-July 1969 with the appointment of the talented Keng Piao
(later head of the PRC's International Liaison Department, in charge of
CCP relations with all other communist parties) to Romania.[96]   Subsequent Chinese diplomacy in Eastern Europe has included a Chinese National
People's Congress goodwill delegation visit to Romania and Yugoslavia in
May 1977,[97] and other enticements to Yugoslavia.[98]   More fundamentally,

---

[93]Speeches to this conference, which convened from June 5-17, are
translated in *CDSP*, July 2, 9, 16, 23, and 30.   The final document
passed by the conference is translated in *CDSP*, August 6, 1969, pp.
14-24.

[94]The anti-China theme sounded by Moscow in anticipation of this
conference is clearly reflected in, for instance, the *Kommunist* Editorial, August 12, 1975, cited in *FBIS/USSR*, September 24, 1975, pp.
C-1-28, which lays out in its fullest form Moscow's critique of current
Chinese domestic and foreign policy.   None of this anti-China rhetoric
found its way into the official documents of the conference when it
convened, however.

[95]Text in the Supplement to *Peking Review*, No. 15, April 12, 1974.

[96]Gurtov, op. cit., pp. 364-365.

[97]For reviews of this visit, see *New China News Agency*, May 18,
1977, cited in *FBIS/PRC*, May 19, 1977, pp. A-9-11; and *New China News
Agency*, May 26, 1977, cited in *FBIS/PRC*, May 27, 1977, pp. A-9-11.

[98]Sino-Yugoslav relations are treated in detail in A. Ross Johnson, "Yugoslavia and the Sino-Soviet Conflict: The Shifting Triangle,
1948-1974," *Studies in Comparative Communism*, Spring/Summer 1974, pp.

however, the Soviet Union's efforts have stumbled over the desires
of West European communist parties, who for the first time in decades
are within sight of sharing power in their countries, to demonstrate
their complete independence of Moscow's dictates--a *sine qua non* if they
hope to convert their popular following into political participation
in their respective governments. Likewise, almost all the countries
in East Europe retain at least a passive interest in not discouraging
efforts to secure their own freedom of maneuver as they seek to solve
their different economic and social problems, each in their own way.
While some of these countries (such as Poland and Czechoslovakia) have
little incentive to seek a decisive break with the USSR, therefore,
they clearly stand to gain by the efforts of others to widen the scope
of permissible leeway in each country's domestic and foreign policy.
Thus, in the final analysis, Moscow's inability to read China out of
the communist movement stems more from the particular interests of the
communist parties of East and West Europe than from either China's
diplomatic finesse or Moscow's lack thereof. The few minor signs of
a tightening in bloc relations on an anti-China basis--for instance,
Moscow's success in negotiating new treaties with Czechoslovakia,
Romania, and the German Democratic Republic (GDR) that call for mutual
aid in the event of attack on either from *any* quarter[99]--barely warrant
mention beside this larger trend.

The Soviets have likewise enjoyed little success in their attempt
to isolate China from the other ruling Asian communist parties, even
though the communist victories in Indochina seem to have left Moscow
in a stronger position than Peking. As of 1978, the Kremlin enjoys
closer ties to Vietnam and Laos. China, by contrast, has cultivated
its relationship with the Democratic Republic of Campuchea (Cambodia).

184-203. See also the documentation on President Tito's September
1977 visit to the PRC in *FBIS/PRC*: August 31, 1977, pp. A-10-19;
September 2, 1977, p. A-6; and September 9, 1977, pp. A-16-17.

[99]The USSR-GDR treaty was signed on October 7, 1975: *New York
Times*, October 8, 1975. The USSR-Czechoslovakia treaty was signed
on May 6, 1970: *New York Times*, May 7, 1970. The Soviet-Romanian
treaty was signed on July 8, 1970: *New York Times*, July 9, 1970.
The preamble to the Soviet-Romanian treaty leaves somewhat ambiguous
whether the treaty could cover a Sino-Soviet military conflict.

Fundamentally, however, the winner in Southeast Asia is neither Moscow nor Peking but Hanoi. China's relations with Hanoi are somewhat strained, especially concerning Vietnam's treatment of overseas Chinese, sovereignty over the islands in the South China Sea,[100] and China's position regarding the Vietnam-Cambodia border dispute.[101] Nevertheless, Hanoi's closer relationship with the Soviet Union seems to be built on the dual considerations of Moscow's greater ability to provide Vietnam with reconstruction aid and its greater distance from Vietnam itself. The Soviet Union almost certainly hopes Hanoi will grant it major port facilities for the Soviet Navy--but the Vietnamese leadership has remained unwilling to permit this.[102] Laos, in turn, is far more responsive to the desires of Vietnam than to those of Moscow, and there is almost no chance of significant change in this sphere in the foreseeable future.[103] Thus, although Hanoi--especially in league with Moscow--is likely to deny China major direct influence over the states of Indochina, the end of American involvement in this area has not allowed Moscow to establish a presence that is directly threatening to the People's Republic of China.[104]

---

[100] On Hanoi's power in the post-Vietnam War era in the region, see Pauker, op. cit. Some of the documentation on the PRC's dispute with Vietnam over the overseas Chinese is presented in *Peking Review*, No. 27, July 7, 1978, pp. 27-30. China has repeatedly made forceful comments about its sovereignty over the Hsisha, Nansha, Tungsha, and Chungsha Islands in the South China Sea, and it has evidently tried to increase the permanent PRC presence in some of these islands over the past few years. See, for example, *Peking Review*: No. 3, January 18, 1974, p. 3; No. 4, January 25, 1974, pp. 3-4; No. 14, April 5, 1974, p. 8; and *New York Times*, November 27, 1975. China seized control of the Paracel Islands in a combined arms operation from South Vietnam on January 20, 1974. Hanoi claims these islands, now that it exercises control over all of Vietnam.

[101] *New York Times*, February 23, 1978.

[102] *New York Times*, December 3, 1976.

[103] Hanoi's forces have enjoyed a major presence in Laos in recent years, and the Laotian communist leadership is generally responsive to the desires of their Vietnamese compatriots. See, for example, *New York Times*, December 14, 1976.

[104] For an analysis that generally parallels that in the text, see Sheldon W. Simon, "Peking and Indochina: The Perplexity of Victory," *Asian Survey*, May 1976, pp. 401-410. A further brief but informative summary of Soviet relations with the three Indochina states during

In Northeast Asia, both China and the Soviet Union have courted
Kim Il-sung, each achieving a measure of success. Peking has often
accorded North Korea pride of place among communist countries, and
there is every indication that Sino-Korean relations are on a solid
footing.[105] Moscow, too, has maintained good relations with Pyongyang,
however, primarily through providing it with sophisticated weaponry.
It seems clear that the net sum of this situation leaves neither Moscow nor Peking with any real control over Kim Il-sung, especially as
regards Sino-Soviet relations. Kim would not swing decisively in
Peking's favor because of his dependence on the Soviet Union to match
the sophisticated weaponry that the United States has made available
to Seoul. Likewise, Korea's extremely close economic ties with China,
including use of electricity generated in the PRC and oil flowing
through the recently completed Sino-Korean pipeline,[106] preclude Kim's
shifting dramatically in favor of the Soviets. Thus, throughout Asia
as well as in Europe the Soviet Union has little to show in terms of
concrete successes for its policy of trying to isolate Peking within
the community of ruling communist parties and states.

Non-Communist Asia

The Soviet Union's policy toward non-communist Asia has generally
paralleled its policy toward the West during the 1970s. Moscow has
stressed the theme of détente and the need for all nations to band together to preserve a structure of peace. In Asia, however, this policy

---

1974-1975 is contained in *The Soviet Union, 1974-1975*, C. Hurst and
Company, London, 1976, pp. 254-257.

[105]The Chinese, for instance, listed the condolences from North
Korea first in their coverage of the mourning for the death of Mao
Tse-tung: *Peking Review*, No. 40, September 30, 1976, p. 19. Also,
Hua Kuo-feng made his first foreign tour to North Korea: *Peking Re-
view*, No. 19, May 12, 1978, pp. 6-8.

[106]The Sino-Korean pipeline opened in 1975-1976 and through it
the PRC provides Korea with oil at concessionary rates.

has served goals distinctly different from those in Europe. On its
western front, the USSR has sought through the policy of détente to
firm up the boundaries extant at the end of World War II and to provide a basis for the increased movement of technology and capital from
Western Europe and the United States to the USSR. In Asia, by contrast, the USSR faces the problem of *establishing a legitimate presence*
in the region in the first place. It has used the vehicle of a proposed Asian Collective Security pact to promote this goal.

The Asian Collective Security System. Soviet advocacy of Asian
collective security began in mid-1969 and has had a checkered history
ever since.[107] The declared object of this system is to involve all
Asian states--including the USSR--in a multilateral collective security
system that would guarantee existing state boundaries through some yet-
to-be-explained system of multilateral action. The Soviets have indicated their willingness, moreover, to work toward this multilateral
system through a series of bilateral treaties with the states in the
area. This, for instance, served as the intellectual framework for
the conclusion of the Soviet-Indian treaty in August 1971.[108]

A system of collective security in Asia would hold several obvious
advantages for the USSR. It would serve Moscow as a legitimate vehicle
for injecting Soviet power into any major dispute between Asian coun-
tries--and indeed could provide ample justification for the USSR to
maintain military resources in the region to be used in the interests
of "collective security" when needed. Concomitantly, it would recognize the Soviet Union as an Asian state while excluding the United
States from this sphere, thereby possibly abetting Moscow's effort to

---

[107]The best available short history of the Soviet Union's Asian
Collective Security Proposal is Arnold Horelick, *The Soviet Union's
"Asian Collective Security" Proposal: A Club in Search of Members*,
The Rand Corporation, P-5195, March 1974. Haselkorn treats Soviet
concepts of collective security on a worldwide scale in Haselkorn,
op. cit. See also Robert C. Horn, "Changing Soviet Policies and Sino-
Soviet Competition in Southeast Asia," *Orbis*, Vol. XVII, Summer 1973,
esp. pp. 524-526.

[108]The Soviet-Indian 20-year treaty of peace, friendship, and
cooperation was signed on August 9, 1971, in the rush of Soviet diplomatic efforts that occurred during the month following the announcement
of Henry Kissinger's first visit to China in July 1971.

supplant the United States in Asia in the wake of the U.S. withdrawal from Indochina. In this connection, the PRC in the past has sought to exclude the Soviet Union from participation in Asian forums on the basis that it is a European power.[109] Additionally, in Asia as in Europe the Soviet Union controls territory that is under challenge by others, from the border dispute with the PRC to continuing conflict with Japan over Soviet occupation of the four Kurile Islands--Habomai, Shikotan, Kunashiri, and Etorofu--since the end of World War II. Soviet statements on a collective security system to date use wording that suggests that current boundaries in Asia should generally be presumed to be legitimate as they are. Lastly, the Soviets use China's strong objections to an Asian collective security system as a vehicle for asserting that China's aims in Asia must be expansionist and bellicose--otherwise, why should Peking object to a universal system whose sole purpose is to maintain peace and harmony? The Soviets stress, in this regard, that Peking is welcome to join this system if it pleases.[110] China's leaders, however, clearly recognize the unilateral advantages to the USSR of this system and have opposed the idea as being essentially anti-Chinese from the start.[111]

To date, the Soviets have succeeded in obtaining no more than one or two mildly favorable references to the system by officials in India and Iran, with no indication that the leaders of any Asian country other than the Mongolian People's Republic will move seriously toward forming such a system in the foreseeable future.[112] It bears remembering, however, that as of the mid-1960s the Helsinki Accords

---

[109] The Chinese used this pretext, for instance, to argue against Soviet participation in the scheduled Bandung Two conference in 1965, which was to include only the states of Asia, Africa, and Latin America. On this conference and its eventual cancellation, see Taylor, op. cit., pp. 100-102.

[110] Many of these points are from Horelick, op. cit.

[111] The Chinese castigate the Soviet "collective security" proposal in Asia as a vehicle of Soviet expansionism and hegemonism. See, for instance, "Soviet Social-Imperialists Covet Southeast Asia," *Peking Review*, No. 33, August 15, 1975, pp. 20-21.

[112] Horelick, op. cit.; *The Soviet Union, 1973*, C. Hurst and Company, London, 1975, pp. 157-161.

would have seemed wild fantasy to most leaders of Europe, and thus the Soviets may be viewing the Asian collective security proposal as an idea whose time will come. *Ad interim*, it costs Moscow little to articulate this notion and permits the USSR to pose as the promoter of peace and security in Asia in contrast to a presumably more aggressive Peking.

Bilateral Efforts. The Soviet Union has moved bilaterally as well as multilaterally to improve its relations with various non-communist Asian countries during the 1970s. The most important of these efforts have been directed toward Japan and India, each with mixed results.

The continuing Soviet occupation of the four Kurile Islands that previously belonged to Japan is the major obstacle to warmer Soviet-Japanese relations. These islands are not of major strategic or economic value to either the USSR or Japan. Nevertheless, Moscow remains fearful of the Pandora's box it might open should it relinquish its hold on any of the territories it acquired as a result of World War II, and thus it regards these islands as nonnegotiable. The Soviet Navy may also argue that the islands are important to their position in the Western Pacific. Tokyo, in turn, is trapped by Japanese public opinion, which will not tolerate a peace treaty with the Soviet Union unless the islands are returned.[113] China, naturally, loses no chance to fan Japanese popular sentiment over this territorial issue-- in part, to help justify its own territorial claims against the USSR, but more importantly to maximize friction in Soviet-Japanese relations. Indeed, Peking has gone so far in these efforts that then foreign

_____

[113]The strength of Moscow's desire to improve relations with Japan has quite clearly varied inversely with the Kremlin's fear of Sino-U.S. rapprochement at the expense of the USSR's interests. Soviet warmth toward Japan seemed to peak, for instance, during Gromyko's January 22-28, 1972, trip to Tokyo, virtually on the eve of Richard Nixon's historic first visit to China that February: *New York Times*, January 29, 1972. Since then, Soviet-Japanese relations have faltered largely over the issues enumerated in the text. On Soviet-Japanese relations, see *The Soviet Union, 1973*, pp. 163-164; *The Soviet Union, 1974-1975*, pp. 135-137 and 257-259; Horelick, op. cit., pp. 16-18; and William Barnds, "Japan and Its Mainland Neighbours: An End to Equidistance?," *International Affairs*, London, Vol. 52, No. 1, January 1976, pp. 27-38.

minister Miyazawa on July 9, 1976, protested in the Diet China's
"interference in Japan's domestic affairs."[114] Given the conflicting
interests and issues at stake, it seems very unlikely that either side
can remove this stumbling block to more felicitous Soviet-Japanese
relations in the foreseeable future.

Soviet policy toward Japan also has suffered from historically
induced schizophrenia. On the one hand, Moscow wants Japanese assistance in developing the immense natural resources of Eastern Siberia,
which in turn will strengthen the USSR's position near the China
border. Major Japanese participation in this effort might also provide a strong incentive to make Japan lean toward Moscow should Sino-
Soviet relations deteriorate further. Still, the Kremlin leadership
remains wary of any strong Japanese presence on the Northeast Asian
mainland in view of the repeated challenge that Japan has made to
Soviet interests in the area since the late 19th century. Thus,
Moscow has been inconsistent over time about the terms it will offer
for Japanese participation in the exploitation of Siberian resources.

Japan has adopted a policy of studied neutrality between the USSR
and China--willing to trade and enjoy diplomatic relations with each
but trying to favor neither.[115] Given Japan's tremendous economic
presence in Asia and its strategic location, however, even slight
shifts in Tokyo's position on Sino-Soviet affairs could have important
repercussions, and both the USSR and the PRC will, therefore, continue
to woo their island neighbor.

India has long cast its lot more with the Soviet Union than with
China, and its Soviet connection is now embodied in a treaty of
friendship and alliance that obligates the Soviet Union to come to
India's assistance in case of attack. Soviet-Indian trade has grown
greatly during the 1970s,[116] as India has tolerated the Soviet buildup

---

[114]For an example of China's propaganda over this issue, see
Peking Review, No. 35, August 29, 1975, pp. 10-12; Peking's response
to Miyazawa's criticism is in *Peking Review*, No. 30, July 23, 1976,
pp. 15-16.

[115]Barnds, op. cit.

[116]Soviet-Indian trade grew from 364.9 million rubles in 1970 to
615.5 million rubles in 1974. *The Soviet Union, 1974-1975*, p. 157.

of naval forces in the Indian Ocean. Thus, since the early 1970s, the Soviet Union has viewed India as its major ally in non-communist Asia and has benefited from the military concessions the Indian government has been willing to make. It seems likely, however, that India under Morarji Desai will not allow itself to become dependent on the Soviet Union economically, politically, or militarily. Moscow cannot export needed food to India, and exchange rate disputes between the two countries were severe even under Indira Gandhi's Administration.[117] More fundamentally, moreover, India's past history of maintaining a posture of rough nonalliance--broken perhaps for periods of time by increasing dependence on one great power, only to be reestablished within a half decade--is likely to provide the best guide to Indian actions of the future. Not surprisingly, then, in early 1978 India hosted a Chinese trade delegation[118] and has recently sought closer ties with Washington.

In sum, New Delhi will probably continue to experience friction in its relations with the PRC and may even sanction a Soviet presence in the Indian Ocean indefinitely. But India's willingness to cooperate in larger elements of Soviet foreign policy--such as the USSR desire to form an Asian Collective Security System--will remain very doubtful.

Two other states warrant mention in connection with Soviet efforts to court non-communist Asian powers. In Singapore, the Soviets have use of port facilities that are important for maintaining a naval presence in the area. Lee Kuan-yew will keep a sharp eye on Soviet activities around Singapore, and this limited noncombat use of port facilities is probably all that the USSR can count on there. Lee's China policy, however, which astutely balances off Taiwan and Peking, will not be affected by Soviet pressures and preferences.

---

[117] *The Soviet Union, 1974-1975*, pp. 164-165, 251-252.

[118] *New China News Agency*, February 7, 1978, cited in *FBIS/PRC*, February 8, 1978, p. A-10. India reestablished relations at the ambassadorial level with China in 1976: Hong Kong AFP, April 15, 1976, cited in *FBIS/PRC*, April 16, 1976, p. A-8; Hong Kong AFP, April 16, 1976, cited in *FBIS/PRC*, April 19, 1976, p. A-9.

Taiwan is another object of potential Soviet involvement. There
are periodic hints, some emanating from esoteric communications in the
Soviet media,[119] that the USSR and Taiwan are feeling out the possibility of some sort of relationship. Kuomintang leader Chiang Ching-
kuo's own education in the Soviet Union and marriage to a Russian
provide tantalizing tidbits for speculation about the possibility of
a Soviet-Taiwan connection in the wake of normalization of Sino-U.S.
relations. While this turn of events cannot be ruled out completely,
however, its prospects are remote. A Taiwan liaison would indicate
that Moscow had completely written off the possibility of improving
relations with Peking--not a likely prospect in the near-term future.
Also, Taiwan's anti-communism is too deeply embedded to tolerate such
a radical shift in external alignments easily. Nevertheless, the
Soviet Union will retain a substantial interest (along with Japan) in
preventing reunification of Taiwan with the PRC if this can be done
without paying too high a political price. For if Taiwan does rejoin
the mainland, it will not only contribute significantly to the development of the PRC's economy[120] but will also provide Peking with a powerful incentive to expand its naval capacity to the point where it can
adequately defend the waters between China's coast and its newly
acquired unsinkable (albeit also unmovable) aircraft carrier astride
Soviet and Japanese sea lanes in the Pacific. While Soviet declaratory
policy will almost certainly, as in the past, favor Taiwan's reunification with the PRC, therefore, Moscow will continue to hope that the
day of this reconciliation will remain far in the future. It probably
will not act affirmatively, however, to realize this hope.

In sum, the Soviet Union has tried to increase its presence in
non-communist Asia through both bilateral and multilateral approaches.

---

[119]The Soviet media occasionally deal with affairs in Taiwan in
a way that leaves open the possibility that the Soviets might regard
the Kuomintang government there as in proper and long-term control
of the island. See, for example, the report on a recent Novosti press
bulletin in *Christian Science Monitor*, December 7, 1973. The Peking
media invariably pick up the slightest hint that the Soviets regard
the current situation on Taiwan as legitimate and issue a major propaganda blast in response.

[120]Taiwan would immediately become China's richest province in
both capital and human resources.

It has achieved limited political success, most noticeably with India, and it has acquired naval docking, repair and maintenance, and other privileges around the Indian Ocean. Still, almost all non-communist states in the area view Moscow with suspicion, and no Asian state is likely to structure its own China policy in the future around the desires and/or dictates of the Kremlin. The USSR has thus enjoyed only marginal success in Asia as it has sought to establish a legitimate presence for itself and drive a wedge between the PRC and other states in the area.

The U.S. Connection

China has figured strongly in the Soviet Union's relations with the United States since 1969. Moscow has sought the twin objectives of securing the USSR's western flank so that it could concentrate more resources toward dealing with its adversary to the east while denying the United States to China as an ally in an anti-Soviet axis. The United States has clearly outmaneuvered the Kremlin leaders in this latter quest, however, and on balance Moscow has found itself more a captive of Sino-U.S. politics than a shaper of that relationship.

With respect to the former objective, the balance sheet on the Soviet Union's policy of détente with the United States is mixed, and reasonable and knowledgeable people can and do differ over the costs and benefits of that policy for each side. Nevertheless, there is no question that the Nixon and Ford Administrations made détente a key element in their foreign policies and that the Soviet concern over China and Sino-U.S. relations has made the Kremlin more willing to pursue this policy during these years. Efforts to stabilize boundaries and defuse tensions in Europe formed a natural part of that process.[121]

On a broader scale, there is no question that China has played a major role in shaping the Soviet Union's policies toward the United

---

[121]The Helsinki Conference on Security and Cooperation in Europe marked the culmination of Moscow's efforts in this sphere. The documents of the conference declared that all the participating states agreed that current European boundaries could be changed only by peaceful means. *New York Times*, July 30, 1975.

States. For example, the Soviet commitment to the SALT negotiations was sealed at a meeting between Soviet Ambassador Dobrynin, Richard Nixon, and Henry Kissinger during which the three men agreed to commence the talks.[122] As noted above, this gathering occurred on October 20, 1969--the very day that the Sino-Soviet border negotiations commenced in Peking. Moscow may well have felt that it could not afford to enter into the SALT negotiations with the United States until it had also begun a process of negotiation with the PRC. In the future, each set of talks could be used to try to gain leverage in the other.

As also noted above, moreover, in 1972, 1973, and 1974 Moscow evidently timed its offers to the PRC in the "border" talks according to a calculus based largely on Soviet-U.S. summit diplomacy.[123] More fundamentally, the whole thrust of the Soviet policy of détente with the United States undercut the fundamental premise of those in China who argued for détente with the United States--i.e., that Soviet-U.S. "contention" was so great that one superpower could be used effectively to ward off the danger from the other.[124] It is not clear how accurately the Soviets perceived this debate in China at the time and structured their policy around it.[125] Whether intentionally or not, however, the Soviet efforts over these years to reach an accommodation with the United States weakened the case of Mao Tse-tung and Chou En-lai in China as these leaders argued for maintaining and expanding the opening to the United States.[126]

---

[122] Kalb and Kalb, op. cit., pp. 114-115.

[123] See p. 17 above.

[124] For details of the origins of this debate, see Gottlieb, op. cit. Details of the continuing debate are given in Peter L. Sargent and Jack H. Harris, "Chinese Assessment of the Superpower Relationship, 1972-1974," The BDM Corporation, Virginia, June 1975. The relation of SALT to this debate is explored in Michael Pillsbury, *SALT on the Dragon: Chinese Views of the Soviet-American Strategic Balance*, The Rand Corporation, P-5457, April 1975.

[125] Borisov and Koloskov (op. cit.), for instance, give no hint that they perceived a debate in these terms taking place in Peking. Other Soviet analyses are likewise devoid of explicit treatment of this dimension of the Chinese political debate.

[126] See, for instance, the analysis of the political debate in China during 1973-1976 given in Sec. II of this report.

It was in 1969 and 1972, in any event, that Soviet policy toward the United States seems to have been affected most directly by Sino-Soviet concerns. In 1969, the Soviets had proven reluctant to commence SALT negotiations with Washington until the October 20 agreement just mentioned.[127] Several China-related problems may have dictated both the initial strategy and the subsequent *volte-face*.

First, Moscow may not have wanted to engage in strategic arms negotiations with the Nixon White House while they were so obviously worried about the possibility of imminent war on their eastern front. The beginning of border talks with the Chinese marked a major turning point away from the slide toward war and thus relieved the Kremlin of this concern. Indeed, the start of the Sino-Soviet negotiations re-structured Soviet incentives concerning SALT in several additional ways. It lessened the potential political cost to Moscow of negotiating with the "imperialists" while the USSR was on the brink of war with a country that other socialist states had repeatedly refused to exclude from the communist community.[128] It also provided an additional spur to the Chinese to be accommodating in the border talks lest Peking's two major adversaries--the Soviet Union and the United States--should intensify their "collusion" in the strategic arena to the detriment of the PRC. Thus, in all likelihood the Kosygin/Chou agreement to commence border talks affected the timing of the USSR's agreement to begin the SALT talks even if it did not determine the basic decision to discuss strategic arms limitations with the United States in the first place.

In late 1971-early 1972, the Soviet Union finally lost its ability to deal separately with China and the United States, secure in the knowledge that there would be no major reconciliation between its two major adversaries. The Kissinger trip to China in July 1971

---

[127] See John Newhouse, *Cold Dawn: The Story of SALT*, Holt, Rinehart and Winston, New York, 1973, for the best available summary of the SALT I negotiations.

[128] On the war scare, see Sec. II, footnote 10, below. The most recent refusal had been at the June 5-17 International Meeting of Communist and Workers' Parties in Moscow, as noted above.

and announcement of the forthcoming Nixon journey to Peking in February 1972 plunged Moscow into trilateral diplomacy in which its tie to
Peking formed the weak link. The reverberations in Soviet policy were
clear, as Moscow pushed for its own summit meeting with Richard Nixon
and structured its posture in the SALT negotiations accordingly. The
importance Moscow now attached to consolidating its relationship with
Washington was dramatically illustrated by Brezhnev's willingness to
embrace Nixon at a time when U.S. war planes had just mined Haiphong
Harbor and were ravaging the cities and countryside of the Democratic
Republic of Vietnam.[129]

In the early 1970s, therefore, concern about China strongly affected Soviet-U.S. relations, and the general trend of great power interaction in turn had a major impact on the foreign policy debate in
Peking. In the years after 1974, however, this dual interaction was
much less evident. Essentially, by that time Moscow had gained greater
confidence in the limits of the Sino-U.S. rapprochement--that it could
lead to the establishment of diplomatic relations and to greater Chinese tolerance/encouragement for a continued U.S. military presence
in Asia but was unlikely to produce active military and intelligence
cooperation on a scale that would seriously threaten the Soviet Union.[130]

---

[129] Hanoi, evidently distressed at the sight of U.S. summitry with
its two major benefactors during the spring of 1972, committed all but
four of its remaining 15 divisions to battle in the South on March 31:
Taylor, op cit., p. 183. President Nixon responded by activating
mines in North Vietnam's rivers and greatly expanding the bombing campaign against the North. Brezhnev, nevertheless, did not cancel out
the summit, which took place on May 22-30 and produced seven agreements, including the one on strategic arms limitation (SALT I). Texts
in *Los Angeles Times*, May 30, 1972.

[130] The initial announcement of Henry Kissinger's secret visit to
Peking in July 1971 stunned the Soviets, who did not have a clear
sense of just how far the Sino-U.S. rapprochement might go. The first
official Soviet response to this dramatic turn of events, for instance,
did not come until 10 days after the July 15 Peking/Washington announcement: Aleksandrov article in *Pravda*, July 25, 1971, cited in *FBIS/USSR*,
International, July 26, 1971, pp. D-1-6. By 1974, however, Watergate
had so thoroughly undermined Richard Nixon's political position in the
United States that further dramatic movement on the Sino-U.S. front was
virtually out of the question. The Ford Administration itself approached
the China question with caution, and by the fall of 1975 it was evident
that the President would not take the political risk of normalizing

At the same time, China had seen its thesis about continued Soviet-U.S. contention confirmed repeatedly--in the October War of 1973, the Jackson Amendment that upset the U.S.-Soviet trade agreement, the Soviet intervention in Angola, U.S. concern over the Soviet role in post-Salazar Portugal, Soviet action in the horn of Africa, and so forth. Thus, the components of the triangle are now sufficiently set in place that it is no longer possible (if it ever was) to fine-tune these sets of relationships by the subtle actions of any one power. Peking's conception of the relationship is unlikely to be significantly altered by anything less than a major diminution in U.S. military spending, which clearly will not occur under President Carter.

Competing for the Third World

Turning away from great power interaction, there has been much Sino-Soviet sparring in the Third World, although this is an arena more tangential to Sino-Soviet relations than are the others discussed above. Both the Soviet Union and China portray themselves as natural allies of the Third World countries--the USSR basing this claim on common opposition to imperialism, and China basing it on shared economic and political interests in comparison with the two superpowers and the rest of the industrialized world. Each is generous in the time and energy it devotes to debunking the other's claim to mutual interests with other Third World countries, and the propaganda exchanges in this sphere are legion. The meeting rooms of the United Nations and its agencies have often resounded with the harsh epithets used in these exchanges.

---

relations with Peking in view of the increasingly likely threat of a challenge from the political Right for the Republican Party nomination. Numerous other irritants, discussed below in this report, also had emerged by 1974-1975 to bolster Soviet confidence that fundamental obstacles remained in the way of a Sino-U.S. alliance against the Soviet Union. As Michael Pillsbury has noted, there continues to be disagreement in Moscow regarding the chances for substantial Sino-U.S. military cooperation: Michael Pillsbury, "U.S.-China Military Ties?," *Foreign Policy*, Fall 1975, pp. 52-55. The weight of opinion now, however, seems to lie on the side of those who doubt such a development.

Beyond verbal cannonades, however, it is the Soviet Union that possesses the resources most needed by Third World countries--machinery to export, large-scale credits, military goods, and so forth. Where the Soviet Union chooses to concentrate its resources on a given country, China usually cannot compete--and Peking has shown its *de facto* recognition of this situation in both the Middle East and Africa.[131] Thus, while the Chinese may enjoy the more reasonable claim to interests consonant with those of the other Third World countries, this claim has not easily translated into a preferred position over the Soviet Union within these countries.

In some areas, the Soviet Union is using its aid to Third World countries to increase its global military capabilities in ways that are directly relevant to China's interests. This is most striking in West Asia and Northeast Africa. In the latter, Soviet basing rights for a while provided for far greater potential logistical and military support for India in the unlikely event of a confrontation with China than was the case in the 1960s.[132] Insofar as an increase in the Soviet Union's power anywhere is viewed as a potential threat from

---

[131] The Chinese have *de facto* chosen to concentrate their military and economic resources on countries that Moscow has not made a serious effort to woo in both the Middle East and Africa. On the Middle East, see Jane Lieberthal, "China in the Middle East," Research Paper prepared for the Foreign Policy Research Institute, October 1972. China's policy toward Egypt illustrates this point, in that the PRC did not try to compete with the USSR in Egypt while the latter enjoyed good relations with Cairo. As soon as the Cairo-Moscow connection soured, however, Peking moved in extremely rapidly to try to make the rift more permanent and to benefit from it. On China's actions toward Egypt at this time, see *New China News Agency*, March 15, 1976, cited in *FBIS/PRC*, March 18, 1976, pp. A-24-28; *Jen-min Jih-pao*, March 19, 1976; *New China News Agency*, March 18, 1976, cited in *FBIS/PRC*, March 19, 1976, pp. A-23-30; Peking Domestic Service, March 20, 1976, cited in *FBIS/PRC*, March 22, 1976, pp. A-11-15; *New China News Agency*, April 21, 1976; Paris, AFP, April 21, 1976, cited in *FBIS/PRC*, April 22, 1976, pp. A-1-11; and Hong Kong, AFP, April 29, 1976, cited in *FBIS/PRC*, April 29, 1976, p. A-11.

[132] Haselkorn spells out this argument with particular reference to air supply routes via Egypt with a refueling stop in Somalia and/or the People's Democratic Republic of Yemen or alternatively over Syria with a refueling stop in Iraq. Haselkorn, op. cit., pp. 240-241. The Soviet-Egyptian and Soviet-Somali ruptures occurred after publication

Peking (because it weakens Peking's *de facto* allies in the West), then certainly even the USSR's successes in Western Africa that increase Moscow's capacity to interdict Western oil supplies must be viewed with disquiet in the Forbidden City. China's strongly negative reaction to Washington's decision to pull out of Angola and essentially cede it to the Soviet-backed Popular Movement for the Liberation of Angola highlights the PRC's sensitivity to this indirect but salient dimension of Soviet power.[133]

In sum, the Soviet Union's resources allow it pride of place in the competition with China for influence in the Third World. For the USSR, this competition has both political and military dimensions that are relevant to China's interests. China must devote its energy to trying to limit the USSR's penetration of the Third World through both propaganda and the use of aid on highly advantageous terms where the USSR is not already heavily involved.[134] Where Moscow has suffered a major political setback, such as in the forced withdrawal of Soviet forces from Egypt, China is ready to move quickly to capitalize on this Soviet failure and dramatize the difference between Soviet and Chinese approaches to the country concerned.[135] Overall, however, this Third World arena of Sino-Soviet competition has been considerably less important than the other spheres discussed above.

---

of Haselkorn's article, which may now serve more to highlight one aspect of possible Soviet strategy in aid to developing countries than the real current configuration of Soviet forces and capabilities.

[133] For the PRC's reaction to Angola, see, for example, *New China News Agency*, January 11, 1976, cited in *FBIS/PRC*, January 12, 1976, p. A-2; *Jen-min Jih-pao* Editorial, February 4, 1976; *New China News Agency*: February 4, 1976, cited in *FBIS/PRC*, February 4, 1976, p. A-3; April 1, 1976, cited in *FBIS/PRC*, April 1, 1976, p. A-1; and June 22, 1976, cited in *FBIS/PRC*, June 23, 1976, p. A-2.

[134] On China's policies of foreign aid, see *Communist Aid to Less Developed Countries of the Free World, 1975*, Central Intelligence Agency, ER 76-10372U, July 1976. This aid is usually given on highly favorable terms (frequently with deferred repayment schedules, little or no interest, and few strings attached): Kurt Müller, *The Foreign Aid Programs of the Soviet Bloc and Communist China: An Analysis*, Walker and Company, New York, 1967, pp. 234-237.

[135] See footnote 131 above.

Conclusion

The basic Soviet policy toward the PRC has thus been one of containment, both bilaterally and multilaterally, in the communist bloc, in Asia, among the great powers, and in the Third World. Moscow has scored few major diplomatic successes in this effort, but its generally increasing presence on the world stage--and especially in Asia--has given the Chinese increasing cause for concern. Within this framework of containment, Moscow has offered China a vastly improved bilateral relationship if Peking should choose to move in that direction. The basic contours of this relationship, at least in its initial stages, have been made clear by the Soviets in their border negotiations with China, and they have indicated that the ball is now in Peking's court. The successors to Mao must play this game, however, fully aware that the Soviet presence in Asia has been growing and will continue to increase for the foreseeable future.

II. CHINA'S POLICY TOWARD THE USSR, 1969-1978

Peking's strategy has been formulated in dynamic interaction with the Soviet actions outlined in Sec. I. Additionally, China, unlike the Soviet Union during this period, suffered wrenching domestic political change--the winding down of the Cultural Revolution, the purge of Lin Piao and his followers, a major program of rehabilitation of those who had fallen during the GPCR, continuing battles for the succession between different groups at the Center, and purge and counter-purge during the year surrounding the death of Mao and three other leading members of the Politburo.[1] Thus, on the Chinese side one must pay particular attention to the entanglement of Soviet policy in this domestic political strife. There is no comparable situation--or evidence to suggest major internal disagreement over China policy--in the Soviet Union during 1969-1978.[2]

THE BILATERAL DIMENSION

Setting aside these internal Peking quarrels and treating China as a unified rational actor for the moment, China's bilateral strategy to deal with the Soviet Union has had two prongs: maintain a high state of tension in the relationship short of war; and take extraordinary measures to strengthen the PRC internally to make it, in Chou En-lai's phrase, "a piece of meat [that] is very tough . . . to bite into."[3] The Chenpao Island clashes in March 1969 created a war scare in China. As noted above, the PRC almost immediately commenced an

2 ⌀
priorities

---

[1] K'ang Sheng, Chou En-lai, and Chu Teh.

[2] This is not to say that there is no evidence of any disagreement at all on China policy in the USSR. There probably has been at least some internal debate in the USSR, for instance, about the prospects for a less anti-Soviet posture on China's part after the death of Mao Tse-tung. Still, the degree to which there has been disagreement over current policy as versus over extrapolations into the post-Mao era is rather problematic.

[3] Quote from Chou's Political Report to the Tenth Congress of the Chinese Communist Party, delivered on August 24, 1973: *Peking Review*, No. 35-36, September 7, 1973, p. 22.

emergency buildup in its armed forces and dispersal of its military production facilities out of the vulnerable Manchuria area. This buildup, clearly reflected in the PRC's military procurement budget, lasted through the latter part of 1971.[4] Almost simultaneously, the Chinese leaders greatly intensified their efforts to wind down the Cultural Revolution and to rebuild the governing civilian apparatus. This program, which had begun in 1967 and been renewed within weeks of the Soviet invasion of Czechoslovakia, accelerated dramatically after the Ninth Party Congress. The Congress, meeting in April 1969, convened in the shadow of the island clashes.[5]

Negotiations

As of the time of the Chenpao Island clashes in March 1969, the Soviet Union enjoyed a preponderance of both conventional and nuclear power along the Sino-Soviet border.[6] Given the Soviet threats and

---

[4]On the measures taken during the remainder of 1969 and early 1970, see Lu Yung-shu, op. cit. Jammes, op. cit., provides the data on the surge in military procurement, followed by the rapid decline in this item in 1971-1972. It is unclear why the military procurement fell off so rapidly, but this development probably reflects one or more of the following considerations: Lin Piao's coup attempt may have so undermined the position of the central military establishment that it was defenseless against punitive cuts in defense spending; conversely, the decision to cut defense spending, taken for whatever combination of military and political reasons, may have occurred before Lin's fall and precipitated his final drastic attempt to reverse a situation rapidly slipping out of his control; or the cuts may have been unrelated to the Lin affair and indicated either the natural completion of the rapid military buildup after the Chenpao Island clashes and/or a calculation by the central authorities that it was not cost-effective to continue major investment in increasingly technologically outmoded equipment. Jammes covers several of these points in more detail.

[5]The major review and analysis of this program to rebuild the governing apparatus at the key provincial level is Frederick Teiwes, *Provincial Leadership in China: The Cultural Revolution and Its Aftermath*, The Australian National University, Canberra, 1973. On cadre rehabilitation related to this effort, see Hong Yung Lee, "The Politics of Cadre Rehabilitation Since the Cultural Revolution," unpublished manuscript, 1977, passim.

[6]See Robinson, 1972, op. cit.; *The Military Balance, 1969-1970*, The International Institute for Strategic Studies, London, 1970; and *Washington Post*, July 11, 1969.

demands that the Chinese commence negotiations to settle their differences, why did Peking finally agree to negotiations only six months
later on September 11?

The Soviet Union presented China with three deadlines during the
course of the spring and summer of 1969. On April 11, Moscow called
for negotiations to begin by April 14 or soon thereafter.[7] When the
Chinese remained noncommittal,[8] on June 13 Moscow called for talks to
start no later than two or three months hence.[9] Exactly two months
later the Soviets launched a combined arms incursion into Sinkiang and
orchestrated a serious nuclear war scare against China.[10] Two days
before the three-month deadline of September 13, Chou En-lai and Alexei
Kosygin met in Peking and Chou agreed to start formal negotiations.
Ho Chi Minh's will, which had called on China and the USSR to resolve
their differences,[11] almost certainly made this action more palatable
to the Chinese side. So did several concessions made by Kosygin—his
willingness to travel to Peking, his consent to convene the upcoming
talks in the Chinese capital,[12] and his agreement to call the renewed

---

[7]*Pravda*, April 12, 1969, cited in *CDSP*, Vol. XXI, No. 15, April
30, 1969, p. 18.

[8]The Chinese replied on April 14, "We will give you a reply,
please calm down a little and do not get so excited." *Peking Review*,
No. 22, May 20, 1969, p. 9.

[9]*Pravda*, June 14, 1969, cited in *CDSP*, Vol. XXI, No. 24, July 9,
1969, pp. 9-13.

[10]On the incursion into Sinkiang, see *Peking Review*, No. 33,
August 15, 1969, p. 3. During August 1969 the Soviets took a number
of measures to orchestrate a nuclear war scare against China, among
which were the following: sounded out communist supporters on their
reaction to a Soviet strike against China's nuclear facilities (*New
York Times*, August 29, 1969); sounded out the U.S. government on its
likely response to a Soviet nuclear strike against the PRC (Hinton,
1975, op. cit., p. 44); appointed V. F. Tolubko to head the Far East
Military District, who in turn on August 6 published a major article
on the Soviet invasion of Manchuria in 1945 to rout the Japanese
(*New York Times*, August 8, 1969); and published a *Pravda* Editorial
that made explicit that any Sino-Soviet war would inevitably involve
nuclear weapons (*Pravda*, August 29, 1969, cited in *CDSP*, Vol. XXI,
No. 35, September 24, 1969, pp. 3-5).

[11]Text in *Peking Review*, No. 38, September 19, 1969, pp. 21-22.

[12]All previous Soviet communications had demanded that they meet
in Moscow.

talks "negotiations"[13] rather than "consultations."[14] Still, the Chinese on September 18 added critical new stumbling blocks to the negotiations in the form of agenda items that would have to be dealt with satisfactorily "first,"[15] and the talks as of 1978 still have not progressed beyond these "priority" questions.[16]

Three reasons suggest themselves for this Chinese posture of procrastination. First, the PRC leadership may have been split over the advisability of entering formal talks with Moscow and/or over the position China should take once these talks began. As indicated in Sec. I, Thomas Gottlieb and others have suggested that factional politics in Peking played a substantial role in the initiation of the first Chenpao Island clash,[17] and this notion of serious disagreement over the advisability of formal negotiations may in fact be the most powerful explanation. Relatedly, the fact that Chou En-lai evidently acceded to one set of conditions for negotiations and then the Chinese

---

[13]"Negotiations" implicitly acknowledges that there are legitimate issues at stake.

[14]The Soviets had characterized the 1964 Sino-Soviet boundary talks as "consultations," and they continued to use this terminology until September 1969. "Consultations" can involve very minor issues and the term does not necessarily imply that there need be give and take by both sides.

[15]The Chinese on the 18th seem to have added the stipulation that the "first" item on the agenda at the negotiations had to be securing the status quo along the border by withdrawal of all military forces from the "disputed" areas, defined as the areas in dispute on the maps exchanged by the two sides during the 1964 consultations: *Peking Review*, No. 41, October 10, 1969, p. 4. No text of the September 18 Chinese letter to the USSR is itself available. The Chinese have subsequently claimed that these priority agenda items had been agreed upon at the September 11 meeting of the prime ministers--e.g.; Tokyo Kyodo, January 28, 1973, cited in *FBIS/PRC*, January 29, 1973, p. A-4; Peking in Russian to USSR, November 6, 1974, cited in *FBIS/PRC*, November 7, 1974, p. A-1.

[16]Indeed, as discussed below, the Chinese in March 1978 announced another precondition to substantive border negotiations--that the USSR draw down its troops all along the border to the level that existed in the early 1960s: Paris AFP, March 23, 1978, cited in *FBIS/PRC*, March 23, 1978, p. A-23.

[17]Gottlieb, op. cit.; Brown, op. cit.; and Hinton, 1971, op. cit.

unilaterally added a far more stringent set nine days later would also suggest continuing disagreement over the proper PRC stance in these talks.[18] Second, the Chinese may simply have felt themselves at too great a disadvantage in the spring of 1969. The little available evidence indicates that the PRC sustained heavy casualties in the second Chenpao Island clash,[19] and the Peking leadership may have been reluctant to enter negotiations at a time when the other side had so clearly seized the momentum. Or third, the Chinese may have felt that a major Soviet attack was so unlikely that there was little advantage to participating in negotiations, as this might in some sense lessen Peking's ability to pose as the principled and aggrieved party. The Soviet incursions and war propaganda of the summer may have changed China's assessment of the risks in this policy, as is suggested by the fact noted above that Chou met with Kosygin and agreed to negotiations just two days before the final deadline for such agreement specified in Moscow's demarche of June 13. See p. 51

The bilateral border negotiations have, as analyzed in Sec. I, been a somewhat peculiar forum since their inception on October 20, 1969. While their major focus should be on resolving the border problem *per se*, the Soviet Union in actuality has used these talks to convey a wide range of proposals designed to lay the groundwork for improving state-to-state relations between the two countries.[20] China, for its part, has for more than seven years refused to discuss the border or any other problem on the ground that the negotiations must "first of all" produce an interim agreement that would include a withdrawal of Soviet forces from all "disputed" territories--those areas on which the Soviets and Chinese disagreed on the maps exchanged during their 1964 talks. Thus, at no time since 1969 does the public record show that any aspect of the border problem itself has been seriously negotiated at these border talks.

---

[18]The obvious alternative interpretation would assume that Peking, having secured public Soviet commitment to sit down at the bargaining table, now sought unilaterally to exact a higher price from Moscow and/or to stall the negotiations from the start.

[19]Robinson, 1972, op. cit., pp. 1189-1190.

[20]These are detailed on pp. 9-15.

China's attitude toward the talks has been consistent. Peking has argued that it cannot negotiate "under the gun" and thus that the USSR must pull back its forces from all "disputed" territories and must take other measures to insure the status quo along the border before talks on the border itself can proceed.[21] While the talks have progressed, Chinese leaders have on occasion commented on their substance, usually presenting a highly misleading picture of Chinese flexibility and Soviet intransigence. For instance, Chou En-lai at the Tenth Party Congress implied that the USSR had demanded that China cede all territory north of the Great Wall[22]--a totally inaccurate portrayal of the Soviet position in the negotiations.

Judging from China's unchanging posture in the talks, it seems likely that Peking views these negotiations as a necessary safety valve for keeping alive in the Soviet Union the hope that at some point Sino-Soviet relations can be improved through diplomacy and thus that a military attack on the PRC would be premature. The Chinese are also probably reluctant to shoulder the blame for the failure of these negotiations, and thus would prefer to see them continue sporadically rather than break them off completely. Finally, Chinese actions since 1969 have demonstrated clearly that the PRC has not expected the talks to produce real progress, as China has taken far-reaching and painful decisions in both the international and domestic arenas to contain and deter the Soviet threat since these negotiations began. Perhaps, indeed, China's leaders felt they could more openly prepare for war after these talks had started than prior to October 1969, for they realized that the Soviet Union would from that point on have a somewhat more difficult time painting the picture of a radically deranged Chinese leadership that would be necessary to justify a major Soviet military offensive.

---

[21] Peking Radio, November 6, 1974, cited in *FBIS/PRC*, November 7, 1974, p. A-1. The most thorough available statement of China's view on this issue is contained in Maxwell (unpublished paper), op. cit.

[22] *Peking Review*, Nos. 35-36, September 7, 1973, p. 23.

State-to-State Relations

China has interrupted this generally intransigent line in the border negotiations with some minor measures to place Sino-Soviet relations on other than a wartime footing. During 1970, the PRC exchanged ambassadors with the USSR[23] and agreed to an increase in Sino-Soviet trade by about 300 percent over the previous year.[24] As outlined in Sec. I, in January 1971 the Chinese engaged in the only bit of seemingly serious negotiating known to have occurred in the border talks. On January 15, the Soviet negotiators tabled a full draft of a "special treaty on the nonuse of force," the provisions of which ruled out both the use and threat of conventional, nuclear, and missile forces in solving disputes between them. China refused, as it had done before, to sign a separate treatly on the nonuse of force but proposed instead to include a suitable provision in the text of an intermediate accord on maintaining the status quo along the border. The two sides negotiated a mutually acceptable wording for this article in an accord, at which time the whole enterprise foundered over Chinese insistence that the article on nonuse of force be tied to Soviet acceptance of the PRC concept of "disputed areas."[25]

----

[23]Tolstikov arrived in Peking on October 10 and Liu Hsin-ch'uan arrived in Moscow on November 23: See, respectively, *New China News Agency* Domestic, October 10, 1970, cited in *FBIS/PRC*, October 12, 1970, p. A-6; and *New China News Agency*, November 22, 1970, cited in *FBIS/PRC*, November 23, 1970, p. A-1.

[24]Total Sino-Soviet trade in 1970 equaled 41.9 million rubles; in 1971 it equaled 138.7 million rubles; and in 1972, 210.6 million rubles (figures from successive yearbooks of *Vneshniaia Torgovlia za -- god* (Moscow). The agreement to expand trade for 1971 was signed on November 22, 1970: *New China News Agency*, November 22, 1970, cited in *Survey of China Mainland Press (SCMP)*, No. 4790, December 2, 1970. Trade has remained at roughly the 1972 figure in terms of volume of turnover ever since. See Appendix A, p. 190, for dates of all subsequent Sino-Soviet trade protocols.

[25]*Zycie Warszawy*, June 23-24, 1974, cited in *FBIS/Poland*, June 28, 1974, pp. G-1-10.

On November 6, 1974, the Chinese made what some have interpreted
as yet another show of some flexibility. In their congratulatory
telegram to Moscow on the anniversary of the October Revolution, the
Chinese for the first time publicly called for conclusion of "an
agreement on mutual nonaggression and nonuse of force against one
another,"[26] but Peking linked this, as it had done privately in January 1971, to the simultaneous conclusion of agreements to maintain
the status quo on the border and withdraw troops from "disputed areas."
Thus, this public stance amounted not to a new reasonableness but
rather only to "going public" with a proposal that had been made almost four years earlier and that Peking knew Moscow found unacceptable.

The above signs of Chinese "flexibility" are few indeed and serve
primarily to dramatize the degree to which the Chinese have remained
rigid in their "principled" stand against any sort of compromise with
the Soviet Union. The one potentially significant crack in this wall
of hostility appeared in late December 1975, when the Chinese startled
both Moscow and the West by their unanticipated release of three Soviet
helicopter pilots they had captured in Sinkiang in March 1974. This
latter case is so involved, however, that it is taken up separately
below.[27] Suffice it to say at this point that China's overall bilateral strategy toward the USSR has been to establish minimal levels
of diplomatic and commercial intercourse within the context of unyielding hostility on all broader issues.

The Military Dimension

Peking rapidly redeployed its military forces to cope with its
redesignation of the primary enemy from the United States and its
"running dogs" to "Soviet social imperialism." Initially, the PRC
simply quickly shifted forces north from primarily the Nanking and Canton
Military Regions to the Peking and the southern part of the Shenyang
Military Regions. These shifts were completed by about 1972. In terms
of nuclear missile capabilities, the Chinese evidently decided in about

---

[26] Peking Radio, November 6, 1974, cited in *FBIS/PRC*, November 7,
1974, p. A-1.

[27] Pp. 126-133.

1971 to slow down development of an ICBM capable of striking the continental United States in favor of increased concentration on development and deployment of shorter-range missiles that could reach numerous targets of importance in the USSR from the Pacific to the Ukraine.[28]

CHINA'S MULTILATERAL STRATEGY TOWARD THE USSR, 1969-1978

Multilaterally, China took dramatic actions to prevent the Soviet Union from isolating Peking in the various arenas discussed in Sec. I. This effort began with the reassignment of ambassadors to a range of communist and Third World countries in two batches during the spring of 1969 and spring of 1970, respectively.[29] The startling centerpiece in this counter-strategy, however, focused on détente with the United States as a balance against the Soviet Union in Asia and elsewhere.

The United States as a Counterweight

The question of an opening to the United States had evidently become an issue in Peking politics as early as 1966.[30] Once Richard Nixon came into office, each side moved cautiously to signal its desire for improved relations to the other, always mindful of the tremendous political costs that a misstep could entail.[31] Mao Tse-tung's dramatic invitation to a U.S. ping-pong team to come to Peking in early April 1971 shifted this process into relatively high gear,[32] as vividly conveyed by Henry Kissinger's secret visit to China in July, resulting in an agreement for Richard Nixon to visit the PRC before the following May.[33] Lin Piao's death and the purge of his top colleagues in

---

[28]Jammes, op. cit.

[29]Gurtov provides details on this: op. cit., pp. 364-365.

[30]See Gottlieb's analysis, op. cit.

[31]Some sense of this delicate minuet is conveyed in Kalb and Kalb, op. cit., pp. 216-265.

[32]Chou En-lai made clear that the invitation to the U.S. ping-pong team had been made by Chairman Mao himself. The text of the Chou interview is in *Bulletin of Concerned Asian Scholars*, Vol. III, Nos. 3-4, Summer-Fall 1971, p. 42.

[33]Kissinger visited China on July 9-11, 1971. The official announcement of this visit was made on July 16. The most complete available description of this visit is contained in Kalb and Kalb, op. cit., pp. 266-283.

the military almost certainly removed a significant obstacle to this new policy line in Peking.[34]

The Sino-U.S. relationship has experienced ups and downs since President Nixon's February 1972 visit to the Forbidden City. In the momentum of the early stages of the relationship, Sino-U.S. trade soared, numerous Americans began to visit the PRC, and the Vietnam War was resolved--at least temporarily--at the conference table in Paris. Taiwan remained an issue, but all sides likely felt that with a strong mandate behind him in his second term (secured in part by his well-publicized and widely acclaimed China diplomacy), Richard Nixon would prove willing and able to extricate the United States once and for all from China's civil war. It was such heady thoughts that inspired the Chinese to agree to the establishment of Liaison Offices--viewed as transition vehicles on the path to full normalization of relations--during Henry Kissinger's mid-February 1973 visit to the PRC.[35] Looking optimistically toward the future, the Chinese were anxious to maintain the momentum that would lead to a Taiwan settlement.

Chinese hopes were dashed upon two rocks in the increasingly turbulent waters of U.S. politics. The most important by far was Watergate, which loomed up out of a half-forgotten past to engulf the Nixon Administration in a sea of accusations that eventually dissolved

_____

[34]Gottlieb, Brown, and Taylor, in the works cited above, all argue that Lin Piao opposed Chou En-lai on the opening to the United States. Taiwan has released what is purported to be a March 1973 report delivered by Chou En-lai, in which the late premier noted that Lin Piao considered the Sino-U.S. détente to be "a betrayal of principle, the revolution and Vietnam": Hong Kong AFP, February 23, 1977, cited in *FBIS/PRC*, February 23, 1977, p. E-26.

[35]Nixon evidently stated to Chou En-lai during the President's 1972 trip to China his intention to normalize relations with Peking during his second term in office: *New York Times*, April 11, 1977. The establishment of Liaison Offices was announced in *Peking Review*, No. 8, March 23, 1973, p. 4. That the U.S. side had not expected China's offer to establish these Liaison Offices is made clear in Kalb and Kalb, op. cit., pp. 435-436. The communiqué of this visit, cited above, sets the establishment of Liaison Offices firmly into the context of "accelerating the normalization of relations."

the President's authority and forced his resignation from office. By
June 1973, the revelations of John Dean in front of a nationwide tele-
vision audience watching the Watergate Senate Hearings appear to have
forced Richard Nixon to begin thinking through the terms of a possible
defense, should Dean's accusations lead to serious attempts to impeach
the President. Nixon's past political alignments commended the logic
of depending on conservative support in the House and Senate--the kind
of support that would be damaged by any policy that seemed to "sell out"
Taiwan. Thus, domestic political events with a dynamic force all their
own created pressures for Nixon to move slowly on the Taiwan issue, even
at the cost of some strain in Sino-U.S. relations.

The January 27, 1973, signing of the Vietnam peace agreement in
Paris ironically may also have made a marginal contribution to U.S.
unwillingness to "sacrifice" Taiwan to normalize relations with the
PRC in Nixon's second term. The United States had originally undertaken its new China policy in part to secure Peking's help in bringing
North Vietnam into a final peace agreement. The "success" of this policy
thus removed a part of the Administration's original incentive to pay
a substantial political price if need be to put relations with China on
a more solid footing. The Vietnam settlement added to the effects of
Watergate to produce a Nixon Administration policy of treading water on
the China issue. The rhetoric of normalization remained, but significant initiatives to realize this declared policy proved weak and
unconvincing.[36]

Thus more than five years after the establishment of Liaison
Offices and six years after the Shanghai Communiqué, U.S.-China relations remain frozen at a level shy of full normalization. Exactly how
far the Carter Administration will go to achieve normalization in the

---

[36] This is not to say that the Administration made a conscious decision to postpone full normalization of relations with the PRC indefinitely. Rather, it merely recognizes that the logic of events in
both U.S. domestic politics and in Southeast Asia lessened the pressure
on President Nixon to face the hard choices that would have to be made
to bring about full normalization and indeed, at least in the context
of Watergate, set up important political obstacles to making these
choices.

near future is not clear. The Chinese, however, originally tilted toward the United States because America could act as a counter to the Soviet Union. Seen in this larger context, how strong is the Sino-U.S. relationship and how permanent a part of China's Soviet strategy is the U.S. connection? Much of the answer requires an analysis of Sino-Soviet and Sino-U.S. relations within the context of China's domestic politics, given below. An initial assessment focusing on the larger contextual issues is as follows.

Watergate and the aftereffects of the U.S. defeat in Vietnam have chipped away at the image of an active and aggressively anti-Soviet U.S. foreign policy that originally enticed some in Peking to woo Washington in the late 1960s and early 1970s.[37] As Richard Nixon's power ebbed, he seemed anxious to produce "triumphs" in summit diplomacy to bolster his image and position. This concern contributed toward U.S. steadfastness in pursuing détente with the USSR, even in the wake of the October 1973 Middle East War.[38] Perhaps more importantly, Watergate undercut the ability of President Nixon to employ U.S. power as he felt necessary to counter Soviet probes. This weakened Executive, in turn, lessened U.S. reliability as a bulwark against Soviet expansion in Asia in Chinese eyes.

Years of failure to bring a credible victory in Vietnam also took their toll in Washington. The Congress, with sensitivities concerning Executive dissimulation and wrongdoing heightened by the Watergate revelations, assertively restricted the President's options in committing U.S. forces to foreign ventures. For instance, the Congress forbade the use of U.S. ground forces in Indochina and, in the War Powers Act, placed new restrictions on the President's ability to make a sustained commitment of U.S. armed forces to combat without specific Congressional approval.[39] In the last agonizing days of the

---

[37] Indeed, the Chinese both in their media and privately often chide the United States for having become too "passive" in opposition to the Soviet Union. See, for example, Huang Hua's speech to the U.N. General Assembly on September 29, 1977: *New China News Agency*, September 29, 1977, cited in *FBIS/PRC*, September 30, 1977, pp. A-1-11.

[38] U.S.-Soviet policy during and after the Middle East War is dealt with, inter alia, in Kalb and Kalb, op. cit., pp. 450-499.

[39] See, for example, *New York Times*, February 1, 1975.

war in Cambodia, Congress refused to grant the Administration funds to prolong the bombing.[40] Congress's subsequent refusal to provide continued support for the National Union for the Total Independence of Angola (UNITA) against the Soviet-backed and Cuban-supported Popular Movement for the Liberation of Angola (MPLA) in Angola[41] must have been, for the Chinese, the logical capstone of this series of actions. Would the Chinese, after Angola, still count on U.S. resolve in containing Soviet expansion in Asia?

The answer is "yes," for a number of reasons: first and most obviously, because Peking has little choice in the matter. As long as the PRC sees the Soviet Union as its primary threat and views far-reaching compromise with the Soviet Union as unacceptable, it will have to rely at least in part on a continuing U.S. role in Asia to counter the USSR. No other country has the resources to play this "spoiler" role.

Second, President Carter is pursuing an assertive foreign policy, albeit one perceived as somewhat erratic by foreign observers and domestic critics. Thus, the argument can still be made in Peking that the United States will continue to contain Soviet expansion in most parts of the world. The 1976 National Intelligence Estimate, for instance, took a much harsher view of Soviet strategic goals than had similar estimates of previous years[42] (although PRM-10 of the summer of 1977 took a more relaxed position on this critical issue).[43] Peking is probably examining this dimension of the Administration's policies as closely as President Carter's views toward the Taiwan issue in gauging China's options for the near-term future. Issues such as SALT II, troop withdrawals from Korea, and the general U.S. military posture and capabilities in Asia are probably the concrete indicators to the Chinese of U.S. mettle when dealing with the Soviets.

---

[40]*New York Times*: March 22, 1975; March 25, 1975; March 29, 1975; and April 11, 1975.

[41]*New York Times*, November 25, 1975, points up Kissinger's priority on aid to UNITA; Congress, however, balked: *New York Times*, December 17, 1975, and December 20, 1975.

[42]According to the *New York Times*, December 26, 1976.

[43]*New York Times*, July 8, 1977.

Third, China gains much from the continuing goodwill of the United States even without Washington's strong commitment to stop Soviet expansion by whatever means necessary. Peking has been in the international market for military-related goods for years,[44] and it is clearly pursuing such purchases with greater fervor now that the leading radicals in the Politburo have been purged.[45] Michael Pillsbury's *Foreign Policy* article in the fall of 1975 (op. cit.) and Peking's consummation of the British Spey engine purchases in December 1975 brought this dimension of Chinese dealings in the international market to the fore in the Western press. In fact, however, the Chinese have purchased military-related electronic components at least since 1972 and have been in the market for substantial additional purchases in the electronics field. Washington approved the sale of a major new computer system to the PRC in October 1976,[46] and the potential for Chinese purchases of either weapons or military-related technology remains high.

Peking will probably shy away from making weapons purchases directly from the United States. Washington holds the power, however, to inhibit or to facilitate military-related purchases from other Western countries and Japan. Thus, a serious deterioration in Peking's relations with the United States could produce difficulties for the PRC in obtaining vitally needed military-related goods with which to strengthen the Chinese Army enough to deter and if necessary to combat the USSR.[47]

---

[44]For example, China began discussions concerning purchase of the Spey engine at least as early as 1973; Heymann, op. cit., p. 57.

[45]The basic approach of the victors in the succession to date is outlined below, pp. 86-95, 137-142. On recent Chinese activities related to possible military purchases from abroad, see, for example, *New China News Agency*, September 15, 1977, cited in *FBIS/PRC*, September 16, 1977, p. A-16.

[46]*New York Times*: October 29, 1976; October 30, 1976; and October 31, 1976.

[47]The United States does not have a legal right to veto the military sales of its allies to China. The argument here is, rather, a political one--that the United States can effectively block almost any major military sales through applying strong political pressure to the country concerned. The most probable exception to this among U.S. allies is France.

Likewise, the United States strongly influences the military policy of Japan and of the NATO countries—all of which China rightly views as directly relevant to its own security interests relating to the USSR. For instance, strong efforts by the United States to maintain the viability and power of NATO directly affect the perceived costs to the USSR of deploying its military resources along the Chinese border.[48] Relatedly, the Chinese have claimed since 1973 that the Soviets will not attack China until they have secured their flank in Europe.[49] A weakened NATO increases the chances that Moscow could achieve this enviable and dangerous position. China has therefore, not surprisingly, repeatedly warned NATO of the growing Soviet threat.

In sum, the United States is of great importance to China: as a potential gatekeeper that can bar China from Western and Japanese military-related goods and technology, as a power that to a degree structures the military posture of both Japan and Western Europe, and as a direct counterweight to Soviet expansion in Asia and elsewhere. Both China and the United States have learned since 1972, moreover, that each can continue a relationship that leaves the Taiwan issue unresolved. Seen in this fuller context, there seems little likelihood that China will make a complete *volte-face* in its posture toward the United States in the mid-term future. Relations may warm and cool according to the particular diplomatic and internal political needs of the moment, but the chances of a slide into either a cold or hot war are slim.[50]

---

[48]The Chinese have repeatedly warned the NATO countries about the threat from the USSR. See, for instance, Paris *Le Monde*, November 3, 1976, cited in *FBIS/PRC*, November 4, 1976, p. A-1.

[49]This idea is embodied in the Chinese notion that the Soviets are "making a feint in the East to attack in the West" and that the focus of Soviet-U.S. contention is in Europe.

[50]This is particularly the case since the October 1976 purge of the radicals, as explained below. A perceived lack of good faith on the part of the United States over the Taiwan question could, however, have unpredictable consequences, given the strength of Chinese nationalism and the continuing political jockeying in the Chinese succession crisis.

Wooing Non-Communist Asia

While the United States connection has been the cornerstone of Peking's policy to deal with the USSR since the early 1970s, it has by no means been the only component of that policy. Rather, China has pursued an extremely active diplomacy to restrict Soviet influence throughout Asia. Most dramatically, Peking welcomed Tokyo's overtures in the wake of the PRC's tilt toward the United States.[51] In a sense, however, Sino-Japanese relations have not yet been fully consummated. Although the two countries have established diplomatic relations,[52] Peking and Tokyo have as yet failed to agree on the wording on a clause about "hegemony" (i.e., the USSR) in their discussions of a treaty of peace and friendship. This diplomatic stumbling block has not prevented the development of extensive economic relations between the two countries, however--relations that China regards as vital to its plans for rapid economic development.[53]

Among other non-communist states in Asia, China has wooed the leaders of Australia,[54] Singapore,[55] Malaysia,[56] Thailand,[57] Burma,[58]

---

[51] Barnett provides a wide-ranging assessment of Sino-Japanese relations: Barnett, op. cit., pp. 88-152.

[52] Japan established diplomatic relations with China and broke relations with Taiwan on September 29, 1972: *Peking Review*, No. 40, October 6, 1972, pp. 12-13.

[53] In early 1977 China and Japan signed an eight-year trade agreement that calls for ten billion dollars (U.S.) of trade in each direction over this period: *New China News Agency*, February 16, 1978, cited in *FBIS/PRC*, February 16, 1978, p. A-5.

[54] China and Australia established diplomatic relations on December 21, 1972. On subsequent relations between the two countries, see inter alia, *Peking Review*, No. 45, November 9, 1973, pp. 3-5, 11-12; *Peking Review*, No. 24, June 13, 1975, pp. 6, 16.

[55] *Peking Review*, No. 12, March 21, 1975, pp. 5-6.

[56] Malaysia established diplomatic relations with China and broke its relations with Taiwan on May 31, 1974: *Peking Review*, No. 23, June 7, 1974, p. 8. See also pp. 3-5, 9-10 of this issue.

[57] Thailand established diplomatic relations with Peking on July 1, 1975, and at the same time terminated relations with Taiwan: *Peking Review*, No. 27, July 14, 1975, pp. 8-9.

[58] Teng Hsiao-p'ing paid an official state visit to Burma in January 1978: *New China News Agency*, January 31, 1978, cited in *FBIS/PRC*, January 31, 1978, p. A-8.

New Zealand,[59] Nepal,[60] and Pakistan[61] and has given strong verbal support to the Association of Southeast Asian Nations (ASEAN).[62] The PRC has encouraged trade links with almost all these countries, running a substantial deficit in its trade with Japan and a surplus with the other countries named above.[63] The PRC and India restored diplomatic relations at the ambassadorial level in 1976 after these relations had been scaled down to the *chargé* level for a decade,[64] and efforts are under way to try to bring about wider improvements in Sino-Indian relations.[65] Peking's relations with the Philippines have improved to the point where China dispatched Politburo member and vice-premier Li Hsien-nien on a goodwill journey to Manila,[66] and there are some signs that relations with Indonesia might begin to improve in 1978 after thirteen years of chill.[67]

---

[59]New Zealand established diplomatic relations with China on December 22, 1972: *Peking Review*, No. 52, December 29, 1972, p. 3. See also: *Peking Review*, No. 14, April 6, 1973, pp. 3, 10.

[60]Teng Hsiao-p'ing paid an official state visit to Nepal in February 1978: *New China News Agency*, February 6, 1978, cited in *FBIS/PRC*, February 6, 1978, p. A-16.

[61]On China's long and intricate relationship with Pakistan, see William Barnds, "China's Relations with Pakistan: Durability Amidst Discontinuity," *China Quarterly*, September 1975.

[62]See, for example, *Peking Review*, No. 25, June 20, 1975, pp. 19, 23.

[63]The *Far Eastern Economic Review* provides an annual summary of the PRC's foreign trade. China has run a deficit in its trade with Japan since 1964 and regularly runs a surplus with the countries of South and Southeast Asia. See also Nai-Ruenn Chen, "China's Foreign Trade, 1950-1974," in *China: A Reassessment of the Economy*, Joint Economic Committee of the U.S. Congress, Washington, D.C., July 1975, p. 650; and *China: International Trade, 1976-77*, Central Intelligence Agency, ER77-10674, November 1977.

[64]Hong Kong AFP, April 15, 1976, cited in *FBIS/PRC*, April 16, 1976, p. A-8; Hong Kong AFP, April 16, 1976, cited in *FBIS/PRC*, April 19, 1976, p. A-9.

[65]A Chinese trade delegation, for instance, visited India in February 1978: *New China News Agency*, February 7, 1978, cited in *FBIS/PRC*, February 8, 1978, p. A-10.

[66]*New China News Agency*, March 12, 1978, cited in *FBIS/PRC*, March 13, 1978, p. A-13; *New China News Agency*, March 16, 1978, cited in *FBIS/PRC*, March 16, 1978, p. A-12.

[67]*New York Times*, April 24, 1978.

Support for a United Western Europe

In Europe, as noted above, the Chinese have suggested the need for a strengthened NATO alliance and have lectured European leaders appropriately during their sojourns to Peking. Also, in late 1973 the PRC established formal relations with the European Economic Community (EEC), and China has consistently supported efforts for the political and economic integration of Europe.[68] China has almost certainly used its increased diplomatic and commercial presence in Europe, moreover, as a vehicle for gaining NATO-generated military intelligence on Soviet capabilities.

The Middle East and Africa

In the Middle East and Africa, as noted in Sec. I, China has geared her aid efforts toward those countries that are not also the objects of major Soviet overtures. While Chinese propaganda appeals to all of the Third World against the superpowers (especially against the Soviet Union), concrete assistance has thus been far more narrowly focused.[69] Chinese aid has, moreover, tended to be given on terms more favorable than that granted by any other country, and much of this aid has been channeled into a few major projects (most notably, the Tanzam Railway). Thus, China's policies toward the non-communist world other than the United States have been geared to limit Soviet influence through a continuing barrage of propaganda aimed against the USSR, backed up by offers of aid and trade as China's limited resources permit.

Among Communist Countries

Within the communist world, the PRC has focused its efforts on both East Europe and the Asian parties in power. Albania was the PRC's

---

[68]See, for example, *Peking Review*, No. 52, December 28, 1973, p. 17. China's support of the EEC is in line with Peking's general approval of regional alliances to strengthen the hands of smaller states against the encroachments of the superpowers.

[69]*Communist Aid to Less Developed Countries* (op. cit.) supports this general characterization.

major ally in East Europe during 1960-1976, although friction developed
in the Sino-Albanian relationship shortly after the death of Mao and
purge of the radicals in Peking.[70] Romania has consistently tried to
serve as a mediator in Sino-Soviet relations, and China has taken
special pains to cultivate its ties with Ceauşescu's government since
Peking emerged from its diplomatic shell in the spring of 1969. Among
the other European communist parties in power, China has adopted a
somewhat differentiated approach. It established a joint shipping
company with Poland, although politically the Polish question has
remained ticklish for Peking. Few governments have backed the USSR
so strongly on issues of bloc relations since the early 1960s as has
Poland. Nevertheless, Peking recognizes the underlying Polish/Soviet
friction[71] and does not treat Poland simply as a lackey of the Kremlin
leaders. The PRC's policy toward Bulgaria, Czechoslovakia, Hungary,
and East Germany has been one of almost unremitting hostility, however,
evidently viewing all four regimes as inextricably tied to the Soviet
Union. Also, the PRC has in the past few years cultivated an increasingly significant relationship with Tito's Yugoslavia, one that may
incorporate a military dimension as well.[72] Thus, Peking has focused
its efforts in East Europe on those countries that are either the most
independent of the USSR or, in Peking's view, have the greatest potential for such independence.

In Asia, China competes with the Soviet Union for North Korea's
favor. This has involved Chinese military assistance and extensive
economic cooperation with Pyongyang, dramatized in 1975-1976 by
the opening of an oil pipeline linking the two countries. China has
also provided Kim Il-sung with more consistent ideological support for
the latter's views on reunification of Korea than has Moscow. Nevertheless, as noted in Sec. I, Kim has had to rely on the Soviet Union

---

[70]*Washington Post*, July 26, 1977; *New York Times*, July 26, 1977.

[71]See, for example, *Peking Review*, No. 30, July 25, 1975, p. 12.

[72]See Johnson, op. cit.; *Peking Review*, No. 41, October 10, 1975,
pp. 3-7. *New China News Agency*, August 30, 1977, cited in *FBIS/PRC*,
August 31, 1977, pp. A-10-18; *New China News Agency*, June 17, 1977,
cited in *FBIS/PRC*, June 20, 1977, pp. A-15-16.

for very sophisticated military aid, and neither Peking nor Moscow
can claim predominant influence over the strongly nationalistic and
self-assertive Korean leader.

China also would like to have constructive relations with the new
governments in Cambodia, Vietnam, and Laos. It has succeeded more in
Cambodia than in the other two countries, as indicated in Sec. I. This
has fundamentally been a function of the greater Soviet ability to
direct aid to Vietnam and Hanoi's feeling that Peking poses a greater
potential danger to its goals than does Moscow. Relatedly, the rough
handling of ethnic Chinese merchants in Vietnam and the large-size
military engagements along the Vietnam-Cambodia border starting in the
fall of 1977 have placed major obstacles in the path of Sino-Vietnamese
friendship.

Lastly, just as Moscow has tried to ensnare the countries in Asia
in an Asian Collective Security System, Peking has sought to entice
these countries to declare themselves in the fight against "hegemonism." Peking's success, like that of Moscow, has been mixed in this
endeavor, but the effort has provided a good deal of the rhetoric of
China's relations with other Asian states in the 1970s.[73]

Summary

In sum, Peking's major efforts against Moscow have involved big
power diplomacy and have focused on wooing the United States, Japan,
and the countries of Western Europe. The other countries of Asia and
Eastern Europe have come next in importance, whereas countries in the
Middle East and Africa have lagged behind. The PRC takes advantage
of every possible forum to excoriate Moscow and try to undercut its
influence throughout the world, but in practice China sculpts its aid
and trade policies around a far more highly differentiated and sober
estimate of its ability to limit Moscow's influence. For the reasons

---

[73] An overview of China's success in enticing its neighbors to
declare their opposition to "hegemonism" in the region is presented
in Joachim Glaubitz, "Anti-Hegemony Formulas in Chinese Foreign
Policy," *Asian Survey*, Vol. XVI, No. 3, March 1976, pp. 205-215.

discussed in the remainder of this section, this policy will not change fundamentally in the near-term future.

THE "POLITICS" OF SOVIET POLICY IN PEKING, 1973-1978

Political Instability and Sino-Soviet Relations

In contrast to the relative unanimity on China policy within the Kremlin, Soviet policy has been part and parcel of the issues that have kept Chinese politics bitterly divided in recent years. The reasons for these great differences between the two countries on this issue are not difficult to fathom.

The Soviet Union's policy toward China survived one succession largely intact during 1964-1966. Although the new Brezhnev leadership decided almost immediately upon assuming office to try to improve relations with China, this new momentum quickly dissipated and hardened into the posture analyzed in Sec. I. Since that time, the Soviet leadership itself has been remarkably stable, and thus policy toward China has not become ensnared in the politics of a succession. On the China side, Mao Tse-tung launched the Great Proletarian Cultural Revolution in part out of concern for his own mortality,[74] and policy toward the Soviet Union after the GPCR was inescapably trapped in the context of succession politics. Put differently, the stable leadership in the USSR and the basic consensus at the top on China policy have not provided much incentive for subordinates to argue for major changes in this policy. The unstable leadership in Peking and the possibility that dramatic changes in the highest level leadership in China could occur at almost any time made the potential range of options in China's near-term Soviet policy far wider and thus provided greater incentives for discussion and dissent on this issue.

Indeed, in a broader sense the contrast between stability in Soviet politics and instability in Peking during the late 1960s and the 1970s

---

[74] Many of Mao's writings and speeches during 1964 that have subsequently become available contain references to the subject of his imminent death. See also Robert J. Lifton, *Revolutionary Immortality*, Vintage Books, New York, 1968.

explains much about the greater dissension on this issue in Peking than in Moscow. Although the Brezhnev years in the USSR have witnessed serious political infighting, such debate and conflict has taken place, as was the case in the PRC during the early to mid-1950s, within a framework of consensus on basic rules and fundamental policy issues.

China, by contrast, since 1966 has been torn by a seemingly unending series of purges at all levels of the political hierarchy. At the highest levels, these began with the ouster of Lo Jui-ch'ing, Lu Ting-yi, Yang Shang-k'un, and P'eng Chen in May 1966, mushroomed into the sweeping condemnations characteristic of the Cultural Revolution, caught Ch'en Po-ta in the wake of the Second Plenum of the Ninth Central Committee in 1970, felled Lin Piao and his closest followers in September 1971 and other colleagues of Lin during 1972-1973, toppled Teng Hsiao-p'ing in January 1976, and finally(?) engulfed Chiang Ch'ing, Chang Ch'un-ch'iao, Yao Wen-yuan, and Wang Hung-wen in October 1976. A foreign policy issue as sensitive as Soviet policy is likely to remain largely in the province of the Politburo. To illustrate the magnitude of these changes at this level alone, these deaths and purges[75] claimed: 59 percent of the 1966 Politburo by April 1969; 38 percent of the Politburo selected in April 1969 by the Tenth Congress in August 1973; and 43 percent of the Politburo selected by that Congress as of January 1977. This extreme leadership instability set the context for debates and decisions on Soviet policy in China, and this policy debate in Peking can be understood only within the context of the infighting and coalition-building necessary to survive a period of such rapid leadership turnover.

From the Cultural Revolution to the post-Mao purge of the radicals, moreover, it appears that few policies were debated in isolation within the upper reaches of the Chinese Communist Party. Prior to the GPCR, policy coalitions shifted across a range of issues in Peking. The people who lined up together in discussions of, for instance,

---

[75]"Purges," in this context, refers to expulsion from the Politburo between Party Congresses.

agricultural organization, differed from those who fought on the same side during debates over the proper mix of policies for higher education.[76]

Against this background, the distinctive contributions of the Cultural Revolution to the policy debate in China were that it polarized opinion within the leadership and linked policy differences inextricably to considerations of personal power. These two legacies are interrelated. The Cultural Revolution brought to the fore a group of people who disagreed across the spectrum of issues with most of the leadership in power as of early 1966. Their attack on this leadership, moreover, broke almost all previous rules of Party debate, thus introducing immense personal rancor into the conflict over issues. The Leftists and their allies by no means completely agreed among themselves on all issues during the GPCR, as witnessed by the continuing turnover among their leadership during this upheaval. Nevertheless, the end of the Cultural Revolution and the subsequent rehabilitation of many high-ranking cadres that had been victims of the Left during the late 1960s forced the remaining leaders of the Left to close ranks in the face of the increasingly serious danger of revenge from their opponents.

Likewise, the rehabilitated cadres, led by former Party Secretary General Teng Hsiao-p'ing, have not necessarily agreed on all major issues, and tensions have clearly been evident among them in the wake of the purge of the Left.[77] Nevertheless, from 1972 through 1976, these cadres perceived a mortal danger from the continuing power of the Left and consequently closed ranks to ward off this threat. Thus, two major groups formed at the highest levels in Chinese politics and put forward

---

[76]Unfortunately, there is no available analysis that deals with this issue comprehensively for the early 1960s, and many works mistakenly parrot Peking's own contention that these years witnessed a "two-line struggle" that cut across all issue areas. The data for a more differentiated approach are presented in at least an initial way in Byung-joon Ahn, *Chinese Politics and the Cultural Revolution*, University of Washington Press, Seattle, 1976.

[77]These are detailed in Kenneth Lieberthal, "The Politics of Modernization in the PRC," *Problems of Communism*, May-June 1978a, pp. 1-17.

contrasting programs that encompassed a broad range of issues confronting the leadership. Each side portrayed these issues as closely linked to each other--essentially, as a "struggle between two lines." China's policy toward the Soviet Union formed one of these issues.

In sum, the Cultural Revolution polarized Peking politics, linked policy issues inextricably to considerations of personal power, and-- perhaps most insidiously of all--undermined the prior consensus on the "rules of the game" for fighting political battles.[78]

Debates over policy toward the Soviet Union thus swirled within this larger maelstrom of issues and personalities in contention. On the Soviet issue perhaps even more than in other areas, moreover, a third force weighed in--Party Chairman Mao Tse-tung. Substantial evidence points up the fact that Mao had seen the Soviet issue as one of the key questions in China politics since at least as early as the mid-1950s. Several elements coalesced to account for this near obsession of the Chinese Party Chairman: Moscow had consistently backed rivals of Mao within the CCP before 1949 and seemed to do so again in supporting P'eng Teh-huai's challenge to Mao over the Great Leap Forward at Lushan in the summer of 1959; the Soviet model during the first Five Year Plan had produced social and political consequences that Mao found abhorrent; Khrushchev's de-Stalinization speech and subsequent activities in this vein heightened Mao's fear for his own place in Chinese history; and Soviet foreign policy seemed increasingly to diverge from Mao's perception of China's fundamental interests. Moscow's long and intimate involvement in the Chinese Communist Party simply increased Mao's sense of urgency concerning the need to eliminate all pro-Soviet sentiment from within the CCP by minimizing intercourse between the two countries and Communist Parties.

Thomas Gottlieb has traced what little is known of Mao's role in Sino-Soviet relations during the late 1960s. Gottlieb's work supports the impression that the Chairman remained bitterly hostile to the USSR

---

[78]See Kenneth Lieberthal, *Central Documents and Politburo Politics in China*, Michigan Papers in Chinese Studies No. 33, University of Michigan Center for Chinese Studies, Ann Arbor, 1978b.

and placed policy toward Moscow high on China's political agenda.[79]
Indeed, it may well be that during the period 1958-1963 Mao realized
for the first time, based on his analysis of the trends in the USSR,
that a socialist revolution could subsequently degenerate into bureaucratic capitalism--and that this realization in turn had provided a
major part of the impetus for Mao's willingness to take the extraordinary measures he initiated in 1966 to increase the chances that
China would not undergo a similar fate after his passing. Thus, to
Mao the Soviet question went beyond strictly military and international
political issues (although these were strongly in evidence also) and
drove straight to the heart of his most vital concerns about his life's
work in China and his role in Chinese history.[80] Although Mao did not
enjoy absolute power in the Chinese system, his central and deep concern with the Soviet question must, therefore, have affected the terms
of political debate around this issue in Peking.

The Foreign Policy Debate in Peking, 1973-1976

Within this context, what were the arguments about Soviet policy
within the PRC? Gottlieb notes that as of the late 1960s one can
discern three different approaches to the USSR, which he labels the
radical, moderate, and military. Gottlieb stresses, however, that the
institutional rubric he has bestowed on one of these perspectives
should not be taken literally. His evidence supports only the conclusion that Lin Piao and some of his closest colleagues in the Ministry
of Defense--all of whom had been purged by the end of 1971[81]--held the
"military" viewpoint. Indeed, as of 1978 every policymaker whose views
Gottlieb could specify is either dead or stripped of office, with the
exception only of Yeh Chien-ying.

---

[79]Gottlieb, op. cit.

[80]The secondary literature pertinent to this issue is too vast
to warrant citation here. Some of these issues are highlighted in
Kenneth Lieberthal, *Mao Tse-tung's Perception of the Soviet Union as
Communicated in the Mao Tse-tung Ssu-hsiang Wan Sui!*, The Rand Corporation, P-5726, September 1976b. See also Barnett, op. cit., pp. 20-80.

[81]Gottlieb, op. cit., p. 14.

How fundamentally have the changes since 1969--in both the cast of characters and the international environment--transformed the arguments Gottlieb discerned in the Chinese media? The following subsection analyzes in detail the *interrelated* foreign and domestic policy positions put forward by the contenders for power in China during 1973-1976, as revealed by allegorical articles of that period[82] and, in many cases, substantiated since.[83] In so doing, it plumbs the depths of the linkages between foreign policy, domestic policy, and factional power concerns in the wake of the GPCR during the period of acute uncertainty engendered by the imminent succession. Only by tying together these various strands can the debates over Soviet policy of this period, the events since the death of Mao Tse-tung, and China's

---

[82]The "allegorical" articles refer to a major body of writing about Chinese history that had clear contemporary significance. These articles posited contemporary policy views through their explanation and presentation of events from China's incomparably rich history. Naturally, any interpretation of this body of literature is bound to be somewhat controversial, but the importance of this body of literature demands that such an effort be made. For details on why the Chinese turned at this time to allegorical writing and how to "read" these articles, see Kenneth Lieberthal, "The Foreign Policy Debate in Peking as Seen Through Allegorical Articles, 1973-1976," *China Quarterly*, No. 71, September 1977, pp. 548-554. For a listing of allegorical articles written for the campaign to criticize Lin Piao and Confucius, see *Bibliography of Literature Written in the People's Republic of China During the Campaign to Criticize Lin Piao and Confucius, July 1973-December 1974*, Central Intelligence Agency, Washington, D.C., 1975.

[83]Virtually all the evidence from China since the overthrow of the radicals in October 1976 has confirmed the accuracy of the substance of the following "allegorical" analysis, and some details of this corroboration are provided in the footnotes below. The Chinese have, at the same time, repeatedly disclosed that the pseudonymous Lo Ssu-ting articulated the views of the radicals, while my own analysis as presented in the following section uses certain Lo Ssu-ting articles as a source for the moderates' views. A careful review of all available articles that appeared under Lo Ssu-ting's name confirms that Lo spoke for the moderates, although some articles suggest that the writing group at Futan University that produced the Lo Ssu-ting articles eventually tried to straddle both sides of the political fence. This latter effort may explain why the group came under attack after the purge of the radicals. In the politics of China since late 1976, moreover, any public attack on a writing group must of necessity assume the form of associating the group with the nefarious radicals. The internal evidence of the articles used below simply does not support this charge.

future policy toward the USSR be understood. At the same time, it should be noted that the arguments put forward in the allegorical pieces were used in a political debate and thus undoubtedly were somewhat reified so as to present the issues in stark and forceful terms. The *thrust* of the argument of each side as derived from these articles, however, seems to reflect accurately the basic framework of the debate in Peking during 1973-1976.

Three basic arguments emerged out of the allegorical literature as it pertained to foreign policy.[84] The first is completely distinctive and agrees in its basic premises with the perspectives generally

_____

[84]Most of the following analysis is drawn from nine major allegorical articles. I list them together here for ease of reference, given the repetition of articles by a single author:

1. Lo Ssu-ting, "Struggle Between Restoration and Counter-Restoration in the Course of the Founding of the Chin Dynasty," *Hung ch'i*, No. 11, 1973, translated in *Peking Review*, No. 17, April 26, 1974, pp. 7-10 and *Peking Review*, No. 18, May 3, 1974, pp. 19-22. Abbreviated hereafter as "Lo Ssu-ting, 4/26/74" and "Lo Ssu-ting, 5/3/74," respectively.

2. Liang Hsiao, "Study 'On Salt and Iron'--Big Polemic Between the Confucian and Legalist Schools in the Middle Western Han Dynasty," *Hung ch'i*, No. 5, 1974, translated in *FBIS/PRC*, May 21, 1974, pp. 1-9. Abbreviated hereafter as "Liang Hsiao, 5/74."

3. Lo Ssu-ting, "On the Struggle Between Patriotism and National Betrayal During the Northern Sung Period," *Hung ch'i*, No. 11, 1974, translated in *FBIS/PRC*, November 20, 1974, pp. E-1-10. Abbreviated hereafter as "Lo Ssu-ting, 11/74."

4. Liang Hsiao, "The Great Historical Role of Peasant Wars," *Jen-min Jih-pao*, December 20, 1974, translated in *Survey of People's Republic of China Press (SPRCP)*, No. 5765, January 3, 1975, pp. 135-146. Abbreviated hereafter as "Liang Hsiao, 12/74."

5. Workers' Theoretical Group of the Peking Equipment Installation Company and the Editing and Writing Group of "Manuscripts of Modern History of China," "Wei Yuan's Thought Against Aggression," *Wen-wu*, No. 5, May 1975, translated in *Survey of People's Republic of China Magazine (SPRCM)*, 75-27, No. 838, September 15, 1975, pp. 1-14. Abbreviated hereafter as "Wei Yuan."

6. Liang Hsiao, "Criticize Lin Piao's Comprador Philosophy," *Hung ch'i*, No. 8, August 1975, translated in *SPRCM*, No. 835-836, August 25-September 2, 1975, pp. 12-18. Abbreviated hereafter as "Liang Hsiao, 8/75."

attributed to the "radicals"--Chang Ch'un-ch'iao, Wang Hung-wen, Yao
Wen-yuan, Chiang Ch'ing, and their followers. This is, therefore,
termed the "radical" argument, even though "nativist" might describe
it equally well. The other two arguments agree on all critical points
save one--the tactical strategy that China should pursue toward the
Soviet Union. These are labeled the "moderate" perspective below, and
the following analysis distinguishes always between the two variants
of this approach. It is probable, moreover, that some high military
figures supported one of these moderate approaches, as explained below.

All three arguments share certain common perceptions. All sides
agree, for instance, that the stakes are high in this debate--indeed,
that wrong choices will jeopardize the very survival of an independent,
revolutionary China. All concur in the judgment, moreover, that China's
future independence demands a sense of unity and patriotism among her
people and popular support for the national government. All affirm
that foreign and domestic policies are inseparable and that errors
in one will have disastrous repercussions for the other. Here, however, agreement ends.

Two fundamental questions divided the radicals from the others:
What is the nature of the threat confronting China? What types of
programs will unify the Chinese people and win their support?

Both "moderate" approaches perceive the overwhelming threat to
China in military terms, and they insist that China must take appropriate measures to cope with this threat. The radicals saw the *primary*
threat in terms of political subversion (both through espionage and

---

7. An Miao, "Confucianist Capitulationism and the Traitor Lin
   Piao," *Jen-min Jih-pao*, August 12, 1975, translated in *SPRCP*,
   No. 5921, August 22, 1975, pp. 171-180. Abbreviated here-
   after as "An Miao."

8. Liang Hsiao, "The Yang Wu Movement and the Slavish Comprador
   Philosophy," *Li-shih yen-chiu*, No. 5, October 20, 1975, translated in *SPRCM*, No. 7536, December 16, 1975, pp. 1-10. Abbreviated hereafter as "Liang Hsiao, 10/75."

9. Liang Hsiao, "Critique of Lin Piao's Capitulationism," *Jen-
   min Jih-pao*, January 28, 1976. Abbreviated hereafter as
   "Liang Hsiao, 1/76."

Note that in subsequent citations, page references are to the *translations*
of these articles.

more generally through the negative effects of the Soviet model) and reasoned that the most dangerous enemy, therefore, lurks within China-- especially at the highest levels of the Chinese Communist Party.[85] These different perceptions of the dimensions of the threat formed the basis for much of the broader disagreement on policies advocated by these groups.

All sides recognized, moreover, that China must remain strongly unified to ward off the danger facing her, no matter how that danger was perceived. There remained fundamental differences, though, over evaluations of what it is the Chinese people want and therefore over what policies will produce unity. The "moderates" say the people demand an increasing standard of living and relative security and optimism in their life expectations. According to the radicals, however, the material incentives used to provide these benefits would in fact weaken the Chinese state, as they inevitably increase inequality and thus raise the level of tension and strife in society. Only political struggles that clearly identify the internal enemy and maintain the vigilance and patriotism of the people at a high level can thus enhance real unity. The material incentives and other measures advocated by the "moderates," indeed, will simply increase the power of local "bourgeois" elements, who are despised by the masses of the Chinese people and are ultimately disloyal to the Chinese revolution.

In greater detail, these three arguments are as follows.[86]

The Radicals' Argument. The radicals start from the fundamental premise that the major danger to China stems from within rather than from other countries. They therefore emphasize the domestic threat

---

[85]This is not to argue that the radicals perceived no military danger to China, but rather that they stressed the political dimensions of the threat and argued, as explained below, that too much attention to the military situation would actually *increase* the chances that the Chinese revolution would succumb to revisionism.

[86]The leading radicals were purged in October 1976, and their perspective is thus no longer actively represented in the highest ranks of the Party. The "moderate" perspectives, however, still inform Peking politics. To avoid tortuous distinctions in verb tense, all three approaches are presented in the present tense in this section.

and the internal policies necessary to counter this challenge. This
does not, however, lead them to ignore the international arena, for
they argue that China's domestic enemies will inevitably link up with
her foreign foes to suppress the radicals and turn China onto a revisionist course.

The radicals' argument condemns analyses of the international
system that focus on conventional power relationships. Given the
obvious disparity between China's military and economic capabilities
and those of her opponents, any such conventional analysis inevitably
leads to the conclusion that China should now make concessions, for not
only the current situation but even the trends all run against the PRC.
Conventional power analysis, then, is conducive to an air of defeatism,
which in turn engenders policies that amount to appeasement and
capitulation.[87]

This conventional power analysis is simply wrong, according to
the radicals. The difficult policy choices that it produces are, therefore, not only distasteful but unnecessary--and thus traitorous.
"Dialecticians" recognize that the world is not static and that the
seemingly strong powers have now entered a state of decline. Only
the newborn things are indestructible, and accordingly the balance
will eventually tip in China's favor. These trends are inevitable,
unless China capitulates earlier because Peking reads history and its
laws incorrectly.[88]

---

[87] For instance, Liang Hsiao condemns those who argue that "resistance involves the risk of national enslavement." These people
"play up the horrors of war and the strain on manpower and material,
saying that 'the aftermath of a major military operation will last
for generations,' and that 'the mothers can only sob while the wives
will live in anguish.' . . . Therefore, they advocate capitualation-
ism. . . ." Liang Hsiao, 5/74, p. E-6. See also, An Miao (p. 172),
another radical author, who condemns the argument that "The weak
cannot contend with the strong." More than a year after the purge
of the radicals, *People's Daily* confirmed that they had argued that
measures for war preparedness amounted to "intentionally scaring the
people": *Jen-min Jih-pao*, December 1, 1977, cited in *FBIS/PRC*,
December 2, 1977, p. E-13.

[88] For example, An Miao, pp. 174-175: "As the Marxists see it,
the question lies not in whether the country is big or small, but
in whether or not the line is correct. The revolutionary new things
are always small and weak at the beginning, but they are rich in

Those who advocate conventional power analysis, according to the radicals, also err in their view of the sources of imperialist, and especially Soviet, aggression against China. Imperialists, whether Soviet or American, are aggressive as a function of the internal dynamics of the imperialist system itself, and no concessions from China can reduce the chance of imperialist aggression against the PRC.[89] Thus, for instance, a Chinese willingness to convene a summit meeting with the Soviets, reach a border accord with them, increase trade with them, or release the helicopter pilots that had been captured in Sinkiang in March 1974 might demonstrate Chinese weakness but could not bring any relief in the real Soviet danger to China.[90] These measures would, moreover, help to cement an alliance between

---

vitality and can grow from the small to the big and from the weak to the strong. On the other hand, although all reactionary and decadent old things are strong in appearance, they are bound to head from the big to the small, from the strong to the weak and finally to their doom. 'Only the emerging and developing things are invincible.' . . . [The moderates, however,] view the big and the small, the strong and the weak from their static, isolated and outward appearance, advocate capitulationism to the reactionary decadent forces and docilely lead the life of lackeys under the imposing power of the big country. This is an out-and-out reactionary theory of capitulationism." Note: here and elsewhere, words in brackets are my own. Frequently, the only difference between these words and the original text is verb tense. I have taken the liberty of putting past tense into the present and/or future (as appropriate) to highlight the intended contemporary message of these allegories.

[89]An Miao (p. 178), for instance, criticizes Lin Piao for allegedly suggesting that the PRC had been at least partly at fault in exacerbating Sino-Soviet relations in 1960. An Miao contends that "The practice of aggression by imperialism was dictated by the law of necessity of monopoly capital." To argue that China's actions could in any way affect the degree to which the imperialists would commit aggression ". . . is the logic of imperialism and its lackeys."

[90]Liang Hsiao castigated those who would make concessions of this nature in an article written directly after the Chinese received a Soviet ultimatum over the Soviet helicopter pilots captured by the Chinese in Sinkiang: Liang Hsiao, 5/74, p. E-6. In this same piece, Liang Hsiao argues forcefully that concessions cannot possibly diminish the aggressiveness of the USSR against China: See p. E-7. As explained below, the "hard" moderate position parallels the radicals' stance on this issue, whereas the "soft" moderates strongly disagree.

the moderates and the Soviets directed against the radicals--an alliance
that in the long run would produce a traitorous betrayal of the Chinese
revolution. How this would come about is explained in detail below.

Although the Soviets do pose a military danger--a danger that requires adequate defenses on the border and constant vigilance--the
main threat Moscow directs at China is that of subversion.[91] The USSR
hopes to undermine the Chinese revolution through cultivating agents
at high levels of the Chinese Communist Party. China's greatest safety,
then, lies not in building up its military (which, as explained below,
would require various domestic policies that are likely to strengthen
the hands of the same moderate elements who will sell out to the Soviets),
but rather in waging a persistent and vigilant domestic class struggle
so as to identify, isolate, and destroy the potential betrayers of the
Chinese revolution.

If the Soviets should launch a military attack, an eventual Chinese victory would require the PRC to be able to mobilize all of its
resources--political, economic, and military--to defeat the aggressors
through a peoples' war.[92] China's ability to do this will depend on
whether Peking is pursuing the correct political line,[93] for only if it
is doing so can it hope to bring the full range of its resources to bear
to repulse the Soviet attack.

Economically, this type of defense demands that Peking pursue
policies that insure maximum government control over resources. Thus,
the PRC should miminize material incentives, private plots, free markets,
and sideline production--for all of these simply enrich the local

---

[91]The Soviet attempt to conquer China through subversion runs like
a thread through almost all articles that articulate the radicals' views.
It is stated most clearly and forcefully in Liang Hsiao, 1/76--for example, to conquer the PRC, "Soviet revisionism . . . must find and foster
its agents in our Party to push the revisionist line, to subvert the
dictatorship of the proletariat and the socialist system in China and
to restore capitalism. This is its unchangeable imperialist policy."
(P. 18.)

[92]Liang Hsiao, 1/76, p. 18; Liang Hsiao, 8/75, p. 144.

[93]An Miao, pp. 174-175.

"bourgeois" elements, people who will not firmly support the national government in a time of crisis.[94]

In a similar vein, China can import some goods and technology from abroad but it is imperative for the PRC to "keep the initiative in its own hands." Given the country's semi-colonial past, the leaders and people must never again lose their confidence that China can accomplish what foreigners have done. In practical terms, the PRC must limit the importation of foreign goods and should study the negative as well as the positive experiences of other states.[95]

---

[94] I interpret the first section of Liang Hsiao, 5/74, as dealing with the question of whether the government should remove some restrictions (or at least not tighten up restrictions) on material incentives and private economic activities--i.e., wage incentives, private plots, free markets, and sideline production. The first of these issues arose in the form of strike activity by many Chinese workers during the period when this article was published and the others appeared in terms of specific guarantees, which were subsequently attacked in the press, contained in the new state constitution adopted by the Fourth National People's Congress in January 1975. Liang Hsiao (5/74, p. E-3) attacks those who advocate maintaining (and broadening?) these rights (on the pretense that this will raise the standard of living of the people) with the argument that "Obviously, the 'people' for whom those virtuous learned men [that is, the moderates] tried to gain some profit were not the broad masses of working people, but local princes, big businessmen, and slaveowners . . . it would be only those local tyrannical forces who would gain profit; the state would achieve nothing." In nonallegorical terms, the beneficiaries of these politics would be the local "bourgeois" elements, whose interests do not coincide with those of the Chinese Communist state. The guarantees appear in articles 5, 7, and 9 of the 1975 state constitution (text is in *Peking Review*, No. 4, January 24, 1975, pp. 12-17). Major criticisms of these guarantees and their long-term effects are contained in Yao Wen-yuan, "On the Social Basis of the Lin Piao Anti-Party Clique," *Peking Review*, No. 10, March 7, 1975, pp. 5-10; and Chang Ch'un-ch'iao, "On Exercising All-Around Dictatorship Over the Bourgeoisie," *Peking Review*, No. 14, April 4, 1975, pp. 5-11; among numerous other articles. A January 1978 allegorical blast at Mao Tse-tung castigated the radicals' suppression of sideline production in the countryside on the basis that it impoverished the peasantry: *Li-shih yen-chiu*, No. 1, January 1978, cited in *FBIS/PRC*, March 24, 1978, pp. E-1-9.

[95] For example, Liang Hsiao, 8/75, p. 18, and Liang Hsiao, 10/75, p. 9: "When we uphold the policy of 'independence and initiative' and 'self-reliance,' it does not mean that we reject the study and importation of foreign advanced experience and technical equipment. The question is: Do we 'make foreign things serve China' with a view of catching up with and overtaking them? Or do we copy them blindly and crawl

Thus, any pattern of thought that underestimates the wisdom and capabilities of the Chinese people is wrong and dangerous. In the economic realm, such thinking produces a "comprador" philosophy that may make China dependent on Western countries for its development. Militarily, this attitude will engender concessions and defeatism, with consequences for the revolution that in the long run are disastrous. Some segments of the leadership and masses in China unfortunately retain an inferiority complex from pre-Liberation days; the radicals stress that Peking must recognize the urgency of avoiding all policies that may enhance this dangerous mode of thinking.[96]

Militarily, properly motivated soldiers can fight with a tenacity that more than matches a larger but less spirited army.[97] China's defense thus requires mobilizing all the country's resources to repel an invader and relying primarily on those armed forces whose performance most varies with the degree of dedication of their men (presumably the militia). Placing exclusive stress on advanced weaponry such as aircraft, missiles, and nuclear weapons inevitably leads to the incorrect conclusion that China is weaker than it, in reality, is. Lin Piao, for instance, committed this major strategic error, and it in turn provided much of the incentive for his turning traitor and seeking refuge in the technologically superior Soviet Union.[98]

The underlying premise upon which the radicals base the above arguments states that China's strength is a function of the degree of its unity and popular support for the government.[99] These are secured

---

behind others at a snail's pace?" Hua Kuo-feng firmly identified this perspective with the radicals in his speech to the National Science Conference on March 24, 1978: *New China News Agency*, March 25, 1978, cited in *FBIS/PRC*, March 27, 1978, pp. E-6, E-8.

[96] The most comprehensive and cogent formulation of this argument appears in Liang Hsiao, 10/75, passim.

[97] An Miao, p. 174.

[98] An Miao (p. 178) castigates Lin Piao's belief that, "We cannot depend on the infantry but have to rely on the air force, atomic weapons and missiles." He argues that this led Lin to worship Soviet nuclear power to the degree that Lin's ultimate betrayal of China and flight to the USSR became a virtual certainty. (P. 179.)

[99] China's real security resides in her "revolutionary people who are united and persist in struggle." An Miao, p. 179.

by a correct political line--one that stresses class struggle to weed out alien class elements and unify the people. The radicals insist, moreover, that the programs of the Cultural Revolution enjoy mass political support, and that any attempt to reverse them would breed popular disunity and split the country in dangerous ways.[100]

Analysis makes clear, then, that the radicals argue that China's national security depends on her leaders' pursuing the proper domestic political course. In this sense, domestic and foreign policy are in-extricably linked in the radicals' program. More subtly, the radicals argue that the fusion of domestic and foreign policies is equally characteristic of their opponents' position,[101] as is apparent in the following wide-ranging radical critique of the moderates' program.

Both moderate approaches view the threat from abroad in military terms and call attention to the fact that China is falling further and further behind its enemies in military power. According to the radi-cals, the moderates' program to reverse this disastrous (as the mod-erates perceive it) trend entails: making concessions to the USSR so as to decrease the chances of attack;[102] importing economic and mili-tary goods and technology from the West to the point where China com-promises its independence from the Western countries;[103] and assigning top priority domestically to economic production and military develop-ment. These latter require the large-scale rehabilitation of cadres and the elimination or cutback of programs that trace their origins to the Cultural Revolution.[104]

---

[100]All radicals argue that the system emerging from the Cultural Revolution enjoys broad popular support, and any attempts at "restora-tion and retrogression" would cause popular strife and dissension. The linking of one's attitude toward the GPCR to foreign policy is por-trayed most explicitly in Liang Hsiao, 1/76; see, for example, p. 19.

[101]In Liang Hsiao's words, "One who practices revisionism will invariably be a capitulationist." Liang Hsiao, 1/76, p. 13. The moderates likewise argue that domestic and foreign policies are in-separably linked, as explained below.

[102]Liang Hsiao, 7/74, p. E-6.

[103]Liang Hsiao, 10/75.

[104]Liang Hsiao, 5/74, pp. 172-173.

As previously noted, the radicals feel the moderates err fundamentally in viewing the international system in relatively static balance of power terms, with power measured by physical military and economic strength. The "soft" variant of the moderate approach compounds this error through arguing that China can modify the Soviet Union's behavior through softening the PRC's anti-Soviet propaganda, adopting a more flexible position in the border negotiations, agreeing to higher levels of Sino-Soviet trade, and making other concessions. The sources of Soviet aggression stem from the Soviet system itself, and no Chinese concessions can affect this situation. Even more egregious, policies such as retreating from the vociferously anti-Soviet stand of the PRC would have the side effect of making the Chinese people less vigilant against Soviet subversion, thus increasing China's vulnerability while doing nothing to lessen the probability of Soviet aggression against the PRC.[105]

Importing military and economic goods and technology on a large scale from abroad simply undermines the Chinese sense of confidence which is fundamental to the long-term success of the Chinese revolution. It also gives Westerners a toehold in China that they can use to nurture Chinese agents among those who retain a "comprador" mentality. Instead of augmenting China's ability to defend itself, therefore, these import policies will sap the country's strength and make it less able to preserve its independence.[106]

The radicals also argue that the imperialists want the moderates to suppress the radicals as a price for imperialist aid in developing China.[107] This, in turn, fits in well with the domestic goals of the moderates, who want to promote the cadres who were purged during the Cultural Revolution and pursue domestic economic and political policies that will undermine the position of the radicals at all levels. Thus,

---

[105] Ibid.

[106] Liang Hsiao, 10/75, p. 5.

[107] For example, Liang Hsiao (10/75, p. 2) argues that the *Yang Wu* program, which the author uses as a surrogate for the contemporary program of the moderates, "was entirely a product of the collusion between the feudal forces [that is, moderates] and the imperialists."

for instance, the moderates want to increase the use of material incentives, private plots, sideline production, and free markets, all of
which--as noted above--will enhance the resources available to their
natural constituents among the local "bourgeoisie" at the expense of
central control over the country. This will aggravate tensions and
create dissatisfaction at the local level and thus in effect will
weaken national unity.

The radicals contend that the moderates are extremely isolated
in the country and the Party, and that their realization of this
weakness at home inevitably makes them turn abroad to sell out the
country's interests in return for foreign support for their policies.
The moderates thus naturally become agents for the countries that seek
to defeat China.[108] This bond, by implication, is formed initially
through mutual convenience--the moderates need external cooperation
and backing to implement their anti-popular policies domestically;
and imperialists seek to cultivate people who will suppress the radicals (the true guardians of China's independence) and become imperialist agents in China. If the USSR actually attacked, moreover, the
moderates would almost certainly yield because their incorrect analysis
of power and its sources would lead them to urge capitulationism in
preference to suffering the hardships of war and inevitable defeat.
In lieu of this type of clear aggression and capitulation, a more
gradual process of undermining the revolution would occur. First, as
noted above, the moderates would use their analysis of the international dangers to justify their policies aimed at undermining the
position of the radicals.[109] Then, given the centralized nature of

---

[108]As An Miao (p. 179) put this case in discussing Lin Piao, "Because he wanted to practice revisionism in China, he was extremely
isolated among the people. Awed by the strong might of the dictatorship of the proletariat, he felt that his own strength was inadequate
and had necessarily to form an alliance with international revisionism."
See also, Liang Hsiao, 5/74, p. E-6: ". . . people advocating split-
tism and retrogression will, because of their own unpopularity and
weakness, invariably look for backstage bosses or seek assistance from
foreign aggressive forces by serving as traitors or lackeys in order to
undermine the country's solidarity."

[109]In Liang Hsiao's (5/74, p. E-2) words, they would try to "carry
out a struggle against the political and economic interests of the
newly-emerging forces."

China's system, the Party leaders who had turned traitor could and would change the nature of the system along the path of revisionism.[110] At the critical moment the hidden traitors in the Party would emerge and show their true colors[111]--and thus it is in anticipation of this event that it is necessary to wage repeated class struggles to ferret out these traitors before they can irreparably damage the cause of the revolution.

To sum up: The radicals argue that the moderates think in conventional balance of power terms. This leads them to stress the military threat to China and the PRC's weakness in relation to this threat; this defeatism in turn provides the basis for a range of policies that will in fact split and weaken the country and invite imperialist subversion and conquest. This theory is anti-Marxist and, moreover, this incorrect theory invites and justifies traitorous action. Both moderate programs amount, therefore, to capitulation at home and abroad and to inevitable national betrayal.

The Moderates: "Soft" and "Hard." Not surprisingly, the moderates plead "innocent as charged!" to the portrayal of their program given by the radicals--that is, the radicals do accurately represent most of the specific elements in the moderate program but they completely misunderstand the real dynamics and consequences of the program and its fidelity to the real problems confronting the Chinese revolution.

The moderates cast their glance at the international sphere and conclude, together with the radicals, that China faces great perils from abroad and that only a strongly unified country enjoying great popular support for the government can maintain China's long-term independence. They strongly disagree, however, on the nature of the external threat and on the formula for achieving strength through unity

---

[110] This fear partly explains the prominence, given in the spring of 1975 and afterwards, to Mao's quote, "Our country at present practices a commodity system, the wage system is unequal, too, as in the eight-grade wage scale, and so forth. These can only be restricted under the dictatorship of the proletariat. So if people like Lin Piao come to power, it will be quite easy for them to rig up the capitalist system." *Peking Review*, No. 14, April 4, 1975, pp. 7-8.

[111] Liang Hsiao, 1/76, p. 17.

at home. The radicals see the external threat as political, while the moderates view it overwhelmingly as military;[112] concomitantly, the radicals see China's unity in terms of maintaining the political line of the Cultural Revolution, while to the moderates unity can be achieved only by abandoning the harshly divisive GPCR policies in favor of an economic program that raises the standard of living.[113]

The moderates pull no punches in asserting that it is military power, not ideology, that determines the strength of nations in any meaningful sense in the near term. Even commercial relations are ultimately backed by political power, according to their argument.[114] Those who do not see this obvious truth are doomed to follow policies that will leave China critically deficient in the means to defend itself. When the USSR actually commits aggression against the PRC the radicals will realize the bankruptcy of their program, but it will then be too late to maintain China's independence.[115] The moderates cannot allow China to learn this lesson in so costly a way.

---

[112] Lo Ssu-ting (11/74, p. E-1) describes this threat as that of "predatory, aggressive wars" launched from the north of China. The radicals, however, ". . . give no thought to the threat of national extinction . . ." (p. E-6).

[113] Lo Ssu-ting (11/74, p. E-2) castigates those whose program "squeezes the people without reservation . . . [which] sharpens the class contradictions and confronts [the government] . . . with the grave situation in which 'it has to worry about the society being destroyed at home and about invasions by the barbarians abroad.'" Since the overthrow of the radicals, the Chinese moderate coalition in power has made clear its view that the Chinese people are unified in their desire for a higher standard of living. See, for example, Hua Kuo-feng's report to the Eleventh Party Congress: *New China News Agency*, August 22, 1977, cited in *FBIS/PRC* Supplement No. 9, September 1, 1977, pp. 32, 36-38.

[114] For example, imperialists have an "'unscrupulous profiteering' nature which makes them commit economic aggression with the backing of violence, 'accompanying commercial activities with military activities, making trade and armed force accompany each other.'" Wei Yuan, p. 2.

[115] The Wei Yuan article, for instance, notes that those who oppose importing foreign military technology and who cling to the current system "once faced with the armed armada of the foreign powers [will be] scared out of their wits and fall on their knees." (P. 5.) *Liberation Army Daily* put the point this way more than a year after the purge of the leading radicals: "In order to defend our motherland from aggression, we must have the latest techniques and equipment. . . . Didn't

Given China's military weakness and vulnerability to potential Soviet aggression, the moderates demand a number of important measures to help assure national survival. In foreign policy, they contend that the PRC should take full advantage of the contradictions among countries in the international sphere so as to augment China's security through diplomatic means.[116] The moderates also favor imports of goods and advanced technology from the West (including, at least for some, military goods and technology) that can alleviate China's critical deficiencies in these areas as quickly as possible. They insist, moreover, that the PRC can borrow from the West without letting the initiative slip from China's own hands and that those who would argue otherwise underestimate (one might even say "disparage") the wisdom, strength, and creativity of the Chinese people.[117]

To the moderates, then, the PRC must tilt toward the West to increase its chances of national survival. Some of these same people—those who pursue the "soft" variant of the moderate approach—also argue, however, that China should make some compromises with the Soviet Union so as to lessen the chances that the USSR will launch an attack in the first place. These moderates are fully convinced that any war with the USSR in the near future would be disastrous for China, involving extremely high casualties, the loss of much treasure, and untold suffering for the Chinese people. Thus, for instance, after the Soviets warned China in May 1974 that if the PRC did not immediately release the three Soviet helicopter pilots China had captured in Sinkiang in March 1974, "it thereby assumes full responsibility for the inevitable consequences of such provocational action."[118] The radicals claimed that

---

the 'Gang of Four' dish up the fallacy that the army's main task was the so-called 'opposing restoration'?. . . The consequences [of this policy] would have led to the greatest dangers imaginable when social-imperialism and imperialism impose wars on us": *Liberation Army Daily* Editorial, January 26, 1978, cited in *FBIS/PRC*, January 26, 1978, p. E-12.

[116]Wei Yuan, p. 7. The fullest post-Mao statement of this view is in *People's Daily*, November 1, 1977, cited in *FBIS/PRC*, November 1, 1977, pp. E-1-37.

[117]Wei Yuan, pp. 4-6.

[118]*Pravda*, May 3, 1974.

the "soft" moderates at this time advocated measures to relieve tensions (release the pilots?), along with the acceptance of several major offers that had been tabled earlier by the Soviets in their bilateral negotiations--a summit meeting, more flexible negotiations on the border, and increased trade.[119]

The moderates who advocate a "hard" variant oppose a policy of making concessions to the Soviet Union to decrease the chances of a Soviet attack on the PRC. They believe this approach fundamentally misreads the Soviet mind. The "hard" moderates, as the radicals, argue that the Soviets will take concessions as a sign of weakness.[120] Concessions will, moreover, simply dull the Chinese people's sense of the danger from the North while actually increasing the probability of a Soviet attack. According to the "hard" moderates, the Soviet threat to China *is* military in nature, but the Soviets are physically strong and politically vacillating. If China shows its weakness, the Soviets will muster up the political courage to attack; but if the PRC adopts an active border defense, continues to take a completely uncompromising stand against the USSR, and in other ways strikes a posture of confidence and strength, the Soviets will prove much less likely to summon up the will and the nerve to launch an attack.[121] The "soft"

---

[119]Liang Hsiao, 5/74, p. E-6.

[120]There is some cultural basis for this evaluation of Soviet perception. The Russian word "kompromis" is used in a pejorative sense. It connotes weakness rather than a statesmanlike effort to reach an agreeable middle ground.

[121]". . . foreign aggressors [bully] the weak but [yield] to might. 'Might inspires fear, and only with that [do] they respect us and abide by our rules.' 'Favors [that is, concessions] and righteousness [that is, ideological purity]' . . . only whet their aggressive appetite. To halt aggression, the only way [is] to 'counter armed force with armed force.'" Wei Yuan, p. 4. The available literature on the two major Soviet invasions of neighboring countries provides considerable support for this "hard" view. The Politburo wavered back and forth before launching the invasions of Hungary (1956) and Czechoslovakia (1968) and in each case seems to have opted for military intervention only when the chances of active resistance appeared minimal. On this vacillation see, for instance, *Khrushchev Remembers*, Little, Brown and Company, Boston, 1970, pp. 415-419 (for Hungary); and Jiri Valenta, "Soviet Decisionmaking and the Czechoslovak Crisis of 1968," *Studies in Comparative Communism*, Spring/Summer 1975, pp. 147-173.

moderates, according to this argument, correctly feel that Chinese measures that visibly increase the PRC's military capabilities might in the short term increase the incentives for Soviets to attack before the PLA becomes much stronger. These "soft" moderates err, nevertheless, in trying to ward off this attack through a policy of concessions. What is needed instead is a show of strength.

Thus, all moderates look to foreign policy both to decrease the chances that the USSR will attack and to increase China's ability to cope with Soviet aggression if it materializes. They combine these foreign policy positions, moreover, with a wide range of proposals to strengthen China domestically in the face of the Soviet threat.

The moderates advocate development of a strong military to defend the PRC. They place great stress on a highly professional military force--one that trains its troops rigorously and has cut out all of the fat.[122] It is unclear from the allegorical articles to what degree the moderates favor the more technically sophisticated branches of the military, such as the air and missile forces.

The moderates argue that China should beef up her defenses along the Sino-Soviet and Sino-Mongolian borders. This involves construction of more and better defense works. It also requires the establishment of more "military/farming units" (production and construction corps) in the border areas.[123] And perhaps most importantly, it demands that China win over her national minorities that live near the northern borders through a moderate and tolerant policy toward them. The minorities, according to the moderates, will display great patriotism if only the central authorities are wise enough to cultivate their loyalties. The radicals, by contrast, insist that only the minority "proletarians" can be won over and that harsh class struggle between the

---

[122]The Wei Yuan piece (p. 5) argues that ". . . troops should be enlisted on a highly selective basis, trained strictly and maintained rationally--in other words, only when troops [are] trained regularly in the spirit of fighting courageously and skillfully [can] their combat efficiency be raised."

[123]Lo Ssu-ting, 11/74, p. E-7.

exploited and exploiter within the minority communities is needed to make even the former fully loyal to the Han socialist state.[124]

China's resources are scarce, and the moderates emphasize the long-term dependence of the military on adequate growth in the country's civilian economy.[125] They also see in economic growth--with a concomitant increase in the standard of living--an absolutely essential ingredient for garnering widespread popular support for the government. The moderates assert it is necessary to increase material incentives to induce China's population to put out the effort required for rapid economic growth. The increased productivity spawned by material incentives will, in turn, engender the expansion of resources necessary to provide China with an adequate base for both a strong defense and a contented populace.[126] Few allegorical articles provide a clear picture of the authors' preferred distribution of material incentives and investment priorities, and there is evidently dissension within the moderate camp on this issue. Some evidence does suggest, however, that the moderates have argued for a policy of placing defense-related

---

[124]This issue was first raised on the moderate side by Lo Ssu-ting, 11/74, pp. E-1-2, E-7-8. The radical rejoinder appeared in Liang Hsiao, 12/74, pp. 143-144. The Wei Yuan piece then refuted the radicals' argument in Wei Yuan, pp. 7-9. In 1978 the Chinese media castigated the purged radicals for the harsh policy toward nationalities that they advocated; see, for example, *New China News Agency*, January 28, 1978, cited in *FBIS/PRC*, January 30, 1978, p. E-14.

[125]Lo Ssu-ting (11/74, p. E-2) castigates the radicals for allowing a "decline in the . . . relations of production" and argues the need to increase the economic *and* military might of the country. This same theme has been articulated by key moderate leaders since the purge of the radicals. See, for example, Yeh Chien-ying's speech to the National Conference to Learn from Taching in Industry: *Peking Review*, No. 21, May 20, 1977, pp. 15-19; and Hua Kuo-feng's report to the Fifth National People's Congress: *New China News Agency*, March 6, 1978, cited in *FBIS/PRC*, March 7, 1978, pp. D-4-6.

[126]Liang Hsiao (5/74, p. E-8) sarcastically sums up this argument by saying that "According to them, 'good deeds to people [are] rewarded by heaven' so that even the weather [is] always fine." This policy has in fact been a centerpiece of the moderates' program since they seized power in late 1976.

industries under civilian management to maximize the beneficial spin-off of military production for the civilian economy.[127]

The moderates stress the importance of a manpower policy appropriate to the tasks of technological development and sound management. They advocate placing the most skilled persons in charge regardless of their backgrounds. Put differently, the moderates contend that cadres should be promoted only on the basis of demonstrated skills and that past political blemishes on a person's record should not rob China of that person's skills in the future. All cadres, moreover, should receive the most rigorous and advanced training appropriate to the tasks they must perform.[128] By implication, then, the moderates call for the large-scale rehabilitation of cadres tarnished by the Cultural Revolution, the demotion of people previously promoted on the basis of political criteria who lack necessary technical and administrative skills, and the curtailment of educational and vocational programs that do not provide the most rigorous professional training for their participants.

In short, the moderates believe Peking can most effectively rally the Chinese people around a program of material incentives, promotion by merit,[129] and national strength defined in terms of rapid economic development and military power. They explicitly charge, moreover, that China cannot strengthen itself sufficiently to maintain its independence as long as the radicals retain access to the levers of political power.

----

[127]Wei Yuan (p. 5) insists that "The armaments industry should be turned into civilian industries . . . the development of big industry [has] wider prospects with civilian production."

[128]In the words of the Wei Yuan article (p. 12), "By training and using capable and talented people, the military and political establishments of the nation will be greatly improved. . . . [The moderates] actively advocate the idea of educating the people and cultivating talents." The radicals, by contrast, suffer from two diseases which must be cured: "ignorance of the people" and "waste of human talent" (ibid.). See also Lo Ssu-ting, 4/26/74, p. 9. Teng Hsiao-p'ing struck this same theme in his speech to the National Science Conference on March 18, 1978: *New China News Agency*, March 21, 1978, cited in *FBIS/PRC*, March 21, 1978, pp. E-4-15.

[129]". . . a wise ruler . . . must reward those who render meritorious service and appoint the capable to official posts. Those who work hard get bigger emoluments, those who render more meritorious service enjoy superior rank, and those who can govern a larger number of people become higher officials." Lo Ssu-ting, 4/26/74, p. 9.

To support their argument, the moderates point to the Cultural Revolution and events during 1974-1976 and charge that bringing the radicals into power means, *ipso facto*, plunging China into a period of internal strife and dissension. Neither the people nor the cadres will accept the radicals' programs, and thus these programs stand no chance of success.[130] The moderates know from experience, moreover, that the radicals personally will never compromise on their fundamental ideas. They will and have concealed their ideas while they are under a cloud so as to retain some access to the highest levels, but in their hearts they are merely awaiting the proper time to seize power and reverse the programs of the moderates (and wreak vengence on their sponsors).[131] Neither the moderates nor their programs, therefore, are safe as long as any radicals retain high positions in the government and Party. The danger of a radical restoration would be greatest, moreover, in the wake of Mao Tse-tung's demise, when especially Chiang Ch'ing would move to take over.[132] Relatedly, in the years before his death Mao Tse-tung had so surrounded himself with sycophants that he

---

[130]The moderate argument asserts that China needs unity to maintain its independence but that there can be no unity as long as the radicals retain a toehold in the political system: Lo Ssu-ting, 5/3/74, pp. 19-22.

[131]According to Lo Ssu-ting (5/3/74, pp. 20-21), restoring the radicals to executive positions throughout the bureaucracy would produce a situation where cadres "would attack one another like enemies and the former situation of division and chaotic fighting . . . would be restored. . . . [Moreover, the radicals are] reluctant to quit the stage of history of [their] own volition. . . . They should be suppressed because they [are] creating public opinion for staging a restoration. . . . [The only proper solution is] disbanding their gang." The other elements in this argument are contained on pp. 19-22; they also suffuse the other articles that present a moderate perspective.

[132]Lo Ssu-ting (11/74, p. E-5) warns of this by recounting that "After the death of the Emperor . . . the diehards . . . came back to assume the reins of power with the support of the Empress Dowager. . . ." Subsequently, the victorious moderates claimed that the radicals headed by Chiang Ch'ing did try to seize power in the month after Mao's death: *New China News Agency*, August 22, 1977, cited in *FBIS/PRC* Supplement No. 9, September 1, 1977, pp. E-17-18.

no longer understood the real situation and would not himself move decisively to eliminate the continuing danger from these radicals.[133]

The moderates' portrayal of the radicals becomes considerably less flattering than even the above would suggest, for they believe that radicals often act on the basis of personal motivations rather than fundamental principles. Thus, for instance, they charge that the radicals' overwhelming desire to retain power keeps them preoccupied with bureaucratic intrigue more than with substantive issues of merit.[134] Indeed, the radicals are ignorant of the people and their programs engender great popular suffering.[135] They are ignorant of the foreign military threat facing China[136] and so completely throw affairs into confusion in the PRC with their ridiculous innovations that they undermine both China's ability to resist and the foreigners' incentives not to attack. Thus, their stress on ideology rather than power will lead to the doom of the state,[137] and their overweening personal ambitions and stubbornness mean they will remain a threat until they are physically eliminated from positions of power.[138]

---

[133]"The 'Son of Heaven' [cares] only for his own personal power and interests, and [gives] no thought to state affairs; officials, civil and military, [open] the doors and [bow] with hands folded. . . . How [can] victory be won with such corrupt politics? How [can we] avoid being humiliated by the enemies?" Wei Yuan, p. 8.

[134]The Wei Yuan piece (p. 12) accuses the radicals of ". . . deception, cowardice, conspiracy and manipulation of power" and castigates ". . . the bureaucratic practices of officials who were unrealistic and hypocritical." Lo Ssu-ting (4/26/74, pp. 7-10) makes many of the same points.

[135]Wei Yuan, p. 11. Lo Ssu-ting (11/74, p. E-2) charges that the radicals "squeeze the people without reservation. This sharpens the class contradictions and national crisis and confronts the [government] . . . with the grave situation in which it has to worry about the society being destroyed at home and about invasions by the barbarians abroad."

[136]The radicals argue that "the trouble lies not without but within . . . [and thus they] guard against the people with greater care than against bandits." The moderates know, by contrast, that "The principal enemies [are] . . . not the people but the foreign aggressors." Wei Yuan, p. 7.

[137]Stressing ideology "to rule our state . . . will lead to its doom." Lo Ssu-ting, 4/26/74, p. 8.

[138]This is the major theme of Lo Ssu-ting, 5/3/74, pp. 19-22.

It is thus the radicals, according to the moderates, who undermine China's independence and have earned the epithets "capitulationists" and "traitors."[139]

The moderates, in sum, stress the overwhelming importance of the imperialist threat confronting China and the essentially military nature of that threat. They advocate major initiatives in both the international and domestic spheres to ward off this threat, fully affirming (as do the radicals) that domestic and foreign policy are inseparable. They argue, moreover, that the radicals so misperceive reality and sap China's strength with their programs that they will inevitably eventually invite Soviet aggression. A possible Soviet attack will then--too late--make the radicals realize the failure of their policies, at a time when they will have no choice but to sell out the interests of China to sue for peace.

SUCCESSION POLITICS AND SINO-SOVIET RELATIONS, 1973-1978

Identifying the Factions: Initial Considerations

The preceding section raises almost as many questions as it answers. Given that Chiang Ch'ing, Yao Wen-yuan, Chang Ch'un-ch'iao, and Wang Hung-wen and their colleagues were the "radicals," who were the "soft" and "hard" moderates? How does this debate over fundamentals mesh with the major events in Chinese politics and Sino-Soviet relations during this period--especially the changing Chinese attitude toward the Soviet helicopter pilots captured in Sinkiang in March 1974? What are the full implications of these arguments for China's relations with the United States?

The available evidence provides no firm basis for indentifying the "soft" versus "hard" moderates in the Chinese leadership. The "soft" moderate position, however, does parallel the position that the PLA under Lin Piao articulated in the late 1960s. As Gottlieb summarized it, the military believed that ". . . if China were to adhere to a

---

[139]The Wei Yuan piece (p. 19) expresses this as follows: "They [choose] to capitulate and resort to treason rather than change 'the laws of their ancestors,' the slightest tampering with which was absolutely forbidden."

policy of not provoking the Russians, and instead occasionally remind them of the traditional friendship between the two countries, then at least they could postpone a confrontation. At best they could prevent a showdown."[140] But, as noted earlier, all of the people Gottlieb identified as espousing the military position have now either died or been purged. The only remaining top military official from that period, Yeh Chien-ying, is the one military figure Gottlieb placed in the moderate camp.[141]

Indeed, the basis for the "military's" opposition to confrontationist politics with Moscow has now in substantial part eroded. The military took their stand in the belief that the United States remained the primary enemy and that the USSR should be regarded as a long-term threat, at best. There was wisdom, therefore, in not providing the Soviet Union with strong provocation that might encourage the leaders in the Kremlin to make decisions that would substantially increase the threat to China from her north in the near term.[142] Events since 1972,

---

[140]Gottlieb, op. cit., p. 125.

[141]Ibid., pp. 14, 17.

[142]Ibid., pp. 125-126. Obviously, there may have been a more subtle calculus centered around the domestic political concerns of the major military figures that contributed to this "military" estimate. Hong Yung Lee has presented data that suggest that by 1968 Lin Piao and Chou En-lai opposed each other on almost all domestic issues-- indeed, that Chou had chosen to side, when necessary, with the Cultural Revolution group radicals to oppose Lin. Thus, the personal rivalry between Lin and Chou must have been keenly perceived by all the highest leaders by 1969-1970 at the latest. Gottlieb (op. cit) has shown that the opening to the United States was a Chou initiative *par excellence*. It may well be, then, that Lin seized on this issue, on which he perceived Chou to be quite vulnerable, to maneuver successfully against his political enemy rather than to put forward the results of his strongly felt military estimate of the dangers confronting China. The other top military leaders, as shown by the purge directly following Lin's demise, had sided with Lin in the factional power struggle. To an unknown degree, then, the "military" viewpoint analyzed by Gottlieb may itself have been a tactical political maneuver in the domestic power struggle rather than a sincere disagreement over strategic policy. Hong Yung Lee's data are presented in "Cleavages and Coalitions in the Cultural Revolution," unpublished paper presented to the Columbia University Seminar on Modern China, February 10, 1977. From a somewhat different perspective, Lin's position on this issue may have been designed in part to wean the radicals away from their alliance with Chou En-lai.

however, have taken the edge off this argument. The Vietnam War has ended, the United States no longer holds a strong position in Southeast Asia, U.S. military strength throughout the Far East has visibly ebbed, and the United States has demonstrated its willingness to break bread with China as a counter to Soviet expansionism. It is a hard argument to make in Peking in the late 1970s that the United States poses the primary military threat to the PRC.[143]

Paradoxically, however, the top military leadership may still be among the "soft" moderates in China, albeit for a rather different set of reasons. Now the Chinese military view the United States and the West as a source of vitally needed technology that will significantly strengthen the PRC against the Red Army. Purchases of such technology and related military equipment, however, might well themselves provoke Moscow, thus necessitating affirmative Chinese action to undercut the hard-liners in the Kremlin as they press for a more aggressive policy while China is still weak. Under this new set of circumstances, therefore, there is a reasonable rationale for China's military leaders to lobby for some ameliorative gestures toward the Soviet Union, coupled with a major program of strengthening the PLA.[144]

The military, of course, could not carry out this diplomatic approach alone. Unlike the situation in early 1969, when Lin Piao and his military colleagues held tremendous independent power in the political hierarchy, by the mid-1970s the military had long since been cut down to size. The Party leadership under Mao and Chou En-lai had decapitated the highest echelon of the central military establishment in the wake of the Lin Piao affair, and the subsequent criticism of Lin had

---

[143]Morton Abramowitz has presented an insightful summary of the broad outlines of U.S. policy in East Asia, in which he argues that the United States has reduced its military presence there out of the recognition that the Soviet Union is now its major military adversary, and thus the United States now needs a capacity to fight 1-1/2 wars rather than the 2-1/2 wars previously planned for: Morton Abramowitz, "Chinese Military Capacities," *United States--Soviet Union--China: The Great Power Triangle*, Hearings Before the Subcommittee on Future Foreign Policy Research and Development of the Committee on International Relations, House of Representatives, April 6, 1976.

[144]This argument is spelled out in detail below.

tainted the entire PLA. In December 1973, moreover, Mao rotated eight
key military region commanders out of their previous bailiwicks, not
allowing them to take along either retainers or troops. All held
lesser positions in their new locations than they had in the old.[145]
Thus, the military by 1975 needed allies among the civilian leadership,
and identification of the other "soft" moderates requires that the
search be carried on within this context.

The military was not alone in searching for allies during these
years. All parties in Peking realized by 1974 that the succession
could begin at any moment. Mao Tse-tung was frail, and Chou En-lai
had been stricken with a terminal cancer. It became increasingly clear
during 1973-1974 that Chou had decided to groom Teng Hsiao-p'ing as
Mao's successor, and this decision in turn greatly excited the politics
of the capital.

The Rehabilitation of Teng Hsiao-p'ing

Teng Hsiao-p'ing had been the second most prominent victim of the
Cultural Revolution. He was, moreover, a strong-willed man who brooked
little opposition to his views. Given the humiliation and vilification
he had suffered during 1966-1968, there is little question that Teng
could not hold ultimate political power in the PRC and still maintain
the delicate balance between radicals and moderates that Mao Tse-tung
had cultivated. In view of his background and the earlier investiga-
tions into his political errors, Teng probably felt that he could not

---

[145]Gottlieb, op. cit., discusses the power of the military in the
Chinese political hierarchy as of 1969. The first major blow to military power came with the fall of Lin Piao in September 1971, followed
almost immediately by the purge of Huang Yung-sheng, Chiu Hui-tso, and
Wu Fa-hsien. The second visible step occurred in December 1973 when,
as noted in the text, eight of China's eleven military regional commanders were rotated out of their home bases and separated from the
troops and provincial political apparatuses with which they had enjoyed
long relationships. In general, the process of rebuilding the Party
and government apparatuses included a gradual shifting of the military
out of the administrative tasks throughout the society that it had
assumed during the later stages of the Cultural Revolution. Two interesting treatments of various aspects of this process are Bridgham, op.
cit., pp. 427-449; and Ellis Joffe, "The Chinese Army After the Cultural
Revolution: The Effects of Intervention," *China Quarterly*, No. 55, July-
September 1973, pp. 450-477.

survive in power as long as his chief enemies remained in the top echelons of the Party. Likewise, Teng could find no means to give adequate assurance to those who had toppled him during the Cultural Revolution that he would not seek revenge when power gravitated into his hands. Chou's choice of Teng, therefore, greatly increased the chances of a major purge directly following Mao's death--and concomitantly heightened the intensity of the maneuvering on all sides prior to the Chairman's demise.

The Politics of the Tenth Party Congress

Teng Hsiao-p'ing's rehabilitation occurred in the spring of 1973, at the same time that Watergate began to sap Richard Nixon's strength. In mid-June, Leonid Brezhnev journeyed to Washington for a summit with the increasingly beleaguered U.S. President. This Brezhnev trip to the United States produced concrete cause for concern in Peking. One of the less noticed but more important clauses of the Shanghai Communiqué that Richard Nixon and Chou En-lai had signed in February 1972 stipulated that both the United States and the PRC opposed "hegemonism" by any country in Asia.[146] Given the accepted Chinese definition of hegemonism, this affirmation essentially committed the United States to some form of opposition to any major Soviet effort to flex its muscles in the Asia-Pacific region. Having thus assumed an obligation to Peking to become involved to a degree on the Chinese side if the Sino-Soviet dispute should lead toward war, the Nixon Administration agreed during Brezhnev's June 1973 visit to the United States to undertake a similar type of commitment (albeit in a different form) to the Soviet side. Specifically, Article IV of the agreement on the prevention of nuclear war, signed by Nixon and Brezhnev on behalf of their respective governments on June 22, obligated the two sides to enter into "urgent negotiations" if relations between them, or between one of them and any third country, "appear to involve the risk of nuclear conflict." In short, if the Soviet Union and China should go to the brink of war, the United

---

[146]*Peking Review*, No. 9, March 3, 1972, p. 5.

States had now agreed to consult urgently with the *Soviet Union*.[147]

Word spread that Article IV had been under preparation secretly, more-over, for more than a year.[148] Ironically, just one month earlier, John Newhouse[149] had revealed for the first time in public a Soviet offer to the United States in July 1970 to reach an agreement that closely approximated that contained in Article IV. The Newhouse book noted that the United States had rejected this suggestion immediately. In June 1973, however, the Nixon Administration completed the process of committing itself to both sides to take an active role in the event of Sino-Soviet conflict, thus chipping away at the underlying premises of China's rapprochement with the United States.[150]

The above events occurred, as noted above, within the context of a rapid erosion in the strength of President Nixon's political base in the United States. At the end of 1972 Nixon seemed at the peak of his power, having just won reelection by a historic margin. In June 1973 the Senate committee investigating the Watergate affair and other alleged mis-deeds of the Nixon Administration had to call a recess in its proceedings during the Brezhnev visit so as not to highlight the weakness of the Presi-dent while he engaged in summit diplomacy with the Soviet Union. Events thus now seemed to be moving in favor of the Soviet Union: The Vietnam agreement of January 1973 had removed U.S. ground forces from South Vietnam and had been followed by a Soviet "peace offensive" in Asia; the political difficulties of the Nixon Administration began to call into question the President's ability to act decisively in Asia or else-where should the need arise; and the Administration's desire to keep

---

[147] Henry Kissinger used this specific example in his news brief-ing on the document the day of the signing ceremony.

[148] *New York Times*, June 23, 1973.

[149] Newhouse, op. cit., pp. 188-189.

[150] If, as H. R. Haldeman has asserted, the United States success-fully dissuaded the Soviet Union from launching a surprise nuclear attack against the Chinese in 1969, the Nixon Administration may have agreed to Article IV as a means to try and restrain future Soviet nu-clear action against the PRC; to the leaders in Peking, however, this agreement could be seen as evidence of U.S.-Soviet collusion at China's expense, and the Kissinger explanation conformed to their more sin-ister interpretation. On 1969, see H. R. Haldeman, *The Ends of Power*, Times Books, New York, 1978.

momentum going in foreign relations helped propel movement toward détente in Europe and elsewhere, which fit in well with the Soviet Union's diplomatic concerns of the moment. At this time, on the very eve of Secretary Brezhnev's summit trip to Washington, the USSR offered China yet another package in their border negotiations.

The Soviet package of mid-June, as noted in Sec. I, contained three elements: a "concrete nonaggression treaty that prohibits both the threat and use of any kind of force"; relations based on peaceful co-existence; and reiteration of Soviet willingness to convene a summit meeting at any time.[151] The Chinese did "not even deign to respond" to these offers.[152]

Following the Nixon-Brezhnev summit, the USSR moved rapidly and forcefully to accelerate the momentum toward détente, especially in Europe. In early July, the Conference on Security and Cooperation in Europe ("Helsinki Conference") convened. The Soviet Union urged this conference to adopt a written declaration that would in the future serve to maintain peace on the continent. Alexei Kosygin, in address-ing this meeting, asked "Who could lose from this? No one--or, more precisely, only those, whether near or far from the European continent, who count on maintaining tension and preserving hotbeds of military danger and who are trying to prevent a rapprochement between the states of the East and the West"[153]--a clear reference to Peking which, at that time, based its policy precisely on maintaining Western vigilance against Soviet aggressiveness and subversion. Brezhnev undertook addi-tional summit trips that summer, to France and West Germany, and Kosygin traveled to Austria and elsewhere. A conference aimed at the reduction of military forces in Central Europe, moreover, was scheduled to begin October 30.

At a meeting of East European bloc leaders in the Crimea on July 30-31, Brezhnev received the support of all countries[154]--including

---

[151] *Pravda*, September 25, 1973, cited in *CDSP*, Vol. XXV, No. 39, October 24, 1973.

[152] Ibid.

[153] *Pravda*, July 4, 1973, cited in *CDSP*, Vol. XXV, No. 27, August 1, 1973, p. 3.

[154] Excluding Albania.

such neutrals between Peking and Moscow as Romania--for the policy of
détente in Europe.[155] These international trends in the period before
China's Tenth Party Congress in August clearly argued against the wisdom of a Peking policy that tilted decisively in the direction of re-
liance on the West to make viable a continuing stance of unremitting
hostility toward the Soviet Union. Advocates of this policy--most
notably Mao Tse-tung and Chou En-lai--had to overcome increasing doubts
as to the correctness of their course, which in turn should logically
have made them welcome all signs of increasing Soviet hostility toward
China as additional support for the premises on which they based their
policy. Soviet actions during this summer, however, carefully blended
relatively ominous actions with offers that held out the potential for
a fundamental improvement in Sino-Soviet relations.

Within the context of a continuing propaganda barrage by both sides,
Sino-Soviet bilateral relations experienced both ups and downs during
the month or so prior to the Tenth Party Congress, which convened on
August 24. On August 1, China and the Soviet Union signed their annual
trade protocol.[156] Although the terms of this agreement were not made
public, the actual level of trade remained at almost exactly the same
level as in 1972.[157] Moscow announced that on July 16 negotiations
that had been carried on to establish regular air service between Moscow and Peking were completed successfully.[158] These negotiations had
been in progress in the Soviet capital since March 31.[159] Nevertheless,
on July 19 Ilyichev departed from Peking, effectively breaking off the
border talks.[160] The Soviets were convinced by then that China had rejected Moscow's offers of June, as a speech by Brezhnev in Alma Ata on

---

[155]*Pravda* and *Izvestia*, August 1, 1973, cited in *CDSP*, Vol. XXV,
No. 31, August 29, 1973.

[156]*Pravda*, August 2, 1973, cited in *CDSP*, Vol. XXV, No. 31, August
29, 1973, p. 23.

[157]*Vneshniaia torgovlia za 1973 god*, pp. 243-245.

[158]*Pravda*, July 17, 1973, cited in *CDSP*, Vol. XXV, No. 29, August
13, 1973, p. 25.

[159]*New China News Agency*, Peking, March 31, 1973; *SCMP*, 73-15, No.
5353, April 12, 1973, p. 153.

[160]*New York Times*, July 20, 1973.

August 15 confirmed.[161] In this same address, the Soviet Party leader again strongly endorsed a collective security system for Asia.

Within this context, the Tenth Party Congress, which met from August 24-28, proved the shortest and most secretive in China's post-1949 history. It was, in all probability, preceded by a central work conference of some sort, where most of the major discussion actually took place.[162] The Congress alone might actually have completed all of its work in five days if it had devoted its attention exclusively to rectifying the glaring problem of Lin Piao's designation as Mao Tse-tung's successor in the Party Constitution long after the former defense minister had been branded a traitor for attempting an armed coup d'etat against Mao before perishing during his escape to the Soviet Union. The Congress did correct this problem in the Party Rules, but it also went far beyond this to lay down a major new foreign policy line. In the process, it revealed the strains that recent Soviet and U.S. policies had placed on those who counted on unending hostility between the two superpowers.

Chou En-lai's political report to the Congress[163] dwelled at some length on foreign policy and especially the Soviet threat. Chou took direct aim at the trend toward international détente that had so filled the air over the summer and pointedly noted that "Relaxation is a temporary and superficial phenomenon, and great disorder will continue. Such great disorder is a good thing for the people, and not a bad thing. It throws the enemies into confusion and causes division among them, while it arouses and tempers the people. . . ."[164] Premier Chou thus declared flatly that China would maintain its strongly anti-détente attitude and he cautioned that ". . . when a wrong tendency surges toward us like a rising tide, we must not fear isolation and must dare

---

[161]*Pravda* and *Izvestia*, August 16, 1973, cited in *CDSP*, Vol. XXV, No. 33, September 12, 1973, p. 5.

[162]Liberthal, 1976a, op. cit., pp. 7-8. Additional evidence to this effect is presented in Lieberthal, 1978b, op. cit., pp. 10, 86.

[163]Text in *Peking Review*, No. 35-36, September 7, 1973, pp. 17-25.

[164]Ibid., p. 22.

to go against the tide and brave it through."[165] Lest people be fooled
by the obvious signs everywhere during the previous months that the
United States and USSR were moving toward closer cooperation in the
international sphere, Chou affirmed that the United States and Soviet
Union ". . . contend as well as collude with each other. Their collusion serves the purpose of more intensified contention. Contention
is absolute and protracted, whereas collusion is relative and temporary."[166] That Chou had to focus so much attention on these points
suggests that his foreign policy line, which depended on continued U.S.-
Soviet contention, had come under fire before this Congress convened.

Chou, indeed, went several steps further. Reasoning dialectically,
he concluded that, since Europe had been the focus during the previous
few months of efforts toward détente promoted by both the United States
and the Soviet Union, then Europe must in fact be the focus of their
underlying contention. The Soviet Union, which made menacing noises
toward China but had only soothing words for Europeans of all countries
during mid-1973, was "making a feint in the East while attacking in the
West."[167]

Why should Premier Chou who, as late as July 28, 1973, had characterized the Soviet Union as an "octopus which extends its tentacles in
all directions,"[168] now assert that in fact the major Soviet threat
centered on Europe? If Moscow was in fact "making a feint in the East
while attacking in the West," what was the nature of the threat that
the Soviets continued to pose to China?

At first glance, it appears that Chou En-lai's report conceded the
argument of his opponents on the political nature of the threat. If
the threatening aspects of the Soviet Union's policies toward China

---

[165]Ibid., Chou explicitly applied this to both domestic and foreign
policy, although Western analysts subsequently generally stressed its
domestic context.

[166]Ibid.

[167]Ibid. This phrase is in quotes in Chou's report because it is
one of the "36 stratagems"--traditional Chinese ploys in political and
military warfare.

[168]Emphasis added. Chou made this remark at a banquet for visiting
Congolese: *New China News Agency*, July 29, 1973, cited in *FBIS/PRC*,
July 30, 1973, pp. A-5-7.

amounted to no more than a "feint" to obscure Moscow's real attack on Europe, then surely Chinese preparedness to cope with a military attack--and the domestic and foreign imperatives of placing top priority on such preparedness--was unwarranted. Chou did indeed emphasize the *subversive* aspect of the Soviet threat, noting, for instance, that in 1967 "Brezhnev publicly announced continuation of the policy of subverting the leadership of the Chinese Communist Party"[169] and quoting another Soviet leader to the effect that "sooner or later the healthy forces expressing the true interests of China will have their decisive say . . . and achieve the victory of Marxist-Leninist ideas in their country."[170] The Premier indeed summed up the fifty-year history of the CCP with the assessment that "Enemies at home and abroad all understand that the easiest way to capture a fortress is from within. . . . [Far into the future] there is the threat of subversion and aggression by imperialism and social-imperialism."[171] Chou explicitly agreed, moreover, that, "U.S. imperialism . . . has openly admitted it is increasingly on the decline,"[172] thus casting substantial doubt on the wisdom of its own policy of courting the United States to counterbalance the Soviet Union.

On closer examination, however, Chou En-lai's political report bears all the earmarks of an artful compromise that allowed all sides to derive satisfaction from different aspects of his presentation. For instance, although the Premier introduced China's new assessment that Soviet policy toward China had become no more than a "feint" and that the key component of that policy focused on subversion, he also greatly distorted the record of recent Sino-Soviet interaction so as to magnify the Soviet military threat and stressed the danger of a surprise attack from China's north.

Chou's recapitulation of "recent" Sino-Soviet relations omits completely the offers the USSR had made in the border negotiations and

---

[169]*Peking Review*, No. 35-36, September 7, 1973, p. 19.

[170]Ibid.

[171]Ibid., p. 20.

[172]Ibid., p. 23.

taunts the Soviet Union with an admonition to "show your good faith by doing a thing or two—for instance, withdraw your armed forces from Czechoslovakia or the People's Republic of Mongolia and return the four northern islands to Japan."[173] While the Soviet Union had offered China simultaneous negotiations on various aspects of the border and related issues, a summit meeting, a nonaggression treaty, and so forth—and had indicated that China could show its good faith by responding positively to any of these initiatives—the Chinese Premier implied that Moscow had demanded instead that "China give away all the territory north of the Great Wall to the Soviet revisionists to show that we favor relaxation of world tension and are willing to improve Sino-Soviet relations."[174]

Having thus exaggerated and distorted recent Soviet demands on China, Chou En-lai asserted that China must "maintain high vigilance and be fully prepared against any war of aggression that imperialism may launch and *particularly against surprise attack on our country by Soviet revisionist social-imperialism.* Our heroic People's Liberation Army and our vast militia must be prepared at all times. . . ."[175] Thus, the "feint in the East while attacking in the West" analysis did not, to Chou's mind, mean that China could afford in any way to slacken its preparations against a surprise attack from the north.

In the context of European détente, moreover, Chou could utilize the slogan on "attacking in the West" to support his position that China could counter the overwhelming military threat it faced from the USSR by, in part, employing bold united front policies with the major

---

[173] Ibid.

[174] Ibid. Chou may have been responding to reports of recent banter among Soviet journalists to the effect that the path to Sino-Soviet amity lay in the creation between the USSR and a shrunken China of Soviet-dominated buffer states, formed from current Chinese territory: *New York Times*, September 1, 1973. Journalists' talk and government policy are hardly interchangeable, however, especially as the basis for so important a document as Premier Chou's official report to the CCP's Tenth Party Congress.

[175] *Peking Review*, No. 35-36, September 7, 1973, p. 24, emphasis added. Yao Wen-yuan, by contrast, used his "Report to the Congress to warn against 'surprise attack by imperialism and social-imperialism'" (that is, the United States and the Soviet Union): Ibid., p. 33.

Western countries. He had premised this strategy on the assumption that the West could continue to view the Soviet Union as a threat that had to be stopped and thus would serve to a degree as a counterweight to that threat. The movement of events during the summer of 1973, however, had lent little support to this analysis. Now Chou made acknowledgment of the continuing Soviet danger to the West--and thus the transient nature of détente--into a central accepted doctrine of Chinese foreign policy. In so doing he both justified his own foreign policy program and, possibly, laid the groundwork for China to make the case in the future that the West should continue to aid China against the USSR as part of the strategy of insuring its own survival. The Premier hinted at the seed of this argument in his assertion that "The West always wants to urge the Soviet revisionists eastward to divert the peril towards China, and it would be fine [as far as the West is concerned] so long as all is quiet in the West."[176] By implication, then, the West recognizes that the Soviet Union cannot cope with a war on two fronts--and thus now that the thrust of Soviet policy has turned back toward undermining the West, it is in Western interests to help maintain a credible Chinese presence on Soviet borders in the East.[177] Conveniently, this formulation also fits nicely into the conceptual scheme of the radicals, who had been arguing that Chou and his colleagues had incorrectly exaggerated the Soviet military threat to China to the point where it had become the justification for a whole series of measures that the radicals found unacceptable in both domestic and foreign policy.[178]

---

[176]Ibid., p. 22.

[177]Almost four years later the Chinese were willing to spell out the implications of this argument more directly. Vice Foreign Minister Yu Chan, for example, told a West German interviewer that "The West Europeans should realize that they are being particularly threatened by the Soviet Union. Political unification of West Europe and strengthening the defensive forces first of all will serve Europe's survival. It is serving China only in a secondary way. On the other hand, *a strengthened China will serve the interests of Europe*": *Die Welt*, Bonn, May 14 and 15, 1977, cited in *FBIS/PRC*, May 17, 1977, p. A-4, emphasis added.

[178]See the "radical" argument in the "allegorical" section above.

Chou's political report, therefore, reflected the serious debate in China over the nature of the Soviet threat to the PRC. The documents emerging from this Congress, however, made clear that anti-Sovietism would continue to be a touchstone of Chinese foreign policy,[179] although they were somewhat more ambiguous concerning China's future relationship with the United States and Peking's specific preparations to counter the Soviet challenge. Moscow's policy of détente with the United States had increased the opposition in China to the PRC's opening to the United States, although it did not quite succeed in reversing that policy.

Radical Resurgence: Fall 1973 to Spring 1974

The radicals renewed their attack after the Congress through the campaign to criticize Lin Piao and Confucius, launched in the fall of 1973. In part by the articles in this campaign,[180] they raised the series of issues spelled out above as the radical viewpoint. They particularly focused on Chou's policy of rehabilitating former cadres, such as Teng Hsiao-p'ing, castigating this as the Confucianist strategy of "restoring old families to power." This radical offensive gained momentum during the winter of 1973-1974 and peaked in the spring of 1974.

The radicals' strength may have been increased somewhat in regard to foreign policy during this period by the mushrooming Watergate affair in the United States. The Chinese had agreed to establish Liaison Offices with the United States in February 1973, thereby compromising their principle of refusing to post PRC diplomats to a capital that also housed representatives from Taiwan. Now, Watergate threatened to unravel the Sino-U.S. understanding that the United States would cut its ties to Taiwan in Nixon's second term in office. The obvious success

---

[179]See, for example, the text of the Party Constitution passed by the Congress, which enjoined the Party to "oppose the hegemonism of the two superpowers--the United States and the Soviet Union--to overthrow imperialism, modern revisionism and all reaction. . . ." *Peking Review*, No. 35-36, September 7, 1973, p. 26.

[180]As noted above, the CIA has published a compilation of the allegorical articles produced during this campaign through 1974: *Bibliography of Literature*, op. cit.

of Soviet détente policy through the summer of 1973, moreover, further undermined Chou's position. The time was ripe to argue that neither the United States nor the Soviet Union could be trusted in foreign relations.

Policy toward both the United States and the USSR edged over closer to the radicals' viewpoint during this period. In relations with the Soviet Union, the radicals' predispositions figured increasingly prominently in Chinese strategy. The volume and tone of criticism of Moscow escalated rapidly in the PRC media after the Tenth Party Congress. Clearly, anyone who may have been inclined toward a "softer" position on the Soviet question in view of the waning tempo of Sino-U.S. normalization stayed in the background at this time. Then after the turn of the year the theme of Soviet espionage and subversion in China--the major thesis of the radicals--suddenly dominated the Chinese media, and it was at this very time that the first of two major "espionage" incidents in Sino-Soviet relations since the Cultural Revolution occurred.

Soviet "Espionage": January 1974. On January 15, Chinese public security personnel arrested five members of the Soviet Embassy in Peking on charges of espionage in an episode that seems more akin to fiction than to serious political history. The Chinese seized Soviet First Secretary V. I. Marchenko and Third Secretary U. A. Semenov and their wives, and a Soviet translator named A. A. Kolosov. They were said by the Chinese to have been caught in the act of having a rendezvous on the outskirts of Peking with Li Hung-shu, an agent Moscow had recruited after his defection to the USSR in 1967 and had repatriated to the PRC in June 1972, and Li's unnamed accomplice. Li purportedly had handed over intelligence he had gathered on "the activities of grass-roots Party organizations and military and other activities around Mutankiang and Chiamuszu,"[181] and had received in turn new radio transmitting equipment for future communications with the Soviet Embassy in Peking. The Chinese must have known of this rendezvous in advance, as they caught the culprits red-handed, bringing into play local militia forces as well as public security personnel, and utilizing signal flares, among

---

[181]*Peking Review*, No. 5, February 1, 1974, p. 17. These are sites of former Japanese aircraft manufacturing plants.

other gadgets. Indeed, the Chinese even took the trouble to film the
entire event, presumably for later propaganda use.[182]

The Soviets claim, of course, that no such rendezvous occurred.
Indeed, they assert that the Chinese authorities captured the various
embassy personnel concerned in two different arrests on the streets of
Peking and then took them to designated areas where the Chinese authorities had organized mobs to stage scenes for filming.[183] No facts are
available from disinterested third parties to evaluate these completely
conflicting claims, but the evidence suggests that the Chinese version
edged somewhat closer to the truth.

The excellent preparations that even the Chinese assert they had
made beforehand must give the analyst some pause for thought, however.
There are several indications that the Soviet agents had been "set up"
by Chinese counterintelligence. Peking's own explanation simply notes
that "both the counter-revolutionary activities of the Soviet agent Li
Hung-shu and the espionage activities of the Soviet embassy members in
China had long been noticed by the Chinese people."[184] The Chinese
almost certainly, however, had gone beyond "noticing" these activities
to confronting Li and turning him "back" on the Soviets. How else
would the Chinese know precisely the time and place of the rendezvous?
Relatedly, why should the Chinese expose Li Hung-shu's name and background but withhold similar information on the "accomplice" unless the
latter was a member of the Chinese counterintelligence forces in dis-
guise, there to make certain that nothing went amiss in this operation?
Relatedly, Li is reported to have passed his information to the Soviet
agents in a small container secreted in a gauze mask. The Soviets threw
the mask and container into the stream where the rendezvous occurred
when they saw the signal flare sent up by the Chinese force. Nevertheless, the vigilant Chinese managed to fish the mask out of the water
in the dead of night. This seems possible only if Li or his "accomplice"

---

[182]Facts from *Peking Review*, No. 5, February 1, 1974, pp. 14-17.

[183]*Pravda*, January 22, 1974, cited in *CDSP*, Vol. XXVI, No. 3,
February 13, 1974, p. 4.

[184]*Peking Review*, No. 5, February 1, 1974, p. 16.

had immediately warned the Chinese forces that the mask had in fact
been disposed of in the stream.

Thus, it seems likely that, while the Soviets were really engaged
in espionage, the specific incident of January 15 had been choreographed
by Chinese counterintelligence organs and designed to be used for subsequent propaganda concerning the Soviet subversive threat to China.
All sides agree[185] that Marchenko and the others were held incommunicado for four days and were then expelled from China.[186] The Soviets
retaliated by arresting Kuan Heng-kuang, a PRC attaché in the USSR, on
January 19, accusing him of espionage, and expelling him from the Soviet
Union.[187] The Chinese asserted in a protest note of January 25 that
Kuan had been "set up" by Soviet agents, which may well have been true.[188]
Kuan returned to a very warm welcome in Peking.

The Chinese protest notes in these instances, moreover, used
stronger language than did their Soviet counterparts. For example, each
of the two major Chinese protests concluded with an admonition that the
Soviet Union must desist from the behavior condemned in the protest note,
"Otherwise, the Soviet Government must bear full responsibility for all
the consequences arising therefrom." The Soviet protest note of January
21, by contrast, concluded with the assertion that "The USSR Ministry
of Foreign Affairs expects that the Chinese side will take the necessary steps to prevent actions that could lead to the exacerbation of
Sino-Soviet relations." In point of fact, neither side made much mention of their mutually declared policy of improving Sino-Soviet state-
to-state relations throughout the remainder of the spring.

Antonioni and the Paracel Islands. During this same week of January 15-22, tensions over the Paracel Islands in the South China Sea
had mounted rapidly, culminating in a Chinese combined forces operation

---

[185]On the Chinese side, this is by implication.

[186]Chinese Note of January 19, 1974, text in *Peking Review*, No. 4,
January 25, 1974, p. 3; Soviet Note of January 21, 1974, text in *Pravda*,
January 22, 1974, cited in *CDSP*, Vol. XXVI, No. 3, February 13, 1974,
pp. 4-5.

[187]*Pravda*, January 24, 1974, cited in *CDSP*, Vol. XXVI, No. 3,
February 13, 1974, p. 5.

[188]*Peking Review*, No. 5, February 1, 1974, pp. 4-5.

"of self-defense" to take possession of islands in this group that had recently been occupied by the South Vietnamese.[189] This was the first military operation of this size beyond China's borders since the 1962 Sino-Indian border conflict. That it was directed most immediately against Saigon and involved the inadvertent capture of one U.S. military adviser suggests that it was viewed in Peking primarily within the context of Sino-Vietnamese-American relations. As a demonstration of China's willingness to employ military force to bolster its territorial claims, however, it also had relevance for the Soviet Union. The fact that both the espionage and Paracel Islands incidents occurred in the same week suggests very strongly that radicals anxious to take a very hard line on both the Soviets and Americans had at least temporarily come to the fore in Peking. There were other indications of a radical "upsurge" at the time, such as the subsequent appearance of a heroic ode to the operation in the Paracels commissioned by Chiang Ch'ing,[190] and great intensification of the campaign to criticize Lin Piao and Confucius.

The criticism of Lin Piao in the Chinese media focused in part on Lin's role as a Soviet spy, thus highlighting the espionage element that had recently been brought into the foreground in Chinese critiques of the USSR. The Chinese in late January also condemned a film of China done by Italian artist Antonioni. This action seemed partially aimed at cultural contacts with the West, which had laid the basis for Antonioni's exceptional opportunity to make his documentary of the PRC. Much of the criticism, however, focused on the parallels between

---

[189] China's version of these events given in *Peking Review*, No. 4, January 25, 1974, pp. 3-4.

[190] *Jen-min Jih-pao*, March 16, 1974; *Kuangming Daily*, March 15, 1974; *New China News Agency*, March 16, 1974, cited in *FBIS/PRC*, March 22, 1974, pp. B-1-14; *New York Times*, March 17, 1974; *New York Times*, March 22, 1974. It is possible that the radicals did not encourage the attack on the Paracels but merely tried to benefit from it. Articles in the Chinese media of 1977 make this case, arguing essentially that Chiang Ch'ing tried to increase her stature with the military *ex post facto* by closely identifying herself with the Paracel Islands operation and its success. She did this through personal letters of commendation to the units concerned and by commissioning the ode to the Paracels triumph mentioned in the text. See, for example, *Jen-min Jih-pao*, March 19, 1977, cited in *FBIS/PRC*, March 31, 1977, pp. E-3-7.

Antonioni's portrayal of China and that in the Soviet media, linking
these together with Lin Piao's activities as a Soviet agent in China.[191]
During the spring, moreover, the Chinese media began to carry numerous
articles on U.S. complicity in pre-1949 atrocities in China,[192] implicitly criticizing the willingness of some in Peking to establish a
close relationship with Washington. The speeches at the ceremony com-
memorating the February 28 uprising in Taiwan also conveyed a harder
line on this key issue in Sino-American relations in 1974 than had been
the case in 1973.[193]

Capture of the Soviet Helicopter Pilots: March 1974. All indicators in bilateral Sino-Soviet relations marked a continued downturn
during these months. The nineteenth session of the border river navigation talks convened on February 5 but broke up without agreement on
March 21,[194] the shortest negotiating session in this forum since the
Cultural Revolution. Foreign Minister Gromyko "deplored" the current
state of Sino-Soviet relations on February 23 in Italy,[195] and three
days later the Soviet government announced special decorations awarded
to troops stationed along the Sino-Soviet border.[196] On March 10

---

[191]See, for example, Hua Yen, "Whose Instrument Is He?," *Hung ch'i*,
No. 3, 1974, abridged translation in *Peking Review*, No. 16, April 19,
1974, pp. 27-28.

[192]Kweichow Provincial Service, March 2, 1974, cited in *FBIS/PRC*,
March 25, 1974, p. E-1; Szechwan Provincial Service, March 12, 1974,
cited in *FBIS/PRC*, March 15, 1974, pp. E-4-5; *New York Times*, March
22, 1974.

[193]The 1973 speeches stressed the degree to which world trends
were turning against an independent Taiwan and the resulting need for
the authorities there to realize this and act accordingly: *Peking
Review*, No. 10, March 9, 1973, pp. 10-11 and 21. The 1974 speeches
assumed a more aggressive tone, arguing that ". . . a handful of diehards abroad, not reconciled to their defeat [on the Taiwan issue],
are still vainly trying to stick their finger in the pie of Taiwan.
Such plots by them absolutely will not succeed. . . . The Chinese
People's Liberation Army will heighten vigilance a hundredfold, defend
the motherland and is ready at all times to destroy enemy intruders and
liberate Taiwan." Ibid., No. 10, March 8, 1974, pp. 18-20.

[194]*New China News Agency*, March 22, 1974, cited in *FBIS/PRC*, March
25, 1974, p. A-13.

[195]*Los Angeles Times*, February 23, 1974.

[196]*New York Times*, February 27, 1974.

Brezhnev reiterated the point he had made in the wake of the Tenth Party Congress--that the USSR had gone as far as it would go, and now the next move was up to the Chinese.[197]

This move came four days later in the form of the second major espionage incident in Sino-Soviet relations since the Cultural Revolution. A Soviet helicopter carrying three crew members crossed the Chinese border in Sinkiang and landed in PRC territory. The USSR asserts that the crew was on a medical mercy mission, sent to pick up a seriously ill serviceman. It "encountered difficult meteorological conditions, lost its bearings and, having used up its fuel supply, made a forced landing near the border in CPR territory."[198] The Soviets immediately informed Chinese border representatives of this accident and on March 15 formally requested through Peking's Embassy in Moscow that a search for the crew be launched and that craft and crew be returned immediately.[199]

However, a Chinese force of frontier guards and militiamen had already located and captured the crew. A quick investigation revealed, according to a Chinese protest note of March 23, that the helicopter was an Mi-4 armed reconnaissance craft that had landed on more than one occasion in China's Habahe County and had carried out espionage activities. It was a strange "medical" mission, indeed, according to the Chinese, that would be undertaken by a helicopter that lacked both medical equipment and trained medical personnel on board. All the Chinese could find that related to the task of the helicopter were arms, reconnaissance equipment, and compromising documents. Thus, the Chinese concluded, "With the culprits and material evidence at hand, the case is conclusive. It is impossible for the Soviet authorities to shirk their criminal responsibility of sending this helicopter to intrude into China for espionage."[200]

---

[197]*Pravda*, March 11, 1974, cited in *CDSP*, Vol. XXVI, No. 10, April 3, 1974, p. 6; *New York Times*, March 11, 1974.

[198]*Pravda*, March 29, 1974, p. 4, cited in *CDSP*, Vol. XXVI, No. 12, April 17, 1974, p. 4.

[199]Ibid.

[200]Chinese Note of March 23, 1974, text in *Peking Review*, No. 13, March 29, 1974, p. 5. As detailed below, the Chinese subsequently

The helicopter incident quickly became a central and festering
issue in Sino-Soviet relations. Moscow submitted its own protest
note to the Chinese Embassy on March 28, noting that "One gets the
impression that the Chinese side, deliberately distorting the facts,
is seeking to use the forced landing of the Soviet border helicopter
to aggravate an atmosphere of hostility toward the USSR in China and
further to exacerbate Soviet-Chinese relations."[201] The Soviets
escalated the pressure five weeks later as the crew remained in Chinese
hands and continued to be held incommunicado. L. F. Ilyichev, the
head of the Soviet delegation to the border talks, met with Chinese
Ambassador to Moscow Liu Hsin-ch'uan and read him a statement that
included the following:

> . . . judging by everything, the CPR authorities are try-
> ing to exaggerate the incident of the unplanned landing of
> the Soviet border guard helicopter on Chinese territory
> and to use this to further complicate Soviet-Chinese rela-
> tions. . . . The Soviet government insists on the immed-
> iate return of the three-man crew and the border guard
> helicopter. We would like to draw attention to the fact
> that if the Chinese side intends to detain the helicopter
> and its crew even further and to make a mockery of the
> Soviet people, *it thereby assumes full responsibility for*
> *the inevitable consequences of such a provocational*
> *action.*[202]

This last Soviet threat sparked debate in Peking, and some hint
of the nature of this discussion appeared in the allegorical article
in the Chinese media mentioned above that ostensibly dealt with a
Han dynasty conference on salt and iron monopolies by the state.[203]
According to this article, some Chinese leaders advocated a positive
response to several of the proposals Moscow had put forward in the

---

reversed their position, declared the helicopter pilots innocent and
returned them to the Soviet Union in late December 1975.

[201]Text in *Pravda*, March 29, 1974, p. 4, cited in *CDSP*, Vol.
XXVI, No. 12, April 17, 1974, p. 4.

[202]*Pravda*, May 3, 1974, p. 4, cited in *CDSP*, Vol XXVI, No. 18,
May 29, 1974, p. 15, emphasis added.

[203]*Hung ch'i*, No. 5, 1974, cited in *FBIS/PRC*, May 21, 1974, pp.
E-1-9.

bilateral negotiations to decrease the possibility that the Soviets would use the helicopter incident as a *casus belli*. These advocates of compromise were, however, overruled. Chinese policy continued to take a hard line on this and related issues in Sino-Soviet relations.

Moderate Comeback

The radicals soon suffered a major setback, however--albeit from domestic rather than from international developments. The campaign to criticize Lin Piao and Confucius tore the still fragile political fabric in many locales, unleashing political storms that harkened back to the days of the Cultural Revolution in their ferocity. Economic production plummeted and finally on July 1 the central authorities issued a directive that effectively took the teeth out of this radical political campaign.[204] The Chinese media would echo with the call to criticize Lin Piao and Confucius for well over another year, but these noises barely rippled the surface of Chinese politics after the July 1974 directive. The radicals had to sit back and lick their wounds, and debate now turned toward the major program of the moderates under Chou En-lai--an attempt to develop China into a modern, powerful socialist country by the end of the century.

The Four Modernizations. Chou's plan, harkening back to the declaration by Chairman Mao in 1964, called for the "four modernizations" of China--that is, rapid development of the PRC's industry, agriculture, military, and science and technology.[205] This plan had potentially far-reaching consequences for the radicals, for it involved stressing economic growth over ideological purification. The priorities in this plan thus would lead naturally to dismantling some of the radicals' cherished reforms in the educational system and would create pressure

---

[204] On the economic disruption, see Robert Field, Nicholas Lardy, and John Emerson, *Provincial Industrial Output in the People's Republic of China, 1949-1975*, U.S. Department of Commerce, Foreign Economic Report No. 12, September 1976, pp. 16-17. The text of the July 1 decision (Chung-fa #21) is in *Issues and Studies*, Vol. XI, No. 1, January 1975, pp. 101-104. For analysis of this directive, see Lieberthal, 1978b, op. cit., pp. 59-68.

[205] Chou formally unveiled his plan in his report to the Fourth National People's Congress, which convened in January 1975: *Peking Review*, No. 4, January 24, 1975, p. 23.

for measures to bring rapid rises in output: stress on discipline in
the factories, reducing costs of production, technological reform, and
material incentives.[206] All of these flew in the face of the radicals'
programs.

In agriculture, this new plan translated into a three-pronged program: rapid mechanization; major increments in the use of chemical
fertilizers, with importation of foreign fertilizer technology a key
component of this effort; and massive efforts to level the land and
carry out water conservancy projects.[207] Mechanization simply added
to the impetus for rapid increases in industrial production, with the
consequences noted above. The fertilizer question highlighted China's
increasing utilization of foreign technology, which rankled the nativist
sentiments of the radicals. Only the land leveling and water conservancy projects were consonant with the radicals' political preferences,
with their implications for the organization of mass labor efforts on
the principle of local self-sufficiency. Even this aspect, however,
seems to have come under fire from the radicals for factional political
reasons--Tachai brigade in Shansi Province became the national model
for such efforts, and Tachai's leader Ch'en Yung-kuei had evidently
increasingly thrown his weight in the Politburo behind the moderates
in opposition to the radicals.[208] Thus, the radicals touted a

----

[206]These are indeed precisely the foci of China's modernization
program now that the Gang of Four has been overthrown. See, for
instance, Hua Kuo-feng's major programmatic speech to the Second
National Conference on Learning from Tachai in Agriculture: *Peking
Review*, No. 1, January 1, 1977, pp. 40-41; and Hua's Report to the
Fifth National People's Congress: *New China News Agency*, March 6, 1977,
cited in *FBIS/PRC*, March 7, 1977, pp. D-1-37.

[207]See Hua Kuo-feng's summing up speech at the First National Conference on Learning from Tachai in Agriculture: *New China News Agency*,
October 20, 1975, cited in *FBIS/PRC*, October 23, 1975, pp. E-1-11. The
Chinese have contracted for the construction of eight large ammonia
plants, worth a total of $215 million, from the M. W. Kellogg Company
of Houston. The ammonia is to be used in the manufacture of urea for
fertilizer, and when all of these plants have come on stream in the late
1970s, they will make a major contribution to China's ability to manufacture chemical fertilizer.

[208]Ch'en Yung-kuei survived the purge of the radicals amid charges
that they had tried to knock down the Tachai model. Some sense of the

different agricultural model--Hsiaochinchuang brigade near Tientsin--
on the basis of that unit's continuing stress on political study and
local self-reliance.[209]

It was in the military and science and technology spheres, however, that Chou's plan most clearly had implications for China's foreign
policy. Given his plan's stress on all-around industrialization and on
the mechanization of agriculture, rapid modernization of China's military would almost certainly entail importation of key components and
technologies from abroad; otherwise, military modernization would
command too large a share of China's scarce resources. Likewise,
science and technology could advance rapidly only with direct reversals
of the radicals' most cherished programs in the educational realm, combined with more active Chinese participation in the international scientific community. Both of these prospects frightened the radicals
who, as explained in the explication of their program above, felt that
foreigners would like to support the moderates in China at their expense. On an even more fundamental level, the radicals remained extremely sensitive to the psychological dimensions of China's semi-
colonial past and placed high priority on avoiding even the semblance
of the PRC's again "trailing behind the West at a snail's pace" and
"believing that the moon is rounder in the West."

Thus, the radicals became alarmed at Chou's program, which en-
dangered both their own goals and their personal political careers.
The January 1975 convening of the first National People's Congress in
a decade, with its attendant appointments to fill major ministerial
positions, provided the focus for the radicals' efforts during the
latter months of 1974. They fought to have Chang Ch'un-ch'iao appointed
as First Vice-Premier, thus giving him a preferred position in vying

---

personal animosity involved in this dispute is conveyed in the subsequent revelations of Chiang Ch'ing's contacts with Tachai during 1975-
1976; see, for example, *Peking Review*, No. 46, November 12, 1976,
pp. 6-9; Peking Domestic Service, November 8, 1976, cited in *FBIS/PRC*,
November 10, 1976, pp. E-6-8.

[209]Chiang Ch'ing escorted Madame Imelda Marcos to Hsiaochinchuang
during the latter's late September 1974 trip to the PRC: *Peking Review*, No. 40, October 4, 1974, p. 13. On Hsiaochinchuang's political
virtues, see also Peking Domestic Service, February 25, 1976, cited in
FBIS/PRC, February 27, 1976, pp. E-6-8.

for the premiership after Chou En-lai's death. They also argued
against the program of the four modernizations, raising particularly
the potential social costs of these efforts as against the radicals'
egalitarian ideals. They nevertheless lost out in this debate, as
Mao Tse-tung himself sided with Premier Chou.[210]

The October 1974 Telegram. It was during this period of heated
controversy that China sent its noteworthy 1974 October Revolution
anniversary messsage to the USSR. As mentioned above,[211] this message for the first time stated publicly that China wanted a nonaggression treaty with Moscow, at the same time coupling this assertion with
the need to conclude "first of all" an agreement on interim measures
along the border, including the demilitarization of all "disputed"
areas along the border. It is simply unclear whether this should be
interpreted as a sign of conciliation or one of hostility by the
Chinese. The Soviets had previously offered a nonaggression treaty,
and thus Peking's acknowledgment that it desired such a pact added
legitimacy to Moscow's efforts in this direction. The necessary preconditions were, however, clearly known in Peking to be unacceptable
to Moscow. In all probability, it was this very ambiguity of the Chinese action that commended it to the various factions battling in the
Forbidden City. The "soft" moderates desired it to create at least
the appearance of some movement in the relationship after the low point
that had been reached with the arrest of the helicopter pilots and
subsequent exchanges in March-May. The radicals, in turn, desired it
because it committed the PRC on the public record to a set of preconditions to which the Soviets would almost certainly never agree, and
it clearly gave both Mao Tse-tung's and Chou En-lai's imprimaturs to
these preconditions. The "hard" moderates supported this effort for
reasons similar to those of the radicals.

The Fourth National People's Congress. The documentation from the
January 1975 National People's Congress (and from the preceding Second

---

[210] These dimensions of the pre-National People's Congress political debate were revealed in the wake of the purge of the Gang of Four.
On the personnel aspect, for instance, see *Peking Review*, No. 6, February 4, 1977.

[211] Page 56.

Plenum of the Tenth Central Committee) shows clearly that the moderates under Chou En-lai dominated the proceedings of both gatherings.
These meetings strongly endorsed Premier Chou's "four modernizations,"
and the ministerial appointments that issued from them suggested that
the radicals had succeeded only in capturing the ministries of culture,
sports, and health. All others fell to the moderates and military.
At the vice-premier level, only Chang Ch'un-ch'iao gained appointment
from among the radicals, while Teng Hsiao-p'ing captured the coveted
position as first vice-premier. The radicals had to content themselves
with having Chang emerge as the man directly behind Teng in the military, Party, and government hierarchies and with having a platform at
the National People's Congress to raise obliquely some of their concerns
about the four modernizations.[212]

Why had the radicals lost out? In part, because Mao Tse-tung had
learned during the Cultural Revolution--and had been reminded again by
the disruption of the spring of 1974--of the high costs of putting the
radicals in charge of the government. Mao sought to keep the radicals
a viable force in Chinese politics so as to serve as a check on the
aspirations of the moderates, but he knew better than to allow all
power to gravitate into the Left's hands. Thus, Mao seems to have
tipped the balance in favor of Chou En-lai and his allies.

At the same time, Mao faced a continuing problem in that others
twisted his decisions to suit their own preferences. The Chairman as
of late 1974 was no longer the active and dynamic leader of the 1950s.
Indeed, as noted in Sec. I, a full decade earlier Mao had seen himself
as so old and infirm that he would likely be passing the revolution on to
the hands of his successors within the very near future.[213] It seems
entirely possible that Mao basically weighed in on the side of the

_____

[212]The appropriate documentation is available in *Peking Review*,
No. 4, January 24, 1975, pp. 6-25. For a more detailed analysis, see
Kenneth Lieberthal, "China in 1975: The Internal Political Scene,"
Problems of Communism, Vol. XXIV, May-June 1975.

[213]This theme emerges strongly from Mao's writings and speeches
during 1964-1965 as conveyed in the *Mao Tse-tung ssu-hsiang wan-sui!*.
A contemporary analysis that captures this dimension on Mao's thinking
of the time is Lifton, op. cit., especially Chapter 2.

moderates in the disputes of late 1974, but that Chou En-lai and Teng Hsiao-p'ing then carried this mandate considerably further than the Chairman desired. Mao, in turn, publicly signaled his displeasure with the proceedings of the National People's Congress and subsequently supported the radicals in their attacks on the potential consequences of some of the policies passed there.[214]

The Battle Is Joined: 1975

The Second Plenum and the National People's Congress clearly positioned Teng Hsiao-p'ing to make a run for capturing the succession after the deaths of Chou and Mao. Teng held the posts of Party vice-chairman, chief of staff of the army, and first vice-premier of the government. On the Party side, Teng was hedged in by the radicals, who retained a number of seats at the apex of the hierarchy--the second-ranking vice-chairmanship and two of the other eight positions on the Politburo Standing Committee (five of which were held by non-contenders: Mao, Chou, Chu Teh, K'ang Sheng, and Tung Pi-wu. The sixth was septuagenarian Yeh Chien-ying). Chang Ch'un-ch'iao alone among the radicals breathed down Teng's neck in the military and government hierarchies from his respective positions as the head of the military's General Political Department and the second vice-premier of the government.

The radicals used the positions in their grasp to try to undo Chou En-lai's succession plan through both mass campaigns and bureaucratic intrigue. This effort began with a campaign to study the dictatorship of the proletariat and restrict "bourgeois right" in the spring of 1975, aimed at criticizing the likely social impact of the four modernizations program, and then in August blossomed into a campaign to study the novel *Water Margin* with the focus on the related questions of class and national capitulationism. These campaigns and other actions signaled that the radicals were prepared to go all out to prevent Teng from succeeding Mao and Chou.[215]

---

[214] See Lieberthal, 1975, op. cit., for greater detail on this line of reasoning.

[215] For an analysis of the radicals' use of mass campaigns to weaken Teng during 1975-1976, see Kenneth Lieberthal, *Strategies of Conflict*

Teng struck back. He viewed this as his only chance at achieving, by the time of Chou En-lai's death, a position of such overwhelming power and prominence that the radicals would then prove unable to unseat him. His plan included the consolidation of ties with coalition partners, rehabilitation of needed allies, and forceful measures to undercut the radicals' programs in various fields. The military was a key object of Teng's maneuvers during this period. Even under a cloud, only the PLA had the coercive power available to tilt the succession decisively in one direction or another if all else failed.

Teng could offer the military the following package. He would encourage a program of rapid military modernization, including importation of some foreign military technology and equipment. He would also support greater discipline in the army, stressing conventional training and undercutting Chang Ch'un-ch'iao's efforts as head of the GPD to expand the role of politics in the PLA.[216] Judged by later events, Teng likewise seems to have allowed the possibility of some conciliatory gestures toward the Soviet Union, appropriately timed so as to ameliorate the impact of any major Chinese military purchases from abroad. And lastly, Teng may well have offered to unseat the radicals and place full emphasis on the rapid development of heavy industry and on law and order. The allegorical articles suggest that this bundle of issues--especially those concerning military modernization--peaked in the late spring of 1975,[217] and it is probably at that time that Teng consummated his arrangement with Minister of Defense Yeh Chien-ying and other military leaders.

---

in China During 1975-1976, The Rand Corporation, P-5680, June 1976c, pp. 7-8. On the bureaucratic intrigues employed by the radicals, see Lieberthal, 1978b, op. cit., pp. 26-50, 75-82.

[216] Teng made part of this appeal to the PLA at an enlarged Military Commission conference in June-July 1975: *Liberation Army Daily* Editorial, January 30, 1978, cited in *FBIS/PRC*, January 31, 1978, especially pp. 1-3. A speculative and interesting account of the decision to streamline the military is given in Victor Zorza, "China's Scrutable Struggle," *The Washington Post*, April 11, 1976, pp. C-1, C-4. The Chinese media subsequently revealed that the radicals had launched a severe attack on the PLA in the spring of 1975.

[217] See the analysis of the allegorical article on Wei Yuan that appeared in *Wen-wu* (Cultural Relics), May 1975, discussed in the "allegorical" section.

Teng also moved rapidly in the educational, science and technology, industrial, and agricultural fronts. In the educational sphere, he backed Minister of Education Chou Jung-hsin to attack many of the Cultural Revolution reforms in education during August and October 1975.[218] In the other fields, Teng sponsored the drafting of major documents calling for far-reaching adjustments in the direction of greater discipline, professionalism, and expertise. These documents were as fundamental in scope as were the 70 Points in Industry and 60 Points in Agriculture that had been passed by the Chinese communists in the early 1960s. They were intended to provide guidance for the basic thrust of advance for entire fields.[219]

Teng also rehabilitated additional cadres who had been purged during the Cultural Revolution, including some in the highly sensitive field of culture. These rehabilitations surged forward in August 1975, and it appeared that Teng intended within a matter of months to call back into good grace such high-ranking members of the pre-GPCR hierarchy as P'eng Chen and Lu Ting-yi, surely sounding the alarm bells for the new doyens of the cultural realm, Chiang Ch'ing and Yao Wen-yuan.[220] Thus, during the summer and fall of 1975, when cancer wracked Chou En-lai's body and sapped his energy, a rapidly escalating battle commenced in which all sides began a determined struggle for the upper hand.

Hua Kuo-feng evidently played a key role in support of Teng's efforts to solidify a ruling coalition during 1975. Hua was a natural for this position. His newly acquired post of Minister of Public Security

---

[218]See Lieberthal, 1978b, op. cit., p. 39.

[219]The three major documents are: "On the General Program for All Work of the Whole Party and the Whole People," "Certain Questions on Accelerating the Development of Industry," and "Outline Summary Report on the Work of the Academy of Sciences." The most complete available texts are in, respectively, P'an-ku, No. 103, Hong Kong, April 1, 1977, cited in SPRCM, No. 921, April 25, 1977, pp. 18-37; Lieberthal, 1978b, op. cit., pp. 115-140; and Lieberthal, 1978b, op. cit., pp. 141-154. For a detailed analysis of the drafting of the latter two documents and their fate, see Lieberthal, 1978b, op. cit., pp. 33-50.

[220]Name lists of rehabilitated cadres (with their pre-Cultural Revolution offices supplied) are presented in China News Summary, No. 586, October 8, 1975, and No. 587, October 15, 1975.

gave him a bureaucratic interest in the public order and discipline aspects of Teng's program.[221] Moreover, Hua had had extensive prior experience in both agriculture and science and technology.[222] Thus, for instance, Hua was able to assume charge of work in science and technology in the Politburo and to play an important role in drafting the key programmatic document in this sphere in mid-1975. He did this in close coordination with Teng Hsiao-p'ing.[223] Hua also gave the major concluding address to the Tachai Conference of September-October, a conference that placed the regime's seal of approval on a package of programs very much in Hua's interest: mechanization of agriculture and increased discipline among the populace as a whole and especially within the Party at the critical county level. This concluding address revealed another aspect of Hua's abilities--that he is a consummate diplomat, able easily to blend the seemingly irreconcilable into a mixture that gives the substance of the issue to one side while graciously bowing in the direction of the other.[224]

Hua had one final attribute of considerable potential importance to Teng during this period--his close personal ties with Chairman Mao Tse-tung. Teng's relations with Mao had been strained for some time before the Cultural Revolution, and surely neither man could fully put aside the traumas of the late 1960s in their subsequent relationship with each other. Hua, by contrast, seems to have cultivated the Chairman's trust and affection as far back as the 1950s. In Hunan in 1955 Hua was a leading advocate of Mao Tse-tung's plans for agricultural collectivization, and Hua clearly came to Mao's attention at this early date.[225]

---

[221] Hua acquired the Public Security portfolio at the Fourth National People's Congress in January 1975.

[222] On Hua's background, see Michael Oksenberg and Yeung Sai-cheung, "Hua kuo-feng's Pre-Cultural Revolution Hunan Years, 1949-1966: The Making of a Political Generalist," *China Quarterly*, No. 69, March 1977, pp. 3-53.

[223] For details, see Lieberthal, 1978b, op. cit., pp. 37-38.

[224] For the text of Hua's speech, see *New China News Agency*, October 20, 1975, cited in *FBIS/PRC*, October 23, 1975, pp. E-1-11.

[225] See Oksenberg and Yeung, op. cit., pp. 3-53.

The strongest bond in their relationship during the 1950s, however, was probably forged in 1959, when Mao Tse-tung faced what he considered to be the greatest challenge to his personal position since the founding of the People's Republic. P'eng Teh-huai questioned Mao's leadership of the Great Leap Forward at the Lushan Conference in July 1959, and P'eng was evidently joined in this attack by three other major figures. One of these, Chou Hsiao-chou, was the top-ranking Party secretary of Hunan Province, a man who had evidently been Hua's supporter as the latter had moved up the ranks within the province during the previous nine years. P'eng based part of his challenge to Mao on the fact that the latter had been fooled as to the degree of success of the Great Leap Forward even in his home village, which Mao had inspected in early 1959. P'eng contended that the state had poured more resources into this village than Mao had realized, and that the village's production figures given to Mao were inflated besides.[226] These accusations struck at the heart of one of Mao's basic claims to power in China--that he understood conditions in the Chinese countryside better than could any of his colleagues.

Chou Hsiao-chou must have supported P'eng in the latter's assertions about Shaoshan, as an issue such as this would certainly have been followed up at the meeting once Mao had picked up the gauntlet that P'eng had thrown down. Mao successfully beat back P'eng's challenge, and it seems very likely that a part of his counterattack consisted of Hua Kuo-feng's assertion, with closer knowledge of the concrete conditions in Shaoshan, that Mao was correct and P'eng (and Chou) mistaken. Two bits of evidence exist for this hypothesis: Hua was one of the extremely few people who would have the information available to challenge Chou Hsiao-chou on this issue; and at Lushan Chou was purged whereas "Mao person-ally promoted Hua to become a Party secretary of Hunan province."[227] If the circumstantial evidence that Hua came to Mao's rescue at Lushan is accurate, it is highly significant. For this would indicate that at

---

[226] Documentation on the Lushan Conference and Plenum is detailed in Lieberthal, 1976a, op. cit., pp. 141-148.

[227] Hunan Provincial Service, November 26, 1976, cited in *FBIS/PRC*, November 30, 1976, p. H-3.

a critical point Hua turned against his local patron[228] to support Mao. The Chairman was not one to forget such loyalty, as was shown when Mao subsequently turned to Hua at two junctures when he desperately needed someone he could trust completely--in the immediate wake of the Lin Piao affair in 1971, and when the Party Politburo locked in a stalemate over the succession to Chou En-lai in early 1976.

As just noted, Hua played a pivotal role under Teng Hsiao-p'ing as the latter cemented the coalition that would allow him to ride out the inevitable storm over the succession, with Hua especially active on the agricultural and science and technology spheres. In the latter, he may well have become involved in the June-July 1975 bargaining with the military and supported their plans for rapid modernization of the armed forces.

Thus, politics in the various spheres during 1975 all came together and became part and parcel of the succession struggle, and China's policy toward the Soviet Union was fashioned out of the pressures and counter-pressures of this future rivalry. In this context, Soviet policy seems to have become linked to Teng's need to link up with the military establishment--and to the need of the radicals to sever this tie.

The Helicopter Pilot Release

Did some significant concession to the USSR in the wake of major military purchases from the West form a part of this package? The limited available evidence suggests strongly that it did, and that Teng Hsiao-p'ing and Hua Kuo-feng played the two pivotal roles in this aspect of the affair, thus clearly identifying these two leaders as "soft" moderates as of late 1975.

The most striking event of 1975 in Chinese foreign policy was Peking's sudden release of the three Soviet helicopter pilots four days before the end of the year. Without public warning, China announced on December 27 that it was turning the pilots free, feting them in Peking, and then returning both the men and their craft to the

---

[228]Oksenberg and Yeung (op. cit.) make the case for Chou Hsiao-chou having been Hua's patron until Lushan.

Soviet Union. No gesture of this nature had been made by China toward the USSR since 1960. Who promoted it, who opposed it, and why? What was it intended to accomplish?

Available evidence indicates that Teng Hsiao-p'ing and Hua Kuo-feng promoted the release of the helicopter pilots, and that this was done as part of their package with the military that had been tied together the previous June-July. The radicals, Mao Tse-tung, and possibly leading "hard" moderates opposed this gesture, as shown by the following evidence.

The announcement that accompanied the release of the pilots[229] first reviewed the capture of the three and then declared, "Now things are clear after investigation by the Chinese public security organs, and *they* consider credible the Soviet crew members' statement about the unintentional flight into China, and have decided to release the three crew members . . . and to return to the Soviet side the helicopter with all equipment and documents aboard." (Emphasis added.) In striking contrast, the statement issued to accompany the release of former Kuomintang personnel at or above the county or regimental level ten days earlier[230] had explained this action as being "in accordance with instructions from *Chairman Mao and the Central Committee of the Chinese Community Party*" (emphasis added). Both amnesties were startling, as was the important difference in wording as to the authority under which they were carried out.

At some point during 1975, then, Hua Kuo-feng submitted a report as head of the Ministry of Public Security that stated that the pilots who had been declared guilty in the Chinese press of 1974 (before Hua had assumed his post) were in fact innocent and should be released. Teng Hsiao-p'ing, who by mid-1975 had *de facto* taken over as China's premier, must have approved this report (and may, of course, have inspired it), or it could not have become state policy.

---

[229]The text of the announcement accompanying the release of the helicopter pilots is given in *Peking Review*, No. 1, January 2, 1976, p. 7.

[230]Text in *Peking Review*, No. 52, December 26, 1975, p. 10.

It is possible that the major difference in wording of the two accompanying statements noted above stemmed from a policy decision in Peking to remove the helicopter pilot issue from China's agenda while making the gesture as insignificant as possible by leaving it at the ministerial level instead of directly invoking the name of the State Council, premier, or Chairman Mao. The larger context, however, makes this explanation seem unlikely.

First, why release the pilots in late December? Undoubtedly, two factors determined the timing of the release: the need to develop an adequate consensus in Peking on the desirability of this action; and the desire to effect the release at a time when it would best serve other purposes. By late December there was formal agreement (although not consensus) on the release; and the last week of December also perfectly served a range of other purposes of various members of the leadership.

For the military, the significant event tied to the release of the pilots was the announcement in England two weeks earlier that China had purchased British Spey engines and the technology for future production of these engines.[231] Although the PRC had been indicating its interest in making military-related purchases abroad for several years,[232] this latest deal was dramatic in that it provided the PRC with a critical component previously lacking from its air force--a good fighter engine that could be outfitted on the Chinese MIG-21 and F-9 air frames. For the first time since the 1950s, Peking had turned abroad to provide a "quick fix" that would substantially increase its military capabilities in the near term. This decision stemmed, almost certainly from the agreement to modernize the military reached in the late spring of 1975 (it had been contemplated for several years

---

[231]*New York Times*, December 15, 1975.

[232]This goes back to at least 1972, according to the illustrations given in Heymann, op. cit., pp. 66-70. Heymann comments with respect to any actual Chinese military purchases from a NATO country, however, that "China's principal adversary, the USSR, would surely view it as extremely provocative. . . ." (P. 69.)

previously), and this major public purchase of important military technology from abroad boded ill in its potentialities for the USSR. The helicopter pilot release, in this context, could serve as one of those conciliatory gestures the military may have felt necessary to insure that China's "provocation" would not touch off some undesirable Soviet response.

The "soft" moderates outside the military must have been sympathetic to the army's rationale. They could also support the late December release date because it fell during the time when the Soviets were drafting the documents for their Twenty-Fifth Party Congress, scheduled to convene in early February 1976. The Twenty-Fourth Congress had endorsed a line of firmness combined with conciliation toward the PRC, and the "soft" moderates must have been somewhat anxious to nudge the proceedings of the Twenty-Fifth Congress along basically the same path. It was not in China's interest for Moscow, frustrated by years of lack of progress in border negotiations and bilateral relations, to opt for a harder line toward the PRC, one that carried increased risk of Soviet military involvement in China during the upcoming succession in Peking.

Additionally, by late December Premier Chou En-lai lay near death, and the Chinese leadership knew they would lose their second-ranking leader within a matter of weeks.[233] Given the virtual certainty of a period of some fairly overt leadership conflict after the passing of the Premier, why not minimize the chances that the Soviets would attempt to apply pressure and "fish in troubled waters" during this delicate interregnum?

Some among the leadership may have been brought "on board" by the possibility that the United States would take this gesture as a warning that China had other options to play unless the United States proved more forthcoming on the Taiwan issue. President Ford had just completed a journey to Peking in early December during which no perceptible progress was made on the normalization issue.[234] The U.S. government had decided to shelve this question until after the 1976

---

[233]Chou En-lai died of cancer on January 8, 1976.

[234]Chinese documentation of the Ford visit is in *Peking Review*, No. 49, December 5, 1975, and *Peking Review*, No. 50, December 12, 1975.

Presidential election. The timing of the release (after Ford's visit instead of before it) and the fact that the release was followed up almost immediately by an invitation to Richard Nixon to revisit China (discussed below) suggests that this motivation was marginal at best, but it may have weighed more heavily in the thoughts of some who opposed this action on any other grounds.

Last, there were reports in the Western press of a major border incident between China and the Soviet Union earlier in the fall of 1975.[235] There is some possibility that this could have created a situation wherein the helicopter pilot release may have been part of some sort of trade of captives on both sides. If so, the significance of this dimension of the problem cannot be judged without further information. If the Soviets captured some Chinese and then presented Peking with what amounted to an ultimatum for the release of prisoners, then this would have vastly complicated the task of the "soft" moderates in Peking who had argued for giving up the helicopter pilots, for it would have made them vulnerable to the charge of selling out ("capitulating") to the Soviet Union. It seems inconceivable that the Chinese leaders would value the border guards and/or peasants that might have been captured in an earlier skirmish equally with the highly publicized Soviet helicopter pilots. If, however, the Soviets simply communicated that should the pilots be released Moscow would try to make some reciprocal gesture, possibly involving Chinese who had crossed the Soviet border and not been repatriated, this would have posed fewer problems for the "soft" moderates in Peking.[236] In lieu of more specific information both over whether there were Chinese hostages to be exchanged and if so, over the terms of any Soviet declaration, little can be said beyond the fact that almost *any* Soviet input on this issue would almost certainly have increased opposition to the release of the pilots by the Chinese.

There is strong evidence that the helicopter pilot release was opposed by at least one major segment of the Chinese leadership. On

---

[235]*Time*, March 22, 1976, p. 26.

[236]It would still be more troublesome than had the Soviets said nothing on this issue, though.

December 25, two days before the release, Peking University's journal carried a major article by Liang Hsiao, a pseudonym for a writing group sponsored by the radicals.[237] This article ostensibly focused on Lin Piao but in reality zeroed in on the link between class and national capitulationism, arguing forcefully that Lin's domestic policies had led inevitably to his selling out to the Soviet Union. In the context of the helicopter pilot release, this article amounted to a scathing indictment of the entire group of issues that had been agreed upon by Teng, Hua, and the military. The article was reprinted in *People's Daily* on January 27, at a time when debate over the succession to Chou En-lai was tearing apart the central Party leadership. Its reappearance in a paper under the editorial control of the radicals at that time strongly suggests that the radicals had raised the Soviet issue (and the release of the helicopter pilots?) against Teng in the furious discussions of that week, albeit almost certainly as a relatively minor issue alongside of the far more central grievances they held against the first vice-premier.

Two other events worth noting bracketed the helicopter pilot release. First, the Chinese press gushed forth a crescendo of criticism of the Soviet Union and its leadership, the most vociferous barrage of such material since the winter of 1973-1974. A *New China News Agency* article of January 3, 1976, brought together the various strands of this criticism that had been scattered through the media of the previous weeks.[238] It amounted to a truculent and far-reaching indictment of the Soviet system and its leadership, clearly designed to prevent the leaders in the Kremlin from "reading" the helicopter pilot release as a signal that China genuinely desired to improve relations. If the "soft" moderates wanted to send such a signal to the Kremlin (even if only for tactical reasons), others in China wanted to make sure the signal did not come across clearly. In point of fact, the Kremlin did

---

[237] Liang Hsiao, "Critique of Lin Piao's Capitulationism," *Peking University Journal*, Philosophy and Social Science Edition, No. 6, December 25, 1975.

[238] *New China News Agency*, January 3, 1976, cited in *FBIS/PRC*, January 5, 1976, pp. A-5-10.

ponder the meaning of the helicopter pilot release with some bewilderment and, as noted in Sec. I, decided finally to reaffirm its previous offers to China and ask for movement on any of those issues as a clear signal of Chinese readiness to take some of the hard edge off of their bilateral relationship.[239]

Second, four days after the release of the helicopter pilots Mao Tse-tung received David and Julie Eisenhower and publicly invited former President Richard Nixon to revisit China. Much evidence suggests that relatively little thought was given to the impact of this invitation in the American political milieu, even though such knowledgeable analysts of the United States as Ch'iao Kuan-hua, Huang Chen, and T'ang Wen-sheng were present at the meeting.[240] Mao evidently wanted to reassert the priority of the United States connection for an audience inside China and possibly also to add support to the radicals' message to the Soviets in the media that the Kremlin should not make too much of the significance of the helicopter pilot release.

How could an event as potentially significant as this release occur in the face of opposition from the Chairman himself? It probably could not have happened had Mao chosen to take a strong stand on this issue. Mao, however, almost certainly was presented with virtually the full range of arguments noted above. In addition, foreign policy specialists probably stressed that keeping the pilots much longer could only bring China additional trouble and little benefit. The National People's Congress in January 1975 had demonstrated, moreover, that major events could occur without Mao's wholehearted backing-- so long as he did not go over into complete opposition to the action itself. Mao may thus have been unhappy about the release and worried that it might produce a positive response from the Soviets that could in turn set in motion a chain of events leading toward Sino-Soviet détente. Nevertheless, he may have become convinced that China

---

[239]Moscow in Mandarin, December 30, 1975, cited in *FBIS/USSR*, January 2, 1976, pp. C-2-3.

[240]The Chinese media carried Mao's invitation to President Nixon: *Peking Review*, No. 1, January 2, 1976, p. 4. The invitation to Nixon highlighted the issue of the Nixon years at the time of the New Hampshire primary in the United States, much to the embarrassment of Gerald Ford.

had much to gain from the release and that associated actions on his part and that of the radicals could make it virtually impossible for Moscow to interpret the release as a sign of goodwill. Mao seems, in brief, to have been brought "on board" while remaining a reluctant and somewhat disgruntled passenger at best. Given the politics of the period, however, it was most likely the radicals and not Mao who insisted that the blame for this decision be clearly fixed in the statement accompanying the release--i.e., that the statement point a finger toward Hua Kuo-feng and, by extension, Teng Hsiao-p'ing.

Teng's Second Fall and Policy Toward the USSR   1976

Chou En-lai died on January 8, and Teng Hsiao-p'ing gave the funeral oration on the 15th, setting in train his own accession to Chou's position. Teng, however, then dropped from view and was not seen again until his rehabilitation at the Third Plenum of the Tenth Central Committee in July 1977.[241]

Teng's fall stemmed from the broad issues discussed above--the policies toward education, agriculture, industry, cadre rehabilitation, and so forth. Mao had become increasingly suspicious during the course of the fall 1975 that Teng wanted to upset the balance between opposing political tendencies that the Chairman had so carefully nurtured over the years. Teng, in turn, acted extraordinarily rapidly and forcefully to put himself in a position to withstand any attacks from the radicals after Chou's and Mao's deaths. This in part accounts for the fact that he was willing to risk raising Mao's suspicions by backing the release of the helicopter pilots before the Chairman died. It also explains why Teng, in the wake of Chou's death, insisted on being appointed *first* vice-chairman of the Party as well as Premier--so that he would outrank all of the radicals in both the Party and state hierarchies as of the time of Chairman Mao's demise.[242]

---

[241] The text of Teng's memorial speech is given in *Peking Review*, No. 4, January 23, 1976, pp. 5-8. Teng was not formally restored to all posts until the Third Plenum in July 1977: *Peking Review*, No. 31, July 29, 1977, pp. 5-6.

[242] In the criticism of Teng after his ouster, the Chinese asserted that Teng had demanded that he head both the Party Central Committee

Within this context, the radicals raised the issue of capitulation
to the Soviet Union to further undermine Mao's already-shaken faith in
Chou En-lai's handpicked successor. Teng subsequently fell for reasons
that went far beyond the Soviet issue, but the question remains why
the subsequent criticism of Teng in the PRC media never directly focused
on his "capitulationism" to the Soviet Union. Victors in major Chinese
power struggles had not hesitated to spear their victims with this
charge in the past, as witnessed by post-purge denunciations of Kao
Kang, P'eng Teh-huai, Liu Shao-ch'i, Lin Piao, and even Teng Hsiao-p'ing
himself during the Cultural Revolution.[243]

Two explanations bear on this seeming anomaly. First and perhaps
most importantly, Hua Kuo-feng, Teng's successor handpicked by Mao, was
too closely allied to Teng on this issue. It would have been almost
impossible to accuse Teng of capitulationism without also tarnishing the
image of Hua--and Mao could not risk this, given the politics of 1976 in
China. During the spring of 1976 Mao needed Hua, for he had to have
someone he could trust personally who at the same time was acceptable to
both the moderates and radicals. Hua had proven his personal loyalty
to Mao before, as noted above. His record over at least the previous
year had firmly established his credentials for the moderates (including
the military). The radicals were in all likelihood unhappy with Hua's
elevation but had little choice other than to accept Mao's selection.
They had succeeded in blocking Teng's elevation--their primary goal--
and the actions of Yeh Chien-ying and other moderates made it clear
they would have to stop shy of placing one of their own people in the
premiership. Hua, moreover, had been careful not to give blatant
offense to the radicals, as Teng had done on numerous occasions. Rather,
Hua's summing up speech to the National Agricultural Conference in

---

and the government after the death of Chou. Some later reviews of the
period assert that Teng had already been given *de facto* authority to
run the Central Committee during 1975: Shanghai Radio, November 25,
1977, cited in *FBIS/PRC*, November 29, 1977, p. G-8.

[243] Regarding Teng Hsiao-p'ing, see, for instance, *Teng Hsiao-p'ing
fan-tang fan she-hui-chu-i fan Mao Tse-tung ssu-hsiang ti yen-lun chai-
pien* (Excerpts from Teng Hsiao-p'ing's anti-Party, anti-Socialist, anti-
Mao Tse-tung Thought speeches), Peking: First Division of the People's
University Three Red Grab Liu and Teng Group of the Capital's Red Guard
Congress, April 1967, especially pp. 47-51.

October 1975 demonstrated his ability to blend the rhetoric and concerns of different sides in a masterful way. In all likelihood, he remained equally diplomatic and circumspect in his actions "in house," albeit substantively placing himself on the side of the moderates. Given especially the crisis atmosphere that prevailed in the wake of the riot in Tien-an Men on April 5, 1976, the radicals simply did not have sufficient cause to block Hua's appointment. Hua's support of the release of the helicopter pilots, in turn, did not in itself disqualify him from Mao's consideration. But having accepted Hua as the premier and first vice-chairman of the CCP, it was necessary to cease even indirect criticism of Teng Hsiao-p'ing's "capitulationism" to the Soviet Union.

Second, opposition to Teng's purge was strong in the Politburo, as witnessed by the fact that the diminutive Party vice-chairman was stripped of his posts but not of his Party membership.[244] Convicting Teng of treason with the Soviet Union would have foreclosed even a faint possibility of his second resurrection—something his allies on the Politburo probably refused to sanction.

Hua Kuo-feng Constructs a Winning Coalition

In any event, once in office Hua moved carefully to avoid the type of incriminating statement and/or action that would enable the radicals to convince an increasingly enfeebled Mao that the Chairman would have to act against Hua to protect his own legacy. Thus, the period from April through August appeared as a time of slightly shifting balances between moderates and radicals, with the latter trying to turn the campaign to criticize Teng Hsiao-p'ing into a major purge and the former clearly succeeding in undercutting this attempt.[245]

There is a possibility that Hua's relationship with the military slipped somewhat off track during these tense months after January 1976.

---

[244]The Central Committee resolution on April 7, 1976 that drew this distinction is given in *Peking Review*, No. 15, April 9, 1976, p. 3.

[245]Most of this period is covered in somewhat greater detail in Lieberthal, 1976c, op. cit., pp. 13-16.

While Yeh Chien-ying seems to have given Teng Hsiao-p'ing strong support in January-March and then rallied to the side of Hua after April, the actions of important figures such as Ch'en Hsi-lien and Yang Ch'eng-wu are less clear. Indeed, given the degree to which he benefited from Teng's fall, Hua after April may have experienced some tension in his relationship even with leaders such as Yeh, who possibly continued to try to rehabilitate Teng.

If Hua's relations with the military did suffer during the course of the first six months of 1976, however, the catastrophic earthquake that destroyed Tangshan on July 28 provided the vehicle for again cementing these ties. Hua personally led the earthquake relief effort and used it to promote his own image in China. The new premier also gave the military a tremendous role to play in the relief efforts and allowed (encouraged?) the media to heap laurels on the PLA for its contributions. Indeed, Chinese media in the wake of the earthquake used words of praise for the PLA that had not been heard since the fall of Lin Piao. In the aftermath of the quake, therefore, the interests of Hua Kuo-feng and the military meshed neatly. The radicals, by contrast, were anxious to play down Hua's role in the relief effort and thus tried to undercut publicity about the entire relief operation.[246] This went against the interests of the military--who viewed the earthquake at least in part as a vehicle to recoup their lost prestige-- and helped cement again Hua's ties to the central PLA command.

Once Mao died in September, it became possible for Hua to bring "on board" the final person needed to purge the radicals--Wang Tung-hsing, the head of Mao's personal bodyguard and the man who controlled the troops in Chungnanhai. Any earlier attempt to recruit Wang would have been too risky, as Wang's loyalties lay strictly with Mao and he might have felt obliged to inform the Chairman that his putative successor planned to tilt decisively toward the moderates. After Mao's

---

[246]This theme was aired extensively in the Chinese media after the overthrow of the radicals, albeit the radicals' opposition to praise of the relief effort was typically ascribed to their callousness regarding the earthquake victims: see, for example, *Peking Review*, No. 48, November 26, 1976, pp. 17-19.

demise, however, Wang could be contacted.[247] With Wang "in place,"
the October 6 purge and arrest of the radicals in Chungnanhai could
be carried out[248] and Hua could identify openly and forcefully with
the moderates and their cherished plan to carry out the "four modernizations" as China's basic policy line.

Since Mao's Death

The October 1976 purge of the leading radicals brought a moderate
coalition into power. Teng Hsiao-p'ing's rehabilitation to all his
previous posts in July 1977[249] and the appointments to the Politburo
made at the Eleventh Party Congress in August 1977 completed the process of rounding out the members of this coalition at the highest level.

During the months directly following Mao's demise and the overthrow of the radical Gang of Four, the Chinese pursued a rigidly hard
line against the USSR. As noted in Sec. I, they refused to accept any
Party-to-Party communications congratulating Hua Kuo-feng on being named
Chairman of the CCP,[250] and they proved unyielding in the border

---

[247]Wang, in turn, seems to have been alienated from the radicals
by their seeming attempts to tamper with some of Mao's writings and to
preempt Wang's control over the Party archives. These activities suggested the radicals would ultimately be disloyal to Wang's patron. See,
for example, the report on Wang's address to the Politburo meeting that
sanctioned the overthrow of the radicals: *Ming Pao*, Hong Kong, October
26 to November 1, 1976, translated in *FBIS/PRC*, October 28 to November 3,
1976, reproduced in *Contemporary China*, Vol. 1, No. 2, November 1976, pp.
43-55. In this report, Wang reviews the radicals' attempt to forge and
tamper with Mao's writings. Subsequently, the Chinese media revealed
that Wang Hung-wen on behalf of the radicals had appropriated the name
of the General Office of the Central Committee immediately after Mao's
death (cf. *Peking Review*, No. 6, February 4, 1977, p. 12). Wang at
that time held the title of head of the General Office of the Central
Committee, and it was this position that gave him control over the Party
archives.

[248]Wang, as noted above, commanded the PLA unit that provides
security for the leaders in Chungnanhai. This unit came in for unusual
publicity and praise shortly after the arrest of the Gang of Four.

[249]Teng's rehabilitation was agreed upon at a March 1977 Central
Work Conference and effected at the July 1977 Third Plenum of the Tenth
Central Committee: *Peking Review*, No. 3, July 29, 1977, p. 5.

[250]Page 21.

negotiations that convened from November 30, 1976, to February 28, 1977.[251] Indeed, in the middle of these negotiations Vice Foreign Minister Yu Chan demanded that the Soviets admit their own responsibility for the Sino-Soviet dispute and apologize for their past errors before any progress could be made.[252] The Chinese media, moreover, continued to denounce virtually the entire range of Soviet domestic and foreign policies. It is not surprising that China's leaders, preoccupied with domestic problems, would essentially avoid facing seriously the Sino-Soviet issue for the time being unless the Soviets forced the question to the top of the agenda by some dramatic offer or action. No such major Soviet initiative materialized during this period, though.

By the fall of 1977, when conditions in China had become more settled, signs of a more differentiated policy toward the Soviet Union began to emerge. Peking for the first time since the Cultural Revolution reached some agreements with the Soviet Union in the border river navigation talks that concluded on October 6.[253] The Chinese at the same time indicated in a range of ways their desire to have more normal state-to-state relations with the USSR, while all the time maintaining their unremittingly hostile position on the nature of the Soviet system and intentions of Moscow's leaders.

---

[251] On these negotiations, which convened at Soviet request, see Hong Kong AFP, December 14, 1976, cited in *FBIS/PRC*, December 15, 1976, p. A-2; Tokyo Kyodo, December 17, 1976, cited in *FBIS/PRC*, December 17, 1976, p. A-1; Paris AFP, February 9, 1977, cited in *FBIS/PRC*, February 10, 1977, p. A-4; Hong Kong AFP, February 22, 1977, cited in *FBIS/PRC*, February 23, 1977, p. A-3; Hong Kong AFP, February 23, 1977, cited in *FBIS/PRC*, February 24, 1977, pp. A-5-6; and Hong Kong AFP, February 28, 1977, cited in *FBIS/PRC*, February 28, 1977, p. A-3.

[252] Hong Kong AFP, February 6, 1977, cited in *FBIS/PRC*, February 7, 1977, p. A-11.

[253] The talks convened for July 27 to October 6, 1977, and produced agreements on improving border river negotiation conditions and on some shipping rules: *Izvestia*, October 9, 1977, cited in *CDSP*, Vol. XXIX, No. 41, November 9, 1977; *New China News Agency*, October 6, 1977, cited in *FBIS/PRC*, October 7, 1977, p. A-6. This was the first border river negotiating session since 1974 and the first announcement of any agreement in these talks since the Cultural Revolution.

This mix of policies emerged clearly in the events surrounding the celebration of the Soviet October revolution, which is observed on November 7. On November 1, 1977, the new Chinese ambassador to Japan, Fu Hao, met with the Soviet envoy Dmitriy Polyanskiy for a half-hour courtesy call.[254] The following day, the Sino-Soviet Friendship Association in Peking gave a film reception that the Soviet ambassador to China, Tolstikov, attended.[255] In the most striking move of all, on November 7, Chinese Foreign Minister Huang Hua attended the reception given at the Soviet Embassy in Peking, marking the highest level Chinese representation at this annual event since 1966.[256] China also sent a congratulatory telegram to the USSR that was slightly more polite in tone than usual for this occasion.[257]

Against this flurry of hints that China would like a less vitriolic relationship with the Soviet Union, the November 7 joint editorial of China's three major publications (*Jen-min Jih-pao*, *Liberation Army Daily*, and *Hung ch'i*), in honor of the October revolution anniversary, heaped abuse on the Soviet Union as a whole and on the Soviet leadership in particular. This editorial, as many other items in the Chinese media, exceeded a forceful statement of the differences that divide Peking from Moscow. It called the CPSU a "fascist party of the bureaucrat-monopoly bourgeoisie" and termed the Soviet Union an "imperialist superpower" that is "trying to realize hegemonism with all its might" under the leadership of "the Soviet revisionist renegade clique."[258]

Since November 1977, Chinese policy toward the Soviet Union has been on a more consistently hostile note than the treatment of the

---

[254]Tokyo Kyodo, November 9, 1977, cited in *FBIS/PRC*, November 9, 1977, p. A-5.

[255]*New China News Agency*, November 2, 1977, cited in *FBIS/PRC*, November 3, 1977, p. A-5.

[256]*New China News Agency*, November 7, 1977, cited in *FBIS/PRC*, November 7, 1977, p. A-12; Hong Kong AFP, November 7, 1977, cited in *FBIS/PRC*, November 7, 1977, pp. A-12-13.

[257]Text in *New China News Agency*, November 6, 1977, cited in *FBIS/PRC*, November 7, 1977, pp. A-8-9.

[258]*New China News Agency*, November 6, 1977, cited in *FBIS/PRC*, November 7, 1977, p. A-11.

October revolution anniversary suggested. The Soviets again went over to the diplomatic offensive on February 24, 1978, as noted in Sec. I, with a proposal for a "joint statement on the principles of mutual relations." In its March 6 response, the Chinese side for the first time demanded that the USSR draw down all of its forces along the Sino-Soviet border and in the Mongolian People's Republic to the level that existed before the Soviet military buildup of the late 1960s as a *precondition* to significant improvement in Sino-Soviet relations.[259] This Chinese posture went far beyond a mere rejection of the Soviet initiative and posited a requirement that Peking knows Moscow will never agree to meet. The Kremlin quickly registered its dismay-- Brezhnev made an extended tour of the USSR's armed forces along the border[260] and a major *Pravda* editorial appeared on April 1, 1978, that flatly rejected the possibility that the Soviet Union would reduce its forces near the Chinese border in response to this PRC demand.

In sum, Chinese policy toward the Soviet Union since Mao Tse-tung's death and the overthrow of the radical Gang of Four has, much like its policy before September 1976, consisted of a basically very tough, un-yielding, and abusive posture punctuated by occasional signs that Peking would like a somewhat improved state-to-state relationship. This mix is not surprising in view of the fact that the current ruling coalition contains advocates of both the "soft" and the "hard" moderate positions discussed above. While the "soft" moderate position toward the Soviet Union is never openly advocated in the Chinese media, Peking's actions around the time of the October revolution anniversary in 1977 indicate clearly that this position still is heard in the leading councils of the party. Indeed, in late March 1978 Peking radio ex-plicitly denounced the premises of the "soft" moderate position (albeit not attributing this perspective to anyone in the PRC), as follows: "Note must be made of some people who advocate compromise and concessions in the face of Soviet expansion and threats in the belief that peace may thus be preserved. However, this is a naive expectation, because such a

---

[259] *New China News Agency*, March 25, 1978, cited in *FBIS/PRC*, March 27, 1978, pp. A-6-8.

[260] *New York Times*, April 10, 1978.

policy of appeasement will only hasten the beginning of war. The reason is very simple: Aggressors always hurt the weak, are afraid of the strong, and will never rest on their laurels."[261]

Are the "soft" moderates of today the same as those tentatively identified earlier in this section? It is impossible to answer this central question with certainty, but some pertinent evidence is available, primarily but not exclusively from interviews Chinese leaders have given to foreigners during 1977-1978. Hua Kuo-feng has said nothing that would force a reevaluation of his position as a "soft" moderate. The *Liberation Army Daily* has called for rapid modernization of China's weaponry (which will require at least some purchases from abroad) and has warned at the same time that "We must . . . do our utmost to prevent the outbreak of war for several years."[262] Thus, the military, or at least some portions of it, may still be favoring a relatively conciliatory tone toward the Soviet Union as China undertakes a major effort to strengthen her defenses.

Others, however, have articulated key components of the "hard" moderate position. Chi Teng-k'uei told one interviewer, for example, that the Soviet Union bullies the weak and fears the tough and that, therefore, China cannot make concessions to Moscow.[263] Li Hsien-nien demanded that "the Soviets thoroughly acknowledge their faults, all the misdeeds they have committed since Khrushchev's arrival, and that they announce to the entire world that there were errors, faults committed." Li also argued that the Soviets cannot change.[264] Most importantly, Teng Hsiao-p'ing seems to have moved in the direction of the "hard" moderate position, possibly in part because as of 1978 he is not trying to bid for Yeh Chien-ying's support in the way he felt

<hr/>

[261]Peking Radio, March 21, 1978, cited in *FBIS/PRC*, March 23, 1978, p. A-2.

[262]*Liberation Army Daily* Editorial, January 23, 1978, cited in *FBIS/PRC*, January 27, 1978, p. E-6.

[263]Hong Kong *Ta Kung Pao*, May 17, 1977, cited in *FBIS/PRC*, May 18, 1977, p. N-1.

[264]Hong Kong AFP, November 2, 1976, cited in *FBIS/PRC*, November 3, 1976, p. A-5. (Li's identity is revealed in a related item in ibid., p. A-12.)

necessary in late 1975.[265] Teng has argued since his rehabilitation in the summer of 1977 that Japan, China, Western Europe, and the United States must work together to oppose the Soviet Union to prevent Soviet aggression. This requires having Western Europe make advanced military technology available to China. In addition, any concessions to the Soviet Union by any of these countries will simply whet the Soviet appetite for aggression and hasten the outbreak of war. Teng has made clear, therefore, that there can be no reconciliation between the USSR and the PRC during his lifetime, and that he believes any such reconciliation is in fact impossible even in the next generation. The Soviet state does, nevertheless, have weaknesses, especially in terms of its lagging economy and relatively backward technological development compared with the United States.[266] By implication, therefore, China can stay safe and eventually acquire a real deterrent capability if Peking assumes a tough stance toward Moscow and a conciliatory position toward Europe, Japan, and possibly the United States in the coming years.

Nobody else on China's Politburo has expressed himself in a way that makes clear his position as "soft" or "hard" regarding the Soviet issue,[267] and thus our ability to map the existence and terms of this debate remains greater than our capacity to specify the individuals on each side of the issue.

CONCLUSION

Several points warrant particular mention in the summary of the preceding.

---

[265] For details, see Lieberthal, 1978a, op. cit.

[266] Teng has made these comments in two interviews: a September 26, 1977, meeting with Manfred Woerner, head of the Bundestag Defense Committee in the Federal Republic of Germany; and a March 23, 1978, session with Friedrich Zimmerman, chairman of the Christian Social Union caucus in the FRG Bundestag. See, respectively, *FBIS/PRC*, September 26, 1977, pp. A-10-11; *FBIS/PRC*, March 23, 1978, pp. A-22-24.

[267] For non-Politburo officials, see Vice Foreign Minister Yu Chan, Bonn *Die Welt*, November 14 to 15, 1977, cited in *FBIS/PRC*, May 17, 1977, pp. A-3-4; and T'an Chen-lin, Hong Kong AFP, November 2, 1976, cited in *FBIS/PRC*, November 8, 1976, p. A-3.

First, policy toward the Soviet Union has been intricately con-
nected both with a whole range of domestic policy concerns and with
factional infighting in Peking. The purge of one of the main sets of
protagonists at the Politburo level--the Gang of Four--has not eliminated this dimension of the problem.[268] Many issues divide those who
remain, including policy toward the Soviet Union, since both the
"hard" moderates and "soft" moderates remain.

Second, of the three different viewpoints analyzed above, only
that of the radicals posed real dangers for the future of Sino-U.S.
relations. Both "hard" and "soft" moderates placed high value on
maintaining and expanding China's ties with the West, as has been
reconfirmed in the Chinese media since the purge of the radicals.
This does not mean that there is no chance of a cooling in U.S.-Chinese
relations in the future should our own policy become particularly offensive to the new rulers in Peking. It does, however, mean that their
appreciation of the military dimensions of the Soviet threat and the
importance of a balance of power in Asia makes the new leaders of
Peking keenly sensitive to the high cost of cutting off their relations with the United States and driving the United States out of Asia.

Third, the debate over Soviet policy in Peking has revolved around
a set of alternatives that *excludes* the option of a far-reaching rapprochement with the USSR. Rather, the three broad options in Soviet
policy have been to: attack the USSR ideologically and prepare against
subversion; take a hard line on the Soviet Union while rapidly improving China's defenses; and take a tactically somewhat softer line on the
USSR so as to undercut the Kremlin's hawks while rapidly improving
China's defenses. It is possible, of course, that some of the "soft"
moderates may actually have preferred a more far-reaching rapprochement
with Moscow but felt they could not voice this goal even indirectly
while Mao lived. Perhaps they thus opted for a more acceptable rationale
that would still allow them to make the initial steps in the right direc-
tion--in the process possibly eliciting a forthcoming Soviet response

---

[268]On the strains in the coalition as of the spring of 1978 and
the probable lines of tension in the future, see Lieberthal, 1978a,
op. cit.

that would pave the way for subsequent moves toward a genuine reconciliation. While there is no way to eliminate this possibility, there has
also been no evidence whatever, either before or since Mao's death,
that this was the case. There remains the additional chance that a
previously anti-Soviet faction could turn toward rapprochement with
the USSR (perhaps negotiated secretly) as part of the political infighting during the course of the succession. Although unlikely, this
possibility of disgruntled Chinese leaders turning toward the USSR is
examined in the following chapter on future prospects.

Last, it remains extremely difficult to differentiate "hard" from
"soft" moderates in the Peking leadership. A *prima facie* case is made
above for including the PLA central leadership among the "soft" moderates, and PLA participation in Peking politics in the past few years
is analyzed accordingly. Conclusive evidence for this, however, is
lacking. It is certainly possible that Yeh Chien-ying, for instance,
is personally on the "hard" side, while Ch'en Hsi-lien, who had to confront the Soviets over Chenpao and live in the shadow of the Soviet
Union in the northeast for many years, opts for the "soft" approach.
Hua Kuo-feng is, as argued above, almost certainly among the "soft"
moderates. Likewise, since October 1976, Li Hsien-nien, Chi Teng-
k'uei, and T'an Chen-lin have taken the kind of deliberately provocative stand toward the Soviets in various forums that almost certainly
places them in the "hard" camp. Teng Hsiao-p'ing has shifted toward
the "hard" position, but information even on the other members of the
Politburo is not available, and thus one can document with greater
certainty the existence and terms of this split than the personalities
who take either side.

III.   SINO-SOVIET RELATIONS IN THE FUTURE

The preceding two sections provide a solid foundation for analyzing the course of Sino-Soviet relations in the near-term future. Two messages stand out from a review of this relationship from 1969 to date: The basis of the Sino-Soviet conflict is broad and fundamental, and thus no far-reaching rapprochement is in the offing; and the relationship has evolved as part of a triangular interaction involving the United States, and thus any full set of prognoses must take account of possible changes in U.S. relations with either China or the Soviet Union or both and the potential repercussions of these changes on the Sino-Soviet bilateral relationship.

The following pages focus initially on Sino-Soviet relations in primarily a bilateral context to understand the likely continuum of policies that each will pursue toward the other. This bilateral focus is grounded in the recognition that Sino-Soviet relations are a function of a very broad set of concerns and perceptions of the political leaders in both Moscow and Peking. Moderate changes in the international situation are, therefore, unlikely to bring about any major transformation in the dynamics of Sino-Soviet interaction. The political successions in China, the USSR, and the United States may make prediction of the future based on analysis of the recent past somewhat problematic, however, and therefore the middle part of this final section does consider some major possible future alternatives to the picture presented in the subsection below. The section concludes with an analysis of the implications of this report for U.S. policy.

THE BILATERAL DIMENSION: THE PAST AS GUIDE TO THE FUTURE

Both China and the Soviet Union have indicated clearly their intended policies in dealings with each other in the future, and other trends that will provide the context for this bilateral relationship in the coming years are also evident. Analysis of these factors leads to the conclusion that the near-term future in Sino-Soviet relations will almost certainly be bounded by a rather narrow range of possibilities: that is, *within a context of continuing suspicion and conflict* the relationship may exhibit a range of features, from some increased friction and rancor to a partial diminution of tension punctuated by occasional flurries of indications of a more significant improvement in relations. These "flurries," if they occur, will prove to be more shadow than substance, as far-reaching rapprochement between these two continental giants remains beyond the realm of the politically possible.

Soviet Strategy

The Soviet Union hopes to steer the PRC onto a less anti-Soviet course and thereby diminish somewhat the immense national security threat that it perceives looming from across the disputed Sino-Soviet border. To this end, the Soviets have pursued a carrot and stick policy toward China to date, and there is every likelihood that the USSR will continue to utilize both approaches in the future. Thus, Moscow will try to increase its strength in Asia around China's periphery while holding out an olive branch to the Chinese leaders. First, the olive branch, which has five leaves on it. Moscow has stated that clear signs of China's interest in picking any of the five will be taken as a signal that Peking wants to move toward a better relationship in the future. The five are: serious negotiations on all or part of the territorial dispute; willingness to convene a summit meeting; significant increases in bilateral trade; acceptance of offers of Soviet aid and/or cooperation in other spheres; and willingness to conclude some form of nonaggression treaty. Moscow put all of these on the table during the border negotiations in 1969-1973, and all remain viable options.[1] In addition, the Kremlin will continue to probe for signs of a changing Chinese attitude, as it did in sending messages from the CPSU CC and from Brezhnev personally on the death of Chairman Mao and the accession of Hua Kuo-feng to the Party leadership. As noted in Sec. I, these would have been the first Party-to-Party communications in more than a decade, had the Chinese accepted them.

The Soviets may also try to jar the Chinese into a more flexible position through some significant new concession at a time when

---

[1]See Sec. I for details.

they believe such a move would influence the ongoing Chinese succession in a way that would increase the chances of a positive response from Peking. Moscow evidently tried to do this in a very tentative and limited way with its February 24, 1978, offer to Peking just before China's Fifth National People's Congress convened. A more significant gesture would be needed, though. In the border negotiations, for instance, the Chinese have repeatedly called for the Soviets to recognize "disputed areas" between China and the USSR. Moscow has *de facto* recognized the partial validity of this Chinese stance through: noting that changes in geography require some changes in the present demarcation of the border; yielding possession of all islands in the Ussuri up to the middle of the main channel to the Chinese with the sole exception of the area around Hei Hsia Tzu; and acknowledging that the current boundary in the Pamir region may be open to some discussion. Moscow has refused two other aspects of the Chinese demand, however: that the Kremlin formally recognize the existence of "disputed areas" (defined as all those territories that differ on the Chinese and Soviet maps of the border exchanged in 1964); and that Moscow withdraw all its armed forces from these "disputed areas." The Soviets assert that the 1964 map submitted by the Chinese to indicate where Peking felt the Sino-Soviet border should be drawn quite arbitrarily claimed much Soviet territory as Chinese, and thus the Soviets could not possibly recognize even the potential validity of a boundary drawn without a clear historical basis. Unstated but important is the fact that the Soviet leaders feel they cannot possibly officially acknowledge that territory taken by Russia from a weaker bordering country should be subject to future negotiations and compromise--for this would add validity to territorial claims made by Japan and could conceivably fuel border disputes with several East European countries. Thus, the Soviets cannot and will not accept the "disputed areas" concept in principle, although they are willing to go some distance toward meeting Chinese territorial demands in practice.

Within this context, the Soviets could make a strong demonstration of their earnestness by acknowledging that the Thalweg principle places the Sino-Soviet riverine border at the confluence of the Amur and Ussuri rivers rather than through the Kazakevichego Channel. This would put Hei Hsia Tzu Island in Chinese hands, which would not be welcomed by the Soviets but still would hardly pose a major strategic threat to Soviet interests in the area. This concession would also permit the Chinese to send larger ships up the Ussuri to the Amur, thus possibly in turn increasing Chinese interest in maintaining the navigability of the Amur, which itself could lead to greater Chinese willingness to undertake the type of coordinated navigation projects that were formerly worked out in the almost annual navigation talks. These talks reached the first such agreement since the Cultural Revolution in October 1977.

On the withdrawal of forces, the Soviets have already withdrawn from all the islands in dispute on the Chinese side of the main channel of the Ussuri. Moscow may choose *de facto* to thin out its forces in other areas designated by the Chinese as "disputed," although the Kremlin certainly would not announce publicly that it was doing this. Indeed, the Soviets have contemplated withdrawal of divisions from the China theater as a part of a process of rapprochement,[2] although the timing and dimensions of such a move are very likely unsettled in Moscow. Almost certainly, no Soviet leader envisions under even the best of circumstances a drawdown that would come close to matching the condition laid down by T'an Chen-lin in an interview in November 1976 and made official Chinese policy by Peking's March 6, 1978, response to the Soviet initiative of February 24: that the USSR reduce its border troop levels along the entire Sino-Soviet border to those prevailing at the time of Khrushchev's death.[3] Some reduction of Soviet forces in the Far East, especially in air wings that can easily be moved back in case they are needed, could occur within the coming few years.

---

[2] A ranking official of the Soviet Institute of the Far East stressed the feasibility of Soviet troop withdrawals as a part of the process of rapprochement during a conversation with me in early April 1976.

[3] Hong Kong AFP, November 6, 1976, cited in *FBIS/PRC*, November 8, 1976, p. A-3. T'an and Li Hsien-nien also dictated in other interviews that the Soviets would have to admit that they have been completely in error since 1960. *Le Monde*, November 3, 1976, cited in *FBIS/PRC*, November 4, 1976; Hong Kong AFP, November 2, 1976, cited in *FBIS/PRC*, November 3, 1976, pp. A-5-6.

The menu of possible Soviet measures to signal good intentions is indeed extraordinarily varied. Moscow, for instance, halted its anti-China public polemics for a period of months after the death of Mao. In the future it may choose to mute its calls for an Asian Collective Security System. In secret negotiations, the Kremlin could propose some lessening of its support for Vietnam or could accept China's preference that the Indian Ocean become an atom free zone. Indeed, in the context of an improving Sino-Soviet relationship, Moscow might even again invite some Chinese participation in the development of Eastern Siberia, almost certainly through the import of Chinese labor to work on specific projects there. The Chinese accepted a similar offer in the 1950s (while complaining that it smacked of a colonial relationship).[4] Peking might again prove amenable to such an opportunity in the late 1970s--for its value as symbol, as intelligence vehicle, and as a means of holding down somewhat the migration of Soviet workers into this territory.

There are many other forums and vehicles for the USSR to try to communicate to the new Peking leadership its sincerity in seeking to ease tension between the two countries. In the United Nations, for instance, the Soviet delegation might parry rather than return the verbal slings of the Chinese, and the USSR might also seek common ground with Peking on some of the many issues before the world body. Regarding countries on China's periphery, Moscow may place new restrictions on the weaponry it is willing to sell India. It might also fairly conspicuously move back toward a more neutral position in the Sino-Indian and Sino-Vietnamese disputes. It could scale down its intelligence and subversive efforts against China, decreasing for instance the number of flights it sends along the Soviet side of the border to test Chinese radar and to undertake aerial reconnaissance. It could, in addition, radio to the mainland side its intention to cross the Taiwan Straits whenever one of its ships is about to enter this body of water. And it might certainly enlist the aid of such East European "neutrals" as Romania and Yugoslavia to help heal the breach. These

---

[4]Khrushchev, 1974, op. cit., pp. 249-250.

are but a few of the ways that the Kremlin could try to improve relations with the current Chinese leadership. Most of them, moreover,
have the virtue of requiring no formal concession from Moscow, and thus
they serve as signals that can be relatively cost-free if it should
become necessary to reverse them.

The Soviet Union has pursued a carrot and stick policy to date,
and there is every likelihood that it will continue to utilize both
approaches in the future. The "stick" can be wielded as blatantly
and/or as subtly as can the carrot be proffered. For instance, within
weeks of Mao Tse-tung's demise the USSR both asked to resume the border
negotiations (and ceased public polemics) and had Victor Louis publish
an article threatening that the leadership in Peking had to show some
flexibility within a month or irreversible decisions would be taken
in Moscow.[5] Louis holds no official position in the Soviet hierarchy
and his article was not published in the USSR. Yet, his ties to the
KGB are well established, and thus the Soviets had succeeded in threatening China without really doing so. More Victor Louis articles may
appear in the future.

Other Soviet actions designed to pressure Peking might include:
increasing "border" flights, intelligence operations, and subversive
activities; staging military maneuvers and high-level military inspec-
tions in the China theater; continuing activities to increase the
state of readiness of Soviet forces in this theater; strongly supporting Vietnamese and Indian claims against China, and possibly even
supporting the North Korean and Japanese territorial claims on the
continental shelf off China; making significant Soviet concessions to
Japan; increasing the Soviet naval presence in the Indian Ocean and in
the Western Pacific; more aggressive Soviet patrolling along the Sino-
Soviet border; and having Soviet leaders make increasingly threatening
statements on the China question.

_____

[5]These border negotiations commenced on November 27, 1976, and
adjourned on February 28, 1977, with no progress having been made.
New York Times, November 28, 1976; *New York Times*, March 1, 1977. For
comments on the Victor Louis article, see *Hsin Wan Pao*, November 16,
1976, cited in *FBIS/PRC*, November 23, 1976, pp. N-2-3; *Hsin Wan Pao*,
October 26, 1976, cited in *FBIS/PRC*, November 3, 1976, p. N-1.

The Soviets might also make some very indirect gestures toward Taiwan, such as using language in their media that suggests the legitimacy of the current government when reporting events from there, sending an occasional reporter there, and radioing to Kaohsiung or Keelung the intention of any Soviet ship to traverse the Taiwan Straits.[6] The USSR almost certainly will not strike any significantly more forthcoming posture toward Taiwan, however, even in the wake of normalization of U.S.-Chinese relations, for several reasons. Through thick and thin, Moscow has since 1950 maintained China's right to Taiwan, and thus a reversal now would fly in the face of a long and clear public commitment to a pro-PRC stand on the Taiwan question. Also, in shifting positions on Taiwan, Moscow would cancel out any hope for improved relations with the successor government in Peking. Thus, in at least the near-term future, any serious Soviet overture to Taipei seems out of the question. In the longer term, however, the merits of the Taiwan issue might change dramatically as discussed in Sec. I.

The Soviet Union has a substantial problem in trying to "read" the Chinese succession. This is critically important for purposes of timing and selecting the mix of gestures it wants to make toward China, for signals sent when the mood in Peking is wrong may well have effects opposite to those intended. The accuracy of Soviet estimates of the situation in China must remain problematic, as we ultimately have no foolproof way of learning either their own evaluations or the true situation in Peking. We also cannot be confident that we know the Kremlin's level of confidence in its own intelligence on the political situation in China.

This assumes importance in part because at some point the leaders in Moscow are going to have to make a judgment as to when the succession in China has ended. Their own experience in the successions to both Lenin and Stalin has most likely sensitized them to the fact that the leader who seems to emerge in the direct aftermath of the death of the *vozhd'* may be the one least likely to consolidate power

---

[6] The USSR has done all three in the past.

in the new era.[7] The "succession" is likely to take half a decade before it fully works itself out, and a significant Soviet commitment to one coalition of leaders may prove disastrous in the longer run as that group is moved aside by other contenders.

By way of illustration, Hua Kuo-feng enjoys the support of Li Hsien-nien (over 70) and Yeh Chien-ying (80 years old). Wu Teh seems to be in a somewhat sensitive position over his previously too-close relationship with the radicals and as a result of his public role in the suppression of the T'ien-an Men demonstration of April 5, 1976. He may look for other ties that will give him a more secure political future. Wang Tung-hsing may have few strong programmatic preferences but seems to be gravitating toward Hua Kuo-feng as the succession unfolds. Ch'en Hsi-lien's preferences and his political record during the past few years are unknown. Teng Hsiao-p'ing may harbor some resentment against those who postponed his most recent rehabilitation for nearly 10 months after the overthrow of the Gang of Four. And so forth.[8] In the short term, therefore, any foreign government would be foolish to consider the current leadership lineup as unchangeable. Even with the rehabilitation of Teng, the Eleventh Party Congress, and the Fifth National People's Congress, the question of the durability and cohesion of the new leadership must remain unanswered for some period of time--and the Soviets must decide for *what* period of time.

A great deal depends on this decision. For instance, while the Soviets will not seek to strengthen ties with Taiwan as long as they see any possibility of a rapprochement with Peking, they could conceivably act to do so after they have determined that a vehemently

---

[7] Almost no outside observers looked to Stalin as the probable successor to Lenin in 1924, and Stalin did not really emerge as the clear successor until 1928-1929. Likewise, Malenkov seemed the inheritor of the mantle of Stalin as of the fall of 1953, only to be knocked off his pedestal in 1955. Khrushchev assumed the position of primacy by July 1957. In each case, then, the person who came to the fore at the outset (Trotsky, Malenkov) fared badly in the long run.

[8] The political cross currents in Peking as of March-April 1978 are analyzed in Lieberthal, 1978c, op. cit.

anti-Soviet leadership has consolidated its power in China. Once the
latter occurred, the diplomatic costs to the USSR of improving ties
with Taiwan would diminish considerably, and a number of important
Soviet interests in preventing Peking from assuming administrative
control over the island might come to the fore. For instance, reunification of Taiwan with the PRC would give China a strong incentive to
increase its naval power in the Western Pacific to strengthen its ties
with Taiwan. This would also give Peking an unsinkable (albeit also
immobile) aircraft carrier and naval basing facilities 100 miles out
into the Pacific, astride Japanese and Soviet sea lanes. It would
allow Peking to claim the Taiwan Straits as territorial waters.[9] And
Taiwan would immediately become China's richest province, able to
contribute significantly to the technical manpower and material resources available to Peking.

It is conceivable (although quite unlikely), moreover, that in the
aftermath of the normalization of Sino-U.S. relations, if this process
includes abrogation of the U.S. defense commitment to Taiwan, Japan
might prove favorable to having the Soviet Union establish some sort
of relationship with Taiwan if that is what is needed to keep the
island out of Peking's control. Japan clearly would not look with
favor on any major Soviet military presence on the island, but it could
welcome Soviet gestures that would serve as "confidence builders" in
Taipei and prevent the Nationalists from losing the determination necessary for their continued independence. This conjecture about Taiwan
takes us into the less likely contingencies, however.

Basically, past performance would suggest that the Soviets will
continue to follow their established policy--trying to take the cutting edge off Sino-Soviet relations through a mixture of implied
threat and suggestive diplomacy. As the Soviets perceive it, the stakes
are high--the possible difference between having a reasonably friendly
and cooperative neighbor and facing an increasingly powerful and menacing

---

[9] Peking has consistently argued that all international shipping
must request and receive permission of the country through whose territorial waters straits run before using those straits. For an analysis of this and related aspects of China's policy toward the sea, see
Romance, op. cit.

enemy with virtually unlimited available manpower over the indefinite future.

This entire Soviet policy will, moreover, take place within the context of an increasing Soviet presence in Eastern Siberia in the regions to the north of the eastern section of the Sino-Soviet border. The current Soviet Five Year Plan envisages rapid development of this region and construction of transportation facilities appropriate to the role this mining region is likely to play in the national economy. The increasing Soviet presence in this region will inevitably lead to greater Soviet interaction with other Asian countries, especially in the commercial sphere. Thus, the Soviet strategy outlined above will be couched in the broader context of the movement of Soviet citizens and capital into the China theater and increments in Soviet transport capability that will have definite military as well as civilian significance. These larger contextual trends will proceed independently of the near-term future of Sino-Soviet relations, but they will inevitably affect the calculations of both China and the USSR as they contemplate their actions in this relationship.[10]

Chinese Strategy

Within this context, what is the future Chinese policy toward the USSR likely to be? The victors to date in the Chinese succession crisis are, as explained in Sec. II, people who view power in the international arena in terms of military and economic might. The inexorably expanding Soviet presence in Northeast Asia, therefore, must alarm them and will likely make them seek closer relations with the West, possibly including importation of Western military goods and technology in the face of a continually growing Soviet military threat. Perhaps, indeed, the majority of balance of power advocates in Peking feel China must now look

---

[10]China has begun to register its concern over the military and economic dimensions of this "civilian" development of the region in its public media. See, for instance, Peking Domestic Service, March 26, 1977, cited in *FBIS/PRC*, March 29, 1977, pp. A-5-6. On the growth of commerce between the Soviet Far East and the rest of Asia, see *New York Times*, November 25, 1975.

abroad in the short term for the military might that will prevent the scales from tipping decisively in favor of the Soviets.

This concern about the balance of power must be linked with the Peking leaders' conception of the Soviet Union's aims and tactics in international politics to gain insight into China's future policy toward the USSR. The Chinese repeatedly describe the USSR as "hegemonic," by which they mean that Moscow will ceaselessly try to expand its military, economic, and political influence on the world stage at the expense of the sovereignty of other countries. China believes, therefore, that all Soviet compromises are by their very nature tactical and temporary, and that they will be tossed to the wind the minute Soviet interests dictate that they are no longer necessary.[11]

Chinese leaders believe that the Kremlin uses a range of tactics for increasing its power in the international arena, not the least important of which is what the Chinese have called Moscow's "treaty craze." According to the Chinese, the USSR uses treaties as a means by which it can further its expansionist aims. Once it has seduced another country into a treaty relationship, the Kremlin then constantly strives to make the treaty work to Moscow's advantage, applying pressure for the repayment of debts while the receiver country is in financial difficulty, trying to expand Soviet base, port, and overflight rights, and in other ways working to make the country subservient to Soviet interests. Likewise, the USSR periodically proposes international treaties that have the effect of shackling its adversaries in areas where the Soviet Union has already achieved some advantage.[12]

This perspective explains why the Chinese will continue to refuse Soviet proposals for a treaty on nonaggression and the nonuse of force, for Peking believes that Moscow will inevitably try to use the treaty to undermine China's sovereignty. For example, a prohibition

---

[11]Two forceful statements of China's views concerning the domestic and international nature of the Soviet system are "Leninism or Social-imperialism?" *Jen-min Jih-pao*, April 22, 1970, translated in *Peking Review*, No. 17, April 24, 1970, pp. 5-15; and "Social-imperialism Is the Most Dangerous Source of War," *New China News Agency* English, January 3, 1976, cited in *FBIS/PRC*, January 5, 1976.

[12]*New China News Agency*, November 24, 1976, cited in *FBIS/PRC*, November 26, 1976, pp. A-4-6.

on preparations for war may bring subsequent Soviet demands for inspection rights to enforce the treaty. Similarly, given the massive current Soviet conventional and nuclear superiority over China, Moscow may choose to interpret any Chinese efforts to catch up as violations of the letter and/or spirit of the treaty. Strictures against the threat of force lose their meaning in the face of 40 Soviet divisions already deployed in the China theater and Soviet missile-firing submarines in the Western Pacific. And an agreement against the use of force is obviously good only within the context of minor border incidents (in which assessments of blame can be difficult to make), for a major war between the two powers would obviously render the agreement null.

A Soviet treaty with China could, in addition, take much of the sting out of the PRC's claims that the USSR is inherently aggressive and that China (among other countries) lives under the threat of Soviet attack. Taking this series of elements together, it is not surprising that the Chinese have repeatedly rejected Soviet offers of a treaty on nonaggression that prohibits the threat and use of any kind of force and calls for an end to further war preparations. Indeed, this same logic will most likely steer the Chinese clear of *any* major agreements with the Soviet Union, for all Chinese leaders deeply believe that the USSR is bent on expansion and on undermining the states on its periphery.

Additionally, China in recent years has proved willing to foment or at least tolerate territorial disputes with many of its neighbors, in sharp contrast to the PRC's efforts to resolve such issues in the late 1950s and early 1960s.[13] If one includes disagreements over the continental shelf and offshore islands, China currently has unresolved territorial disputes with the USSR, North and South Korea, Japan, the Philippines, Vietnam, and India. Peking has made no effort to settle any of these in recent years and has, indeed, been willing to exacerbate the dispute with Vietnam while holding the issue in abeyance with the other countries. The Chinese leaders evidently believe that China

_____

[13]The Chinese resolved outstanding border issues with a number of their neighboring states during 1959-1962. For a review on a state-by-state basis, see Harold Hinton, *Communist China in World Politics*, Houghton Mifflin, New York, 1966, Chapter 12.

will be stronger in the future than it is now, and thus they can afford to be patient, for history will be kind to them. Given this attitude, Peking will not feel under any strong compunction to settle the Sino-Soviet territorial issue.

Finally, China's leaders may well calculate that any détente between the USSR and the PRC can be better exploited by Moscow than by Peking in their respective relations with the United States in the future. Such a development would likely in fact increase to a degree the bargaining leverage of each with Washington. The Soviet-U.S. relationship is, however, more complex and in many ways more important to Washington than is the Peking-U.S. tie. Thus, it would not be surprising for the Chinese leaders to calculate that any actions of theirs that more fully "triangularize" the relationship between the three countries would in fact serve to strengthen Moscow's rather than Peking's hand, given the current state of Soviet-U.S. and Sino-U.S. relations.

Since both "soft" and "hard" moderates remain within the Chinese leadership, however, Peking's stance toward the USSR will probably include *occasional* hints that the PRC would like to take some of the edge off their bilateral relationship. These hints could crop up in various places: articles in the Chinese media that recall with favor the Sino-Soviet cooperation of the 1950s; Chinese gestures such as allowing the USSR to send representatives to pay homage at the monuments to Soviet martyrs in the Chinese revolution; a possible decrease in anti-Soviet propaganda, perhaps including neglect of an anti-Soviet diatribe on Lenin's birthday in April; seemingly serious Chinese negotiations on one or another of the matters raised in the border talks (negotiations that, as happened in 1971, break down on the verge of reaching final agreement); slight changes in the wording of China's telegram to the USSR on the anniversary of the October Revolution; and so forth. These ephemeral gestures may keep the Soviets at least somewhat uncertain as to whether a determinedly anti-Soviet leadership has consolidated its power in China without at the same time incurring any real costs for the PRC.

These gestures will, however, almost certainly take place within the context of an overall Chinese foreign policy that is strongly

anti-Soviet. If the analysis in Sec. II is valid, all current Chinese
leaders, regardless of their other disagreements, *exclude* the possibility of serious reconciliation with the USSR from their list of
realistic policy options. Debate in China now takes place over how
best to ward off the Soviet threat while rapidly building up the PRC's
military strength--through a hard line in all relations with the Soviets
or by some short-term, tactical compromise(s) to confuse Soviet analyses of China's intentions.

While Mao Tse-tung lived, the hard line approach won out with the
exception only of the helicopter pilot release. Several things have
changed with Mao's death, however, that could eventually shift the
balance somewhat in the direction of a "soft" moderate stance. First,
Mao himself is no longer on the scene to throw his weight behind the
"hard" moderate position. Second, people need no longer fear that
advocacy of a "soft" position will be used to turn the Chairman against
them in the succession struggle. Third, key members of the group that
has at least temporarily come to the fore in this struggle--Hua Kuo-
feng and Yeh Chien-ying--are evidently in the "soft" moderate camp,
although the overall balance between them and such current "hard"
moderates as Teng Hsiao-p'ing, Li Hsien-nien, Chi Teng-k'uei, and
T'an Chen-lin remains unclear and probably fluid. Fourth, until Mao's
death China could take some solace from the fact that the Soviets were
extremely unlikely to attack the PRC before they had some inkling of
whether Mao's passing would produce a less anti-Soviet leader. In this
peculiar sense, Mao was something of an insurance policy for China--
a policy that expired on September 9, 1976. Thus, "soft" moderates in
the Chinese leadership can now argue with greater force that significant
Chinese acts of hostility toward the Soviets (such as major imports of
Western military goods and technology) will greatly increase the chances
of Soviet attack insofar as they signify that China in the post-Mao
era will become an even greater threat to Soviet security and will remain an implacable enemy. While hard-line anti-Sovietism will remain
the touchstone of Chinese foreign policy, therefore, indications of a
more conciliatory approach may occasionally surface.

Western analysts should not be fooled by the types of conciliatory
gestures on China's part listed above. They signify not a strategic

change but only some new tactical flexibility within continuing pursuit of "Chairman Mao's revolutionary [i.e., anti-Soviet] line in foreign policy." Barring any major unforeseen setback, it is extraordinarily unlikely that the Chinese will change the anti-Soviet basis of their global foreign policy, which entails: supporting a united and strong Western Europe; courting Japan and trying to drive a wedge between Tokyo and Moscow over such questions as their territorial dispute; trying to cement China's relations with the other countries of Asia and prevent them from joining any Soviet-supported regional grouping; and adopting an "objective" attitude toward the United States in which, regardless of the state of bilateral Sino-U.S. relations, the Chinese welcome a continued U.S. presence in Asia and prove sensitive to major U.S. interests in the region (other than those centered on Taiwan). Over the next four to five years, these basic contours of Chinese policy should remain fixed. In all likelihood, only when Peking feels the vitality of rapid industrial growth combined with infusions of military hardware and technology will the Chinese leaders dare to contemplate pulling away from the policy outlined above and risk offending important U.S. policy interests across the board in the Pacific region.

Conclusion

In sum, the USSR is ready and anxious to improve relations with the PRC and has already laid an agenda of possible starting points on the table for China to contemplate. Moscow may, at what the Soviet leaders perceive to be an appropriate point in the Chinese succession, decide to sweeten the pot either through indirect gestures that can be rescinded if they do not prove fruitful or even through some fairly significant direct concession, such as a pullback of some forces from the Sino-Soviet border or relinquishment of Hei Hsia Tzu. The USSR will, however, continue to apply the stick to China, both through direct and/or indirect threats and through its broader diplomatic and military activities in the area.

China might possibly move toward greater tactical flexibility than it has exhibited in the past in its bilateral relations with Moscow, fearing its potentially greater risk of suffering a Soviet attack now that Mao Tse-tung is gone. Given a continuing balance of forces in Peking politics, however, most likely the PRC's policy in this sphere will prove mixed, with a steady stream of hard line gestures and insults interspersed by only occasional (and usually indirect) indications of Chinese "reasonableness." Fundamentally, China will continue to construct its foreign policy around the need to counter the Soviet military threat, and this underlying context should remain constant regardless of the seesaw battle between "soft" and "hard" moderates behind the walls of the Politburo quarters in Chungnanhai.

THE BILATERAL DIMENSION: SUCCESSION POLITICS EXPAND THE ALTERNATIVES

Two dimensions of the context in which Sino-Soviet relations will be played out during the rest of this decade may require adjustments in the above prognosis. The first is the political succession currently under way in Moscow and Peking. The second is U.S. relations with the USSR and PRC. Each of these variables introduces uncertainties into the situation that can, at least in broad outline, be anticipated and evaluated. At the same time, the above analysis makes clear that Peking's and Moscow's fundamental attitudes toward each other stem from their respective evaluations of a wide range of issues, including basic economic and military trends, ideological assessments of the nature of each other's systems, foreign policies pursued toward third parties, and so forth. Since most of these dimensions will remain basically constant over time, the underlying perceptions and fears that structure the Sino-Soviet relationship are likely to prove relatively immutable in the near-term future. The uncertainties analyzed in this subsection should, therefore, be regarded as *highly improbable contingencies* rather than as alternatives coequal with the scenarios sketched out in the first part of this section.

Bilaterally, succession politics introduce the greatest unknowns into the Sino-Soviet equation. The analysis in Sec. II concludes that there is no significant group in Peking that would favor a far-reaching rapprochement with the USSR. China's military situation, moreover, virtually rules out the possibility of PRC armed aggression against Soviet territory. Thus, insofar as the political succession brings to the fore people who advocate strategies significantly different from those already analyzed above, these new approaches are likely to surface in Moscow rather than in Peking.

Real Sino-Soviet rapprochement would have to begin with the emergence of a succession leadership in Moscow that proved willing to take "risks for peace" with Peking. One can easily imagine the platform such a group would put forward: that relations with the United States were deteriorating and could improve only if the Soviet Union gained the leverage that an easing of tensions with Peking would bring; that the military containment of an increasingly powerful China drained badly needed resources; and that in any case the danger from a China that rears its youth on anti-Sovietism for another several decades would be so acute that a policy of prudent risk-taking is more than justified to avoid this nightmarish future. At the same time, the soft moderates would have to secure their position in Peking, at least sufficiently to allow a process of reconciliation to begin. The stress here must clearly be on *process*, though, as it is difficult to envision a clear-cut Chinese *decision* in favor of rapprochement with the Soviet Union.

Essentially, then, one would look for a conciliatory gesture by China's soft moderates that brought a far more generous and forthcoming response from Moscow than any Chinese leaders had anticipated. This could cause debate in Peking along the lines of whether or not there should be further probing to see whether China could substantially reduce the short-term threat on its northern border without yielding anything of substance itself. This debate could produce additional gestures, leading to Soviet responses and further discussion in the Chinese councils of state. Almost unintentionally, then, the Chinese might begin to approach reconciliation with the Soviet Union, as the leaders in the Forbidden City became increasingly excited by the results they elicited each time they nibbled at the previously forbidden policy of rapprochement with the Soviets.

The analysis in Sec. II strongly suggests, however, that even were the above unlikely combination of circumstances to occur, Sino-Soviet détente would not in fact develop very far. Taking all factors into consideration, the road to a Sino-Soviet détente is not so much slippery as strewn with obstacles, for a number of important reasons.

First, China's fear of Moscow's intentions is based on its appraisal of a set of factors far broader than Moscow's posture in the Sino-Soviet bilateral relationship. Thus, really significant movement toward rapprochement (that is, movement that would affect the military balance in Asia by freeing both Chinese and Soviet troops for potential use elsewhere) would require that Moscow change its position in the entire international arena in ways that fundamentally altered the Peking leadership's appraisal of Soviet aspirations and capabilities. This would most likely require a long-term scaling down of Soviet defense expenditures, reduction in the overall size of the Soviet military, some significant Soviet defeats abroad and increasing signs of Soviet timidity in the international arena. Short of this, the Chinese will continue to assess the USSR as an imperialist power in the ascendancy and will shape their policy so as to diminish and ward off the Soviet threat. China long ago realized that appeasement will not permanently quiet the appetite of the Russian Bear, and all the alternatives demand a relationship characterized by considerably more rancor and suspicion than a fundamental rapprochement would allow.

These Chinese attitudes toward the desirability of a far-reaching rapprochement with the Soviet Union almost certainly would not be determined, moreover, by the United States' posture on the world stage. Sino-Soviet hostility on the Chinese side is based on Peking's evaluation of Soviet long-term intentions, not the availability of the United States as a counterweight. Naturally, the more clearly U.S. policy conforms to the role of counterweight to the Soviets, the less strain will be evident in the Chinese leaders as they periodically reassess the wisdom of their current Soviet policy. The only U.S. actions that could drive the Chinese back toward Moscow, however, would be actions so threatening to China's territorial integrity or security that Peking felt compelled to reevaluate its designation of China's main enemy in the international arena.[14] Put differently, Peking's strategic thinking

---

[14]The likelihood of a deterioration in Sino-U.S. relations and its possible effect on China's policy toward the Soviet Union is discussed below.

excludes the tactic of uniting with one's greatest immediate enemy to decrease the chances of an attack.

Even if strategic evaluations in Peking changed in a way that could lead to a far-reaching Sino-Soviet rapprochement, moreover, ideological obstacles are likely to arise that will prevent the consummation of any such trend. China unquestionably would not reenter the Soviet bloc except on its own terms--and those terms would demand full equality with Moscow in bloc affairs. Few things could be less congenial to the Soviet leadership. In recent years, Soviet control over its East European communist neighbors has relied more on economic and military levers than on ideological underpinning. Nevertheless, the Soviets have proven jealous of their "leading" role in this group of states, and they would almost certainly find it impossible to accord the Chinese the equality of status and influence that would be necessary to satisfy the Peking leadership.

Thus, even if a combination of political factors in Moscow and Peking augured well for some real improvement in Sino-Soviet relations, it would take a major change in the Soviet Union's world posture to bring about an equally far-reaching transformation in Chinese attitudes toward this bilateral tie--and if even this should occur, there would still remain political limits to the degree of rapprochement that could be effected by these two continental giants. Signs of Sino-Soviet détente, even well short of full rapprochement, might, however, in themselves engender profound effects throughout the remainder of Asia.

Japan and South Korea would feel their security far more threatened than they have in recent years. For South Korea, this would produce greater anxiety about the U.S. security shield, and probably would call forth even more stringent security measures at home, with a clandestine effort to complete development of South Korea's own nuclear weapons capability. Any indication by Washington that the United States might lessen its support for Seoul would almost certainly hasten this nuclear development.

The Japanese have tried to steer a careful neutral course between China and the Soviet Union, albeit evidencing greater fear of the Bear

than the Dragon.[15] Japanese reaction to a Sino-Soviet rapprochement
would depend in substantial degree on the ruling party in Japan at
the time this process unfolded. If the Liberal Democratic Party remains in power, the Japanese are likely basically to seek improved
ties with the United States as the touchstone of their defense. If
the Taiwan issue had not yet been resolved, they would probably increase their (discreet) efforts to encourage the United States to
keep Taiwan independent of the mainland--which in turn might simply
increase Peking's incentives to pursue closer ties with Moscow, as
discussed below. Should the Japan Socialist Party assume power, however, it is possible that Japan would edge closer to the new Sino-
Soviet bloc, seeking security partly through friendship and trade.
In either case, there is every likelihood that such developments
would produce some changes in Japanese attitudes toward military spending, most likely leading to increased investment in submarines and
conceivably in the nuclear and missile technology necessary to give
Tokyo a submarine-based nuclear deterrent.

It is not clear how Vietnam would respond to a Sino-Soviet rapprochement. Superficially, Hanoi would probably cultivate good relations with both Moscow and Peking, but it might also seek a measure
of security through multiplying its international contacts outside the
communist world. The Vietnamese communists may have received less than
what they had hoped for from a united Sino-Soviet bloc in the past,[16]
and it is doubtful that they would forget this lesson of only two decades
ago.

---

[15]A very solid review of this question is presented in Barnds,
1976, op. cit., pp. 27-38.

[16]There is a disagreement over the question of whether the Vietnamese felt their interests were adequately defended by the USSR and
PRC at the Geneva Conference of 1954. Khrushchev argues strongly that
they were (see Khrushchev, 1970, op. cit., pp. 479-483). Some Western
analysts have concluded that the Vietnamese lost at the conference
part of what they had won on the battlefield because of Soviet and
Chinese willingness to compromise their interests. See, for example,
Hinton, op. cit., pp. 253-254. The important element is, of course,
how the Vietnamese really evaluated this situation, and there is no
reliable evidence on this crucial dimension.

The remaining non-communist countries of Asia would probably all tend to turn toward the West should China and the USSR reestablish a relationship of close cooperation in foreign policy. How dramatic this turn would be would depend to a great extent on the role that they believed the United States was willing to play in the region.[17]

Given the current perceptions of the leaders on both sides of the Amur, however, a slide toward *military confrontation* in Sino-Soviet relations seems more likely than does significant progress toward a rapprochement, although it bears repeating that all the scenarios analyzed in this section are highly unlikely to come about.

The Sino-Soviet border is now one of the most heavily armed in the world. The Soviet military threat, moreover, is taken very seriously by most Chinese leaders, and the proper strategy of deterrence has been a subject of acrimonious debate within Peking.

The Soviet Union currently enjoys overwhelming superiority to the PRC in virtually all aspects of military strength. Soviet nuclear warheads and delivery capabilities, conventional firepower, mobility and armored strength, tactical and strategic bombing and fighting capability, and naval capacities are all far ahead of those enjoyed by the Chinese. The USSR now has about one-quarter of its armed forces explicitly committed to the Chinese theater, and it is rapidly increasing its ability to attack China from the sea. In any major military conflict, therefore, the Chinese would suffer far higher casualties and material losses, and indeed for the foreseeable future the Chinese have no realistic possibility of launching a successful offensive operation of any scale against Soviet territory. The PRC's forces are, moreover, deployed well back from the border in a clearly defensive posture.

Still, any Sino-Soviet military conflict would pose immense dangers for the Soviet Union as well as for China, since the potential drain on Soviet resources could prove enormous. What, then, could bring these two countries to engage in military combat?

---

[17]Obviously, a virtually complete abnegation by the United States of any major role in the area would deprive these countries of the option of relying on the United States to counter the thrust of a new Sino-Soviet bloc.

One could contend that Soviet failures in previous attempts to influence significantly Chinese politics by the use of military force should make this an unlikely tactic for Moscow to try again, and recent history would provide strong support for those who make this case. As detailed in Sec. I, for instance, the Soviets pressured Peking into the border negotiations that commenced in October 1969 through an escalating campaign of military threats waged during the spring and summer of that year. Implicit military threats were also used to try to affect the outcomes of several major Chinese meetings during the following three years.

What stands out, however, is the degree to which Peking yielded only the minimum necessary in each instance to alleviate a particularly grave threat (that is, by entering the border negotiations in October 1969) but did not go one inch further. Indeed, since 1970 it is difficult to pinpoint *any* advantage the Soviets have reaped from their military pressure on China's borders, albeit not for lack of trying. Military threats are, by their very nature, double-edged--producing either greater accommodation on the part of an adversary or a more determined effort by him to strengthen himself so as to be relatively immune to the threat in the future--and in China since 1970 the latter response has predominated. Thus, the history of the 1970s has not been kind to those in Moscow who may have argued that the high costs of establishing a major military presence on the Chinese border would pay off in terms of greater ability to wring concessions out of the Peking leadership. Future Soviet attitudes toward the utility of military pressure are, nevertheless, likely to be shaped more by Moscow's reading of the unfolding Chinese succession than by lessons that could be drawn from the recent past when Mao Tse-tung still strongly influenced China's foreign policy.

Under what conditions, then, might the Soviets be persuaded that they should bring their military superiority actively into play against the PRC during the coming years? The answer to this question depends critically on the assumptions the leaders in the Kremlin are making about the evolving situation in China and the prospects that it holds. Two basic assumptions and the military actions they might engender,

therefore, warrant brief consideration. The first stipulates that
although Mao Tse-tung succeeded, through purges and persuasion, in
making many Chinese leaders sincerely anti-Soviet, there nevertheless
remain in China leaders who see the wisdom of a fundamentally better
Sino-Soviet relationship. The second assumption denies the possibility that a pro-Soviet group of "healthy forces" still exists within the confines of Chungnanhai.[18]

A Kremlin conviction that there are leaders friendly to the
Soviet Union battling for the succession in China creates strong incentives in Moscow to try to influence the course of the succession
in Peking. The problem for Moscow, however, is that it is almost
impossible to know with confidence just what the impact of any given
actions will be on the political infighting in China's capital. Should
the Soviets try to project an image of strength? Would aggressive
border patrolling and a further buildup of forces around China's periphery bolster the argument that they think is being made in Peking
that China should seek accommodation with the Soviet Union? Should
they, instead, draw down some forces to strengthen the position of
those in Peking who might be stressing that the Soviets can be quite
reasonable if only China ceases trying to exacerbate relations between
the two countries? Perhaps shows of military strength combined with
indications of diplomatic flexibility will provide the best (or the
worst?) of both worlds. The main point is simply that a Soviet assumption that there remain potentially friendly elements in Peking creates
the rationale and incentives for an activist Soviet diplomatic and
military posture, but specific actions must be contemplated and adopted

---

[18]There is, of course, a third fundamental assessment that the
Soviet leaders could make--i.e., that Mao was almost unique in the
vehemence of his anti-Soviet feeling and thus that *most* Chinese
leaders will want to pursue détente with the USSR as soon as the
political situation in China stabilizes sufficiently to permit this.
The operational consequences of this assessment are not explored here
because there is no evidence available to suggest that any Soviet
leaders in fact hold this view. See the brief but excellent analysis
of this question in Morris Rothenberg, *Soviet Perceptions of the Chinese Succession*, Center for Advanced International Studies, University
of Miami, 1975.

in an environment of inadequate political information. This uncertainty in turn makes small actions more inviting than bold strokes, as the former presumably allow for continued flexibility as more information becomes available.

The problem with even "limited" measures of a military nature during a period of possible political uncertainty in both countries, however, is that they may ignite a process of escalation that neither Moscow nor Peking desires. It is not difficult to envision a situation where, for example, in the context of the succession struggle in China, some in the PRC may seize upon any local difficulties between Chinese and Soviet forces along the border as the pretext for a campaign of bold, nationalistic rhetoric to rally the populace to a patriotic cause. This could even lead to demands for some sort of retaliatory action. A political situation might well exist at the time in Peking, moreover, that would inhibit any potential contender for power from strongly advocating that the Chinese stand down. On the Soviet side, the leadership could interpret the strong Chinese words and actions as a "test of strength" by a contending faction within Peking and could become convinced of the necessity of demonstrating that this sort of approach to the USSR by any new Chinese leadership will meet with a "firm rebuff." The resulting incidents may touch off a process that slips beyond the firm control of the leaders in each country, developing eventually into a situation where Moscow feels compelled to take significant military action. The history of the 20th century, and especially of the origins of World War I and of U.S. involvement in the Vietnam War, suggest that even highly perceptive policymakers can be drawn step-by-step into a major military confrontation by a combination of incorrect premises about the nature of their own security and by the force of a chain of circumstances. Given the succession politics in China, and the fact that the USSR is also entering a succession period, this type of scenario cannot be overlooked or discarded out of hand. Just because it is difficult to see how either the USSR or Peking could possibly benefit from a large-scale military encounter between them, there is no reason to assume that such an encounter cannot take place.

One can, indeed, even envision the possibility that in a bitterly contested Chinese succession (which is still not out of the question) one group or another will actively try to entice the Soviet Union into actions in support of their cause. Although exceedingly unlikely, this scenario cannot be completely ruled out and thus warrants brief consideration. The Lin Piao affair of 1971 demonstrates how this situation could provide a potential basis for Soviet military involvement in China.

After Lin's overthrow, the Chinese circulated a document purported to have been drafted by Lin's son, Lin Li-kuo, and his colleagues. Entitled "Project 571," the document amounted to a contingency plan to be put into effect if the ever-worsening situation should turn disastrous for Lin senior. As detailed in Sec. I, the plan essentially called for a military-based effort to take power in China, relying primarily on air force units in Central and South China. One part of the plan suggested establishing contact with the Soviet Union and offering to renew solidarity with the USSR after Lin's successful bid to put himself in power. During the critical military confrontation within China, the Soviet Union would use its forces along the northern border to tie down troops loyal to Mao (and presumably Chou En-lai) and prevent them from making a successful challenge to Lin's insurgent forces in the south.

The means by which the Red Army was to tie down the PLA in the north are not specified, but almost certainly Lin had in mind a series of border incidents and ominous military moves that would keep Chinese troops in the north. There is, of course, no certainty that Lin's dissident group ever established contact with Soviet forces to make this proposal. Even had they done so, there was no certainty that the USSR, knowing that a military conflict of major dimensions had erupted in Central China, would play its assigned role and resist the temptation to secure even greater leverage over any successor government.

Indeed, one can imagine the problems Moscow would have had in fully authenticating the proposal communicated to it and making sure that it was not a trap being set by people who were in fact pushing for détente with the United States. It is also possible, in this regard, that the

entire "571" document was written (or rewritten) after Lin's demise
to fabricate history in a way that would serve the political interests
of the victors.

The current period of succession, as indicated above, is likely
to witness continuing political infighting. The purge of the radicals
during 1976-1977 is, moreover, the fourth major housecleaning carried
out in the PRC over the past decade. One legacy of this recent history
is that there is no lack of dissidents in China, including possibly
some who are now at very high levels, who are aggrieved over their past
treatment and who might think in terms of desperate actions to recoup
their positions during the succession. At the same time, any side in
the political battle in Peking might be willing to create and/or seize
opportunities to accuse its opponents of Soviet intrigues. Thus, for
the foreseeable future, the conditions will exist whereby some Chinese
faction might invite some form of Soviet armed support to bolster its
position in the succession, while at the same time Moscow will have to
remain sensitive to the possibility that it is being led into a trap
by some wonderfully devious ploy by a Chinese group. Since these contending possibilities render "signals" inherently ambiguous, they may
increase somewhat the chances that the USSR will become militarily
involved in the Chinese succession.[19]

There is a geographical dimension to this issue that bridges the
possibilities stemming from the two basic sets of Soviet assumptions
noted above. The regional variant in Chinese politics has been marked,
especially since the onset of the Cultural Revolution. This dimension
may even have infected the PLA, although the evidence for this hypothesis
remains in dispute. It is certainly within the realm of possibility
that the key leadership of a given border region will feel sufficiently
threatened by political trends in Peking that it will turn to the
Soviet Union for protection. The most likely candidates for this

---

[19] There is a large literature in political science that analyzes
the types of inherent ambiguities in international signalling under even
the best of conditions. See, for instance, Robert Jervis, "Hypotheses
on Misperception," in Morton H. Halperin and Arnold Kanter (eds.), *Readings in American Foreign Policy: A Bureaucratic Perspective*, Little,
Brown, and Company, Boston, 1973, pp. 113-138.

distinction are the Sinkiang-Uighur and Inner Mongolian Autonomous
Regions, with their large minority populations. Saifudin, a Uighur
who formerly enjoyed close ties with the Soviet Union, was purged
from his leadership of Sinkiang in early 1978. Heilungkiang could
also fall into this group, although it seems less likely to do so.

Moscow might honor a local Chinese request for a Soviet presence
in one or more border regions, given the Kremlin's long-evident concern with the concept of buffer states' protecting Soviet national
borders from hostile powers. This is a concern that has, moreover,
been demonstrated by each Soviet leadership since World War II: by
Stalin in the late 1940's, Khrushchev in Poland and Hungary in 1956,
and Brezhnev and Kosygin in Czechoslovakia in 1968.

In sum, an assumption in the Kremlin that the leaders in Peking
remain fundamentally divided over the policy China should pursue
toward the USSR creates a range of incentives for Moscow to adopt an
activist policy toward China, including under certain circumstances
the use of military force. The potential scenarios are numerous, and
only a few are sketched out above. The common factor in all of these
is that the Soviet leaders must act in a situation where their information is inadequate--and these actions in turn may be seized upon by
one or another group contesting for the succession in China and utilized
to help secure their position. Thus, the potential for Soviet mis-
calculation and for "irrational" (in terms of Sino-Soviet bilateral
relations) responses by the Chinese exists and can conceivably produce
a major military conflict that neither side desires.

Should the Kremlin leadership become convinced, on the other hand,
that no "healthy forces" remain in Peking, their views of any military
action against the PRC would differ considerably from those articulated
above. The type of military action they would initiate and the circumstances under which it would take place would also differ accordingly.
Under this second set of assumptions, the perceived opportunity costs
to Moscow of alienating the incoming Chinese administration would diminish greatly, and the focus of Soviet policy would shift instead to
trying to undermine China's ability, now and in the future, to wage
aggressive war against Soviet territory. Diplomatically, the Kremlin

would almost certainly try to utilize whatever leverage it could muster to prevent other countries from accelerating the growth of China's military power through either direct military-related sales or by other assistance that would indirectly hasten the day when the PRC could become a military superpower. It is conceivable that Moscow would make direct overtures toward Taiwan. In desperation, also, the Kremlin might choose to exercise any one of a range of military options against China.

As Moscow witnesses rapid growth in China's conventional military capabilities, the Kremlin might decide that it is necessary to provide non-Russian territory as the battleground should a future Chinese leadership ever risk launching an attack. The rationale for this action in this case is different from that in the "buffer state" scenario above, and so is the military action that would ensue. While, as noted above, the most likely areas of Soviet intervention in support of local Chinese dissidents would be in the sparsely populated and economically marginal Sinkiang-Uighur and Inner Mongolian Regions, a military campaign that aimed instead primarily to weaken China's future ability to fight a war on Soviet territory would almost certainly strike at the three Manchurian provinces above the Great Wall-- Heilungkiang, Kirin, and Liaoning. This region contains 20 percent of China's industrial output capacity,[20] and thus its separation from China would be a major economic as well as security loss.

Alternatively, if the Soviet leaders find themselves confronted with what they perceive to be an irreconcilably hostile and ever-stronger China, they might conclude that the trends in China's military and political development point to the wisdom of a preemptive attack directed against vital military targets. The scope of such a preemptive attack could vary greatly. It would almost certainly, at a minimum, seek to destroy China's nuclear weaponry in hand and China's missile

---

[20]Calculated on the basis of gross value of industrial output by province for 1974-1975 as presented in Robert M. Field, Nicholas Lardy, and John P. Emerson, *Provincial Industrial Output in the People's Republic of China, 1949-1975*, U.S. Department of Commerce Foreign Economic Report, No. 12, Washington, D.C., September 1976, p. 11.

delivery system. It could also have wider objectives, including one
or more of the following: to destroy China's nuclear delivery system
(including bombers) on the ground; to destroy not only the nuclear
weapons in being but also the means for manufacturing and developing
them--the research and production facilities in the nuclear program;
to destroy a large proportion of China's conventional military forces;
to cripple China's ability to wage war through massive destruction of
China's industrial capacity. Naturally, the scope of this type of
attack would determine to a great degree Moscow's options as to the
types of weaponry and modes of operations involved. Specifications
of the degree of assured levels of destruction desired would also
affect the modalities of conflict. For instance, if the Soviets desired to use nuclear weapons to destroy China's nuclear weapons in
being, the number of weapons launched by the Soviets would vary greatly
according to the permissible margin of error in destroying the Chinese
weapons in the initial attack. Overall, of course, the number and type
of weapons employed would also vary with the Soviet Union's quality of
intelligence as to the placement of Chinese weapons and Moscow's degree
of confidence in the accuracy and thoroughness of this intelligence
information.

The logic of the situation would, if a decision to attack is made,
argue in favor of a broad definition of the targets for the Soviet
Union to destroy in the case of preemption. Simply to eliminate
China's nuclear forces in being without destroying the nuclear establishment more broadly defined would at best set back China's military program by a few years--at the cost of assuring the unremitting hostility
of all Chinese throughout the coming decade and longer. Given that
the political costs in terms of Sino-Soviet relations are likely to
be similar even at significantly different levels of preemption, the
Soviet Union would be better off destroying as much of China's nuclear
establishment and air force as possible in a preemptive strike. Attempts to cripple China's economy to the degree that it would significantly undercut the PRC's military potential for a period of years, however, would entail such a dramatically higher level of casualties that
this step of escalation may well be high enough that it would draw the
boundary on the escalation the Soviet leadership would tolerate.

The intermediate area of seeking to destroy much of China's nuclear *and conventional* forces in being would require hard decisions as to the priorities for destruction within limits of casualties that were deemed politically acceptable. Many military forces in the close vicinity of major cities, for instance, perform primarily garrison functions for domestic security purposes and represent little or no importance in China's overall strategic strength. To remove these forces would, moreover, inflict very high levels of civilian casualties. Thus, the "preemption" option would entail pressures to launch an attack more broadly conceived than simply eliminating China's nuclear weapons and missiles in being, but it would probably fall short of any attempt to obliterate China's entire military establishment and/or the industrial base that undergirds it. This type of attack would almost certainly be launched without warning and, ironically, the more rapid the progress of the Hua Kuo-feng administration in building a substantial nuclear force and conventional military capability, the greater are Moscow's incentives to destroy this Chinese capacity before it grows even more threatening. Thus, over the short run, quick growth in Chinese military strength in combination with unremitting hostility to the USSR might temporarily (i.e., until the PRC develops a credible deterrent) heighten rather than decrease the risk of Soviet attack. China is still a very long distance from acquiring the type of assured second-strike capability that is likely to provide protection from this sort of Soviet calculus.[21]

In sum, it is possible, albeit very unlikely, that Sino-Soviet relations may be shunted considerably further toward either the reconciliation or military conflict ends of the spectrum than the prognosis in the first part of this section anticipates. Given the heightened sensitivities, the internal disruption, the possible linking of foreign policies to factional concerns, and the unreliability of

_____

[21]China's lack of a credible second strike capability is posited, in part, on probable Soviet diplomatic warnings that would make clear the consequences for Chinese cities if any surviving Chinese missiles should leave their launch pads. "Credibility" is, however, a psychological factor that cannot be reduced to objective capabilities with complete certainty.

No vote for US. reactors to USSR military action

(U.S. threat won't stop pre-emptive strike; and what would U.S. do post-attack anyway?)

political information engendered by the succession in each country, moreover, one must judge the possibility of significant military conflict to be somewhat greater than that of far-reaching rapprochement among this continuum of improbable relationships between Moscow and Peking. All of the above analysis has, however, drawn on purely bilateral factors to evaluate the probable range of futures in Sino-Soviet relations. While these bilateral concerns will undoubtedly play a major role in sculpting the policy of each country toward the other, the Sino-Soviet relationship obviously cannot be fully insulated from changes in the multilateral setting in which it is nested.

THE MULTILATERAL DIMENSIONS OF SINO-SOVIET RELATIONS IN THE FUTURE

The Impact of Events in Asia

Looking toward the future, other events in Asia can impact on the analysis presented above. A new war on the Korean Peninsula could conceivably create strong pressures for Sino-Soviet cooperation in aiding the Democratic People's Republic of Korea that might in turn set into motion events that will affect the contours of any future Sino-Soviet relationship. Alternatively, massive Soviet involvement in a Korean conflict could raise tensions in the entire area and increase the likelihood of war between the USSR and China. Another Sino-Indian border war might force the Soviets into actions in support of the Indian side that will make Moscow use more of the stick and less of the carrot in its China policy than it would have preferred. A similar situation could arise out of a Sino-Vietnamese military conflict. In any such case, of course, the danger of uncontrolled escalation analyzed above remains ever-present.

Still, the somewhat more likely possibilities (albeit not probabilities) for the near-term future in Asia--development of a nuclear capability by South Korea, Taiwan, and/or Japan, significant increments in Japanese military might, some resurgence of Indonesia based in part on a renewed relationship with the Soviet Union, Vietnamese granting of naval basing facilities to the USSR, and possible Vietnamese aggression against its neighbors--should not significantly alter the basic Sino-

Soviet relationship analyzed in the subsection on the "past as guide to the future" (pp. 145-160). All these are contingencies that provide incentives for one side or the other to maintain the current level of disagreement in Sino-Soviet relations, while none would provide major incentives for either of the two sides to seek rapprochement or to go to war.

U.S. Policy and Sino-Soviet Relations

Thomas Gottlieb argues persuasively that as of the late 1960s, U.S. policies affected the debate in Peking over Sino-U.S. and Sino-Soviet relations in a direct and significant manner. Several U.S. authors have offered prescriptions concerning how Washington can affect the Chinese succession (and thus China's Soviet policy), assuming that in the late 1970s Peking's debate concerning its policy toward the Soviet Union still remains sensitively attuned to relevant U.S. actions. Roger Brown and Donald Zagoria have advocated that the United States normalize relations with China quickly to prevent the emergence of a relatively anti-U.S. and pro-Soviet faction into power during the course of the succession. Michael Pillsbury has likewise warned of a "pro-Soviet" faction in China whose strength in Peking is augmented by signs of U.S. weaknesses and/or conciliation in the face of the Soviet threat. Pillsbury, like Brown, expressed concern that this "pro-Soviet" group might get the upper hand after Mao's demise if China and the United States had not normalized relations by then.[22] The thrust of the analysis in the present report is that too much has changed since the period that Gottlieb so skillfully analyzed to justify the subsequent arguments made by Brown, Pillsbury, and Zagoria. Indeed, one can sum up the current basic context for the Sino-Soviet-U.S. triangle as follows.

The chasm that divides China from the Soviet Union is wide and deep. It is grounded in the perception shared by all Chinese leaders that the

---

[22]Brown, op. cit., pp. 21-22; Pillsbury interview in *Newsweek International*, December 8, 1975, p. 52. Richard Solomon implies a somewhat similar rationale for normalization in his "Thinking Through the China Problem," *Foreign Affairs*, January 1978, pp. 340-341.

Soviet Union is basically aggressive and expansionist--a perception that will not change unless the Soviet Union fundamentally restructures its policy along the lines of decreased emphasis on military affairs and a less assertive role in the international arena. Peking's leaders fully appreciate that the Soviet Union has launched open invasions only against its allied socialist states (Hungary and Czechoslovakia) since World War II, that Moscow has since the mid-1950s devoted massive resources to creating the potential to project the military might of the Kremlin across long distances, that the Kremlin has proved increasingly willing in recent years to use military force either directly or indirectly in more distant places such as Angola, and that the USSR has made considerable efforts to develop a potent military capability almost around China's entire periphery--an effort that continues to grow each year. The Chinese also draw attention to the fact that the USSR does not remain faithful to its allies and friends but rather seeks to turn each relationship to its own advantage, such as in Egypt. It is these larger contextual elements that provide the major impetus for continuing the dispute on the Chinese side. Chinese ideological analyses about the degeneration of the Soviet system into social imperialism provide the intellectual underpinning for this Chinese perspective and make Peking's leaders even more firmly convinced of the accuracy of their prognosis on Soviet foreign policy.

The Soviet Union sees advantages in a Sino-Soviet rapprochement. At a minimum, such a development would preclude the formation of a Sino-U.S. axis against the USSR. More positively in Soviet eyes, it would allow Moscow to decrease somewhat the resources it must currently spend on coping with its perception of a Chinese threat and would provide greater security for the rapidly developing Soviet areas in Eastern Siberia. It might also provide the vehicle for easier Soviet penetration of Asia, as China would no longer devote so much energy to keeping the USSR out of the region. It could even increase Soviet leverage with the United States in the Peking-Moscow-Washington triangle. Nevertheless, the price of any far-reaching rapprochement is likely to prove too high. The Soviet Union has repeatedly demonstrated its inability to treat its friends and alliance partners as equals, and there is little reason to believe the Kremlin leaders in the future will be able to accord China the type of equality the Chinese would undoubtedly demand.

Additionally, the Soviet Politburo seems sufficiently wary of Chinese designs that they will continue to strengthen Russia's military capabilities in the Asian theater during the process of seeking a rapprochement with China. While they may offer token withdrawals as a bargaining ploy with the Chinese, these will not dismantle the military machine they have created. Fundamentally, then, Soviet behavior will continue to provide the proof the Chinese leaders seek about the long-term expansionist trends in Soviet policy even while Moscow holds out an olive branch to the PRC.

Importantly, the Soviet behavior that structures Chinese perceptions is motivated primarily by concerns about the West and other areas of the world. It probably is not, therefore, behavior that can be *significantly* modified in response to the Soviet desire to take some of the tension out of Moscow's relations with Peking. China's essentially defensive responses, in turn, feed Soviet distrust of Peking's motives and make any serious modification of the offending Soviet behavior still less likely.

The United States' relationship with both the USSR and the PRC is now more clearly defined and settled than was the case from 1968-1973, and the rest of Asia has now adjusted in the main to the new configuration of power relationships in the region. Thus, for instance, it is now almost certainly accepted in Peking that there will remain limits on the degree of cordiality in Soviet-U.S. relations and that conflicts of interest will continue to mar that relationship around the globe. The Chinese naturally prefer that these conflicts be greater rather than less and that the limits to détente be sharply drawn, but there is no longer evidence of serious debate in Peking as to whether or not Washington and Moscow will "collude" to pick the fruits of the Chinese revolution.[23]

---

[23]As Gottlieb notes, this was a major focus of the debate in Peking over foreign policy as of the end of the 1960s and early 1970s:

Why should anything happen that might nudge this triangular relationship out of the reasonably well accepted groove into which it has
settled over the past five years? The answer lies in the fact that
the United States' bilateral relations with the Soviet Union and/or
China could conceivably change sufficiently to set in motion significant changes in the Sino-Soviet leg of the triangle.

Normalization of relations between Washington and Peking will
not provide enough of a shock to the triangle to jar it out of its
current track. Similarly, the completion of a SALT II agreement (and
even progress in the MBFR talks) would not force the Chinese to rethink their fundamental assumptions about the nature of the triangle.
Rather, changes significant enough to impact on the Sino-Soviet relationship itself would probably have to stem from a radical *deterioration* in Washington's relations with either Moscow or Peking, or both.
Three major possibilities present themselves in this regard.

First, U.S. relations with *both* the USSR and the PRC may deteriorate significantly. The seeds of this unhappy possibility have
already been sown and could possibly bear fruit. On the Soviet side,
President Carter's commitment to human rights and his style of open diplomacy seem to have seriously damaged the delicate fabric of mutual understanding between Washington and Moscow that was so carefully stitched
together during the Nixon and Ford administrations. Ironically, the
President's desire for meaningful *reductions* in strategic weaponry
may introduce new strains into the coalition of forces that Leonid
Brezhnev put together to allow him to pursue a policy of détente with
the United States. The Soviet General Staff's agreement to support
this policy, for instance, may have been based on an understanding with
Brezhnev that he would never allow détente to go beyond arms control
to actual arms reduction. New technological advances that almost seem
to have a life of their own--such as the cruise missile, the neutron
bomb, high energy antimissile beams, and breakthroughs in missile guidance technology, to name but a few recent examples--can also erode the

Gottlieb, op. cit. Further analysis of this dimension of the debate
in Peking is provided in Peter L. Sargent and Jack H. Harris, *Chinese
Assessment of the Superpower Relationship, 1972-1974*, The BDM Corporation, BDM/W-75-128-TR, Virginia, June 30, 1975.

mutual trust on which the détente relationship depends. There are,
in brief, major threats to the policy of U.S.-Soviet détente, and
there is a realistic (although not likely) possibility that Soviet-
American relations during the remaining Carter years may take on
again the atmosphere[24] of that relationship during the Eisenhower and
Kennedy administrations.

There may be trouble ahead also for U.S.-Chinese relations. As
analyzed in Sec. II, Sino-U.S. relations have remained on a plateau
since 1973 as they became wedded to domestic politics in both capitals.
Mao Tse-tung and Chou En-lai, nevertheless, had the prestige and power
to continue China's relatively cordial relationship with the United
States even in the face of obvious disappointment over their failure
to bring a resolution of the Taiwan issue. Hua Kuo-feng, however,
clearly does not enjoy Mao's or Chou's stature with either his colleagues
or his countrymen. What better way for him to secure his position (and
that of his administration), then, than to move forcefully toward a
resolution of the Taiwan question, especially since China's internal
economic problems are not susceptible to quick and easy solutions? If
Hua has a target date in mind for this, it is probably 1979--the
thirtieth anniversary of the founding of the PRC. He is certainly
anxious not to face that historic benchmark with China's territorial
integrity still questioned by one of the world's two major powers.
While Hua can entertain little hope for *actual* reunification of Taiwan
with the Mainland within two years, therefore, he undoubtedly is in-
tensely concerned to have Peking's sovereignty over Taiwan affirmed in
theory and to have the U.S. military and diplomatic commitment to Taiwan
rescinded. It is not yet certain whether this desire might lead the
Chinese leaders to propose some compromise that Washington can accept.
Should negotiations over this critical issue fail for any reason (including President Carter's relations with the U.S. Congress), however,
there is a possibility that Hua Kuo-feng will feel that he has no viable

_____

[24]The actual substance of the relationship and the points of conflict would, of course, differ greatly from those earlier years.

choice other than to show his determination by taking actions to worsen Sino-U.S. relations, even conceivably to the point of a military attack on Quemoy, more aggressive PRC naval patrolling of the Taiwan Straits, and so forth.[25]

A careful distinction should be drawn here between Sino-U.S. bilateral relations, which could deteriorate significantly, and Chinese sensitivity to the parallel interests Peking shares with Washington relating to limiting Soviet penetration of Asia. Under almost any circumstances, China is likely to continue to refrain from pressuring Japan to break the Japanese-American security treaty, telling the Philippines to deny the United States the use of Subic Bay and other facilities, and so forth. Peking will almost certainly also try to maintain good relations with U.S. allies in both Europe and Asia even should increasing bitterness mark Sino-U.S. exchanges. In brief, given the perceptions of the current Chinese leaders as analyzed in Sec. II and briefly recapitulated above, Peking now has a strong predisposition toward developing a more solid relationship with the United States and, barring that, would probably try to sharply define the areas of difference with the United States so as to minimize the spillover effects of any deterioration in Sino-U.S. bilateral relations engendered by the Taiwan question.

Should the coming year witness the unravelling of both U.S.-Soviet and U.S.-Chinese bilateral relations because of the factors raised above, then, what would be the likely effect of this major change on the Sino-Soviet leg of the triangle? The analysis in Sec. II would suggest that in Peking this situation should work to the benefit of the "hard" moderates, as the deterioration in Soviet-U.S. relations would

---

[25] As Allen Whiting has shown, China's military capabilities in the Taiwan Straits area will remain extremely modest at least in the early 1980s, however: Whiting, "Taiwan: Trends and Prospects," background paper distributed by the China Council of the Asia Society, March 8, 1978, pp. 7-12. Another possible scenario is that failure to resolve the Taiwan impasse will become an issue in political infighting in Peking, with perhaps Hua and Teng each trying to blame this situation on the policies of the other one. The result could, from abroad, look very much like the situation suggested in the text.

focus Moscow's security concerns more directly on Europe and in general would make it far less likely that Moscow would risk becoming bogged down in a military conflict with China. In this situation, moreover, the Chinese would very likely try to purchase military-related goods and technology abroad, albeit not from the United States.

In the Soviet Union, the unravelling of both Soviet-U.S. and Sino-U.S. relations would almost certainly produce a policy consensus in favor of making greater efforts to bring about a significant improvement in Sino-Soviet relations. Now feeling increasingly threatened by the United States and its allies, Moscow would at least try to diminish the possibility that the U.S.-China relationship might again mend and produce a Washington-Peking anti-Soviet alliance (or what would be perceived to be such in the Kremlin). Significant troop withdrawals from along the Chinese border might prove to be the most attractive major Soviet "concession" to jar Sino-Soviet relations onto a more positive course in this eventuality, as the USSR might want at least temporarily to beef up its force dispositions in European Russia and the Warsaw Pact countries.

The net result of these pressures, if the above analysis is correct, will be a Sino-Soviet relationship that differs relatively little from that observed today. The Soviets will appear more forthcoming and the Chinese more obstinate, but the chance of any significant improvement in relations between them will remain as remote as ever. The "hard" moderates can take the Soviet stance toward the U.S. to "prove" the basically bellicose nature of Soviet social-imperialism and the relative security from Soviet attack that China will enjoy as the PRC strives to build its military and economic muscle. Indeed, Chinese attempts to exacerbate relations between the Soviet Union and the West European members of the NATO alliance under these circumstances are almost a foregone conclusion.

There is one significant variation of this scenario that, while extremely unlikely, cannot be overlooked completely. That is, if Peking decides that it must begin to apply military pressure in the Taiwan Straits, it may feel that it first must try to relieve tensions with the Soviet Union to make sure that China will not find herself in a military confrontation with both superpowers at the same time. This calculus might lead to seemingly significant progress toward an improvement in Sino-Soviet state-to-state relations, at least over the short run. Since this would represent a tactical ploy rather than a major strategic reassessment on China's part, though, the chances are great that it would not produce any far-reaching Sino-Soviet rapprochement--unless a process such as that discussed in this section is set in train. A Sino-Soviet border settlement issuing from this attempt at détente could, however, focus the entire brunt of Chinese nationalist feeling against the United States and Taiwan, with potentially very worrisome consequences.

What if, by contrast, U.S. relations with the Soviet Union seriously deteriorate over the coming year but U.S.-Chinese relations are put on a far more solid footing than previously? In the Soviet Union, this would produce fears of isolation on the world stage and concern about concerted U.S.-Chinese military activity against Soviet interests at some point in the future. The reaction this will engender in terms of Soviet foreign policy cannot be predicted with certainty, especially as a succession leadership may take over at any time if Leonid Brezhnev's health (physical or political) should fail. Past experience would suggest, however, that the Soviets are likely to pursue a generally harder line and may increase their military pressure on the PRC to demonstrate the dangers of the course that it believes the Peking leadership is about to take. Paradoxically, it is precisely this kind of military pressure that could force Peking to change its current policy and seek some form of active and explicit security cooperation with the United States. Obvious Soviet military pressure on the PRC, moreover, could conceivably help create a political atmosphere in the United States that would be conducive to a direct, if limited, security relationship with China. Thus, Soviet military pressure on the PRC growing out of Moscow's fear of an impending *de facto* anti-Soviet alliance between Washington and Peking in the wake of a deterioration in Soviet-U.S. relations could actually create the very situation that Moscow fears most. For without Soviet military pressure on the PRC, China is unlikely to seek, and the United States is unlikely to agree to, any form of significant *direct military* relationship, even in the context of a cold war between the United States and USSR.

The Soviet Union's reaction to a budding Sino-U.S. military relationship cannot be predicted. Moscow could conceivably seriously escalate tensions with either the United States or China or both. Conversely, it is possible, of course, that the initial signs of a crystallization of a Sino-U.S. military relationship would produce a major effort by the Soviet Union to improve Sino-Soviet relations and thereby persuade the PRC[26] that the Sino-U.S. military relationship was unnecessary. This in turn might well work to cut off any Sino-U.S. military relationship that had developed--both because Peking would feel that relationship had become less necessary and because the United States might no longer see China as imminently threatened. Naturally, once a Sino-U.S. military relationship of any sort has commenced, however, influential groups on each side could develop a strong interest in maintaining it. There is, therefore, no certainty that this dimension of Sino-U.S. relations would cease as the Soviet threat toward the PRC seemed to diminish.

The third basic possibility for the near-term future of the triangle is for U.S. relations with Moscow to take a turn for the better while Sino-U.S. relations deteriorate. In this case, the Soviet Union's incentives toward China would remain much as they are now--a strong desire to find an accommodation within the framework of an increasing Soviet presence in Asia and guarantees of Soviet security interests in the region. The probable policy outcome, then, would be a continuation of the current carrot and stick approach analyzed previously.

----

[26]Another possibility, of course, would be a Soviet effort to woo the United States away from the relationship--or to threaten the United States with serious consequences if Washington did not rethink its policies. This part of the analysis in the text is, however, concerned only with the possible effects on the Sino-Soviet leg of the triangle.

In Peking, this combination of circumstances would almost certainly heighten fears of Soviet military pressure during a period when China is trying to focus on its own economic and military development. It would in all probability, then, work to the advantage of the "soft" moderates, who would advocate making some overtures toward the USSR so as to decrease the chances of a Soviet attack on China. The Soviet-U.S. détente and Sino-U.S. friction should not give the Chinese leaders any reason to fundamentally reevaluate their assessment of the long-term danger to China from the USSR, and thus the basic "Soviet threat" orientation of China's foreign policy would remain unchanged. Within this context, however, the Chinese would prove more inclined to encourage Moscow with signs here and there of a willingness to patch over differences and might even make some real, albeit very limited, concessions to the Soviet Union. This would be especially true if China, as mentioned above, decided to apply military pressure in the Taiwan Straits.

Basically, then, each of the above three scenarios based on deteriorating U.S. relations with the USSR and/or the PRC involves some change in the dynamics of Sino-Soviet relations, although none of the three anticipates changes of such magnitude that they would fundamentally transform Sino-Soviet interaction. The chances of some major shift in relations between Moscow and Peking stem, rather, from the fact that the relatively small changes induced in their bilateral interaction by their altered relations with the United States could set off either a process of reconciliation or a spiral of military escalation through the mechanisms dealt with in the previous subsection. While very unlikely, these possibilities cannot be completely dismissed.

The fundamental lesson of the foregoing analysis for U.S. policy is clear: The basic contours of the Sino-Soviet relationship are relatively firmly fixed along the lines analyzed at the beginning of this section, and there is little the United States can do to manipulate this Sino-Soviet interaction. United States policies toward each of these communist powers should be based, therefore, primarily on U.S. bilateral interests with each, and should not take as a central concern a desire to produce an effect on the *Sino-Soviet* leg of the triangle.

Whether the United States should base its policies toward Moscow and Peking around a calculus that tries to gain leverage over each by Washington's relations with the other is, of course, a somewhat different matter.

There seems little chance that the United States could increase its leverage significantly in its bilateral relations with the PRC by orchestrating moves toward détente with Moscow. Indeed, should relations between Washington and Moscow become more cordial, Peking is apt to prove even less willing to bend its policies to place Sino-U.S. ties on a firmer footing. Similarly, the fact that the Sino-Soviet-U.S. triangle has been an international fact of life since 1972 has diminished the leverage the United States can gain in its relations with the Soviet Union by manipulating its relationship with Peking. Moscow has by now developed a keen sense of the limits of Sino-U.S. cooperation--limits imposed by the internal political processes of each country, by sharply differing interests concerning Taiwan, and by the fact that many U.S. allies in Asia would feel greatly dismayed if the United States were to provide aid and assistance that would permit China to increase significantly her own ability to affect events throughout the region. The remaining major outstanding issues between China and the United States are, from the Chinese side, the core problems limiting the entire relationship, and therefore in a real sense, Washington's ability to conjure up the ghost of a far-reaching Sino-U.S. relationship in front of Moscow's eyes has diminished during the mid to late 1970s.

A U.S. desire to keep China strong enough to hold to a minimum the chances of a Soviet strike against the PRC is valid enough; although given the full range of U.S. obligations in the Asian area, the most responsible way to pursue this objective is by the quiet encouragement (or at least not the discouragement) of appropriate transfers of technology and goods by friendly third countries. Where sales by other countries involve items that include U.S. components,

Washington should take a prudently flexible stance, keeping a low profile but trying not to deny to China those items that would significantly increase Peking's defensive capabilities while not directly augmenting the PRC's ability to project its power abroad.

Appendix A

SINO-SOVIET NEGOTIATIONS

The Soviets and Chinese regularly engage in three sets of negotiations: the border talks, navigation talks, and trade talks. The border talks are analyzed in Sec. I. The navigation talks concern joint efforts to maintain the navigability of the boundary rivers between the USSR and China. These talks have produced only one set of agreements during the 1970s (that of 1977). The annual trade negotiations result in a trade protocol that stipulates the general amount and composition of bilateral trade for that year.

Border Talks: Known Sessions

Year	Dates Convened
1969	October 20 – December 14
1970	January 4 – April 22
1971	January 15 – summer
1972	March 20 – mid July
1973	March 6 – late June
1974	June 25 – August 18
1975	February 15 – May 5
1976–1977	November 27, 1976 – February 28, 1977
1978	April 26, 1978 –

Border River Navigation Talks: Known Sessions

July 10, 1970   – December 19, 1970
December 6, 1971 – March 21, 1972
January 5, 1973 – March 5, 1973
February 5, 1974 – March 21, 1974
July 27, 1977   – October 6, 1977

Trade Protocols: Dates of Signature

1970	November 22
1971	August 5
1972	June 13
1973	August 1
1974	May 15
1975	July 24
1976	May 21
1977	July 21
1978	April 17

Appendix B

SINO-SOVIET TRADE, 1969-1976[a]

Year	Soviet Exports to China	Soviet Imports from China	Total
1969	25.0	26.1	51.1
1970	22.4	19.5	41.9
1971	70.1	68.6	138.7
1972	100.2	110.4	210.6
1973	100.5	100.8	201.3
1974	108.4	105.5	213.9
1975	92.8 (93.1)[b]	107.8	200.6 (200.9)[b]
1976[b]	179.8	134.6	314.4

[a]All figures in millions of rubles. Figures taken from successive yearbooks of the *Vneshniaia Torgovlia* published in Moscow. The jump in ruble value for trade for 1976 reflects a change in price indexes and not an increase in the actual turnover of goods. Most trade until 1976 was conducted on a barter basis, using 1958 prices.

[b]These figures for 1975 and 1976 are taken from the Soviet publication *Foreign Trade*, No. 3, March 1977 (supplement on "Soviet Foreign Trade, January-December 1976").

BIBLIOGRAPHY OF SECONDARY SOURCES CITED

Abramowitz, Morton, "Chinese Military Capacities," *United States--Soviet Union--China: The Great Power Triangle*, Hearings Before the Subcommittee on Future Policy Research and Development of the Committee on International Relations, House of Representatives, 1976.

An Tai-sung, *The Sino-Soviet Territorial Dispute*, Westminster Press, Philadelphia, 1973.

Barnds, William, "China's Relations with Pakistan: Durability Amidst Discontinuity," *China Quarterly*, No. 63, September 1975, pp. 463-489.

-----, "Japan and Its Mainland Neighbours: An End to Equidistance?," *International Affairs*, London, Vol. 52, No. 1, January 1976, pp. 27-38.

Barnett, A. Doak, *China and the Major Powers in East Asia*, The Brookings Institution, Washington, D.C., 1977.

Borisov, O. B., and B. T. Koloskov, *Sino-Soviet Relations, 1945-1970*, translated and edited by Vladimir Petrov, Indiana University Press, 1975.

-----, *Soviet-Chinese Relations, 1945-1973*, translated by Yuri Shirokov, Progress Publishers, Moscow, 1975.

Bridgham, Philip, "The Fall of Lin Piao," *China Quarterly*, No. 55, July-September 1973, pp. 428ff.

Brown, Roger Glenn, "Chinese Politics and American Foreign Policy: A New Look At the Triangle," *Foreign Policy*, No. 23, Summer 1976, pp. 3-23.

Byung-joon Ahn, *Chinese Politics and the Cultural Revolution*, University of Washington Press, Seattle, 1976.

Central Intelligence Agency, *Bibliography of Literature Written in the People's Republic of China During the Campaign to Criticize Lin Piao and Confucius*, July 1973-December 1974, Washington, D.C., 1975.

-----, *Communist Aid to Less Developed Countries of the Free World, 1975*, ER 76-10372U, Washington, D.C., 1976.

Charles, David, "The Dismissal of Marshal P'eng Teh-huai," *China Quarterly*, No. 8, October-December 1961, pp. 63-76.

Doolin, Dennis, *Territorial Claims in the Sino-Soviet Conflict*, Hoover Institution, Stanford, 1965.

Field, Robert, Nicholas Lardy, and John Emerson, *Provincial Industrial Output in the People's Republic of China, 1949-1975*, U.S. Department of Commerce, Foreign Economic Report No. 12, 1976.

Ginsburgs, George, "The Damansky/Chenpao Island Incidents: A Case Study of Syntactic Patterns of Crisis Diplomacy," *Asian Studies: Occasional Papers Series*, No. 6, Southern Illinois University, 1973.

Glaubitz, Joachim, "Anti-Hegemony Formulas in Chinese Foreign Policy," *Asian Survey*, Vol. XVI, No. 3, March 1976, pp. 205-215.

Gottlieb, Thomas, *Chinese Foreign Policy Factionalism and the Origins of the Strategic Triangle*, The Rand Corporation, R-1902-NA, November 1977.

Grow, Roy, "The Politics of Industrial Development in China and the Soviet Union: Organizational Strategy as a Linkage Between National and World Politics," Ph.D. dissertation, University of Michigan, 1973.

Haldeman, H. R., *The Ends of Power*, Times Books, New York, 1978.

Halperin, Morton H., and Arnold Kanter, *Readings in American Foreign Policy: A Bureaucratic Perspective*, Little, Brown and Company, Boston, 1973.

Haselkorn, Avigdor, "The Soviet Collective Security System," *Orbis*, Vol. XIX, Spring 1975, pp. 231-254.

Heymann, Hans., Jr., *China's Approach to Technology Acquisition: Part I: The Aircraft Industry*, The Rand Corporation, R-1573-ARPA, February 1975.

Hinton, Harold, *Communist China in World Politics*, Houghton Mifflin, New York, 1966.

-----, *Bear at the Gate*, American Enterprise Institute for Public Policy Research, Washington, D.C., 1971.

-----, "The United States and the Sino-Soviet Confrontation," *Orbis*, Vol. XIX, No. 1, Spring 1975, pp. 25-46.

Hong Yung Lee, "Cleavages and Coalitions in the Cultural Revolution," Paper for the Columbia University Seminar on Modern China, 1977.

-----, "The Politics of Cadre Rehabilitation Since the Cultural Revolution," unpublished paper, 1977.

Horelick, Arnold, *The Soviet Union's "Asian Collective Security" Proposal: A Club in Search of Members*, The Rand Corporation, P-5195, March 1974.

Horn, Robert C., "Changing Soviet Policies and Sino-Soviet Competition in Southeast Asia," *Orbis*, Vol. XVII, Summer 1973, pp. 493-526.

Jammes, Sydney H., "The Chinese Defense Burden, 1965-1974," *China: A Reassessment of the Economy*, Joint Economic Committee, Washington, D.C., 1975.

Joffe, Ellis, "The Chinese Army After the Cultural Revolution: The Effects of Intervention," *China Quarterly*, No. 55, July-September 1973, pp. 450-477.

Johnson, A. Ross, "Yugoslavia and the Sino-Soviet Conflict: The Shifting Triangle, 1948-1974," *Studies in Comparative Communism*, Spring/Summer 1974, pp. 184-203.

Kalb, Marvin, and Bernard Kalb, *Kissinger*, Little, Brown and Company, Boston, 1974.

Kau, Michael Y. M. (ed.), *The Lin Piao Affair: Power Politics and Military Coup*, International Arts and Sciences Press, White Plains, 1975.

Khrushchev Remembers, Little, Brown and Company, Boston, 1970.

Khrushchev Remembers: The Last Testament, Little, Brown and Company, 1974.

Lieberthal, Kenneth, "China in 1975: The Internal Political Scene," *Problems of Communism*, XXIV, May-June 1975, pp. 1-11.

-----, *A Research Guide to Central Party and Government Meetings in China, 1949-1975*, International Arts and Sciences Press, White Plains, 1976a.

-----, *Mao Tse-tung's Perception of the Soviet Union as Communicated in the Mao Tse-tung Ssu-hsiang Wan Sui!*, The Rand Corporation, P-5726, September 1976b.

-----, *Strategies of Conflict in China During 1975-1976*, The Rand Corporation, P-5680, June 1976c.

-----, "The Foreign Policy Debate in Peking As Seen Through the Allegorical Articles, 1973-1976," *China Quarterly*, No. 71, September 1977, pp. 528-554.

-----, "The Politics of Modernization in the PRC," *Problems of Communism*, May-June 1978a, pp. 1-17.

-----, *Central Documents and Politburo Politics in China*, Michigan Papers in Chinese Studies No. 33, University of Michigan Center for Chinese Studies, Ann Arbor, 1978b.

Lifton, Robert J., *Revolutionary Immortality*, Vintage Books, New York, 1968.

Lu Yung-shu, "Preparation for War in Mainland China," *Collected Documents on Mainland China*, Taipei, Taiwan, 1971, pp. 895-918.

Maxwell, Neville, "The Chinese Account of the 1969 Fighting at Chenpao," *China Quarterly*, No. 56, October-December 1973, pp. 730-739.

-----, "A Note on the Amur-Ussuri Sector of the Sino-Soviet Boundaries," *Modern China*, Vol. 1, No. 1, January 1975, pp. 116-126.

Müller, Kurt, *The Foreign Aid Programs of the Soviet Bloc and Communist China: An Analysis*, Walker and Company, New York, 1967.

Newhouse, John, *Cold Dawn: The Story of SALT*, Holt, Rinehart and Winston, New York, 1973.

Oksenberg, Michael, and Yeung Sai-cheung, "Hua Kuo-feng's Pre-Cultural Revolution Hunan Years, 1949-1966: The Making of a Political Generalist," *China Quarterly*, No. 69, March 1977, pp. 3-53.

Pauker, Guy, *Prospects for Regional Hegemony in Southeast Asia*, The Rand Corporation, P-5630, April 1976.

Penkovsky, Oleg, *The Penkovsky Papers*, Doubleday and Company, New York, 1965.

Perkin, Linda, "The Chinese Communist Party: The Lushan Meeting and Plenum, July-August 1959," M.A. Essay, Columbia University, 1971.

Pillsbury, Michael, "Patterns of Chinese Power Struggles: Three Models," Paper for the Modern China Seminar, Columbia University, 1974.

-----, *SALT on the Dragon: Chinese Views of the Soviet-American Strategic Balance*, The Rand Corporation, P-5457, April 1975.

-----, "U.S.-China Military Ties?," *Foreign Policy*, Fall 1975, pp.

Robinson, Thomas (ed.), *The Cultural Revolution in China*, University of California Press, Berkeley, 1971.

-----, "The Sino-Soviet Border Dispute: Background, Development, and the March 1969 Border Clashes," *American Political Science Review*, Vol. LXVI, No. 4, December 1972, pp. 1175-1202.

Romance, Francis J., "Peking's Counter-Encirclement Strategy: The Maritime Element," *Orbis*, Vol. XX, Summer 1976, pp. 437-459.

Rothenberg, Morris, *Soviet Perceptions of the Chinese Succession*, Center for Advanced International Studies, University of Miami, 1975.

Sargent, Peter L., and Jack H. Harris, "Chinese Assessment of the Superpower Relationship, 1972-1974," The BDM Corporation, BDM/W-75-128-TR, Virginia, 1975.

Simmonds, J. D., "P'eng Teh-huai: A Chronological Reexamination," *China Quarterly*, No. 37, January-March 1969, pp. 120-138.

Simon, Sheldon W., "Peking and Indochina: The Perplexity of Victory," *Asian Survey*, May 1976, pp. 401-410.

Snow, Edgar, *The Long Revolution*, Vintage Books, New York, 1973.

Solomon, Richard, "Thinking Through the China Problem," *Foreign Affairs*, January 1978, pp. 324-356.

The Soviet Union, 1973, C. Hurst and Company, London, 1975.

The Soviet Union, 1974-1975, C. Hurst and Company, London, 1976.

Taylor, Jay, *China and Southeast Asia: Peking's Relations with Revolutionary Movements*, Praeger, New York, 1976.

Teiwes, Frederick, *Provincial Leadership in China: The Cultural Revolution and Its Aftermath*, The Australian National University, Canberra, 1973.

-----, "The Dismissal of P'eng Teh-huai and the Campaign Against 'Right Opportunism,' 1959-1960," Seminar Series Paper for the Contemporary China Centre of the Australian National University, Canberra, 1976.

Thornton, Richard, *China: The Struggle for Power, 1917-1972*, Indiana University Press, Bloomington, 1973.

The Case of P'eng Teh-huai, Union Research Institute, Kowloon, 1968.

CCP Documents of the Great Proletarian Cultural Revolution, Union Research Institute, Kowloon, 1968.

Whiting, Allen, *The Chinese Calculus of Deterrence*, University of Michigan Press, Ann Arbor, 1975.

-----, "Taiwan: Trends and Prospects," (background paper distributed by the China Council of the Asia Society), 1978.

P.24 " in over ɛ̄ past 8 yrs, the USSR has developed ā
capacity ... to menace China from ɛ̄ east
and south as well as from the north."

P.24 " moscow has combined its diplomatic overture & to ɛ̄z
with highly visible and clearly threatening actions to
bring military force to bear in this relationship "

P.35 SU Asian collective security system

P.35 Footnote # 108 _____ SU–Indio–treaty

P.42 SU–US détente undermine Sino–US détente

P.42 20 oct 1969 Sino–SU border negot'n Commune same day as
US–SU agreem't talk on SALT negot'n

P.42 Sino–SU border talks & SU–US treaty

P.46 WEB Nixon– China Can't Couple with SU

P.47 Third word not seen as shameful !

P.50 In 1969 when ɸ attack SU — SU had greder assertion border

P.52 aft 10 yrs (by 1978) negotiation stalled 3 reasons (P52–53)

(P51) SU give China ɛ 3 mth deadline to enter talks
June 13

P.53 border never seriously discussed !

P.64–65 China's dale of estb relations with Amer fed's

P.64 "China actions since 1969
have demonstrated that ɸ PRC
has not expected ɛ̄ talks to
produce real progress